Europe and the Sea

B

The Making of Europe series is the result of a unique collaboration between five European publishers – Beck in Germany, Blackwell in Great Britain and the United States, Critica in Spain, Laterza in Italy and le Seuil in France. Each book will be published in all five languages. The scope of the series is broad, encompassing the history of ideas as well as and including their interaction with the history of societies, nations and states, to produce informative, readable, and provocative treatments of central themes in the history of the European peoples and their cultures.

Europe and the Sea

Michel Mollat du Jourdin

Translated from the French
by Teresa Lavender Fagan

BLACKWELL
Oxford UK & Cambridge USA

First published in 1993 by Blackwell Publishers and simultaneously by four other
publishers: © 1993 Beck, Munich (German); © 1993 Critica, Barcelona (Spanish); ©
1993 Editions du Seuil, Paris (French); © 1993 Laterza, Rome and Bari (Italian).

Blackwell Publishers
108 Cowley Road
Oxford OX4 1JF, UK

238 Main Street, Suite 501
Cambridge, Massachusetts 02142, USA

British Library Cataloguing in Publication Data
A CIP catalogue record for this book is available from the British Library.

Library of Congress Cataloging-in-Publication Data
Mollat, Michel.
    [Europe et la mer. English]
    Europe and the sea/by Michel Mollat du Jourdin: translated from the
French by Teresa Lavender Fagan.
        p.   cm. — (The Making of Europe)
    Includes bibliographical references and index.
    ISBN 0–631–17227–0
    1. Navigation–Europe–History.
    I. Title.   II. Series.
    VK55.M65   1993
    623.89′094–dc20   92–37706
                                                                        CIP

Typeset in 11 on 12½ Garamond by TecSet, Wallington, Surrey
Printed in Great Britain by T. J. Press (Padstow) Ltd, Cornwall
This book is printed on acid-free paper

Contents

Illustrations

Series Editor's Preface

Europe is in the making. This is both a great challenge and one that can be met only by taking the past into account – a Europe without history would be orphaned and unhappy. Yesterday conditions today; today's actions will be felt tomorrow. The memory of the past should not paralyse the present: when based on understanding it can help us to forge new friendships, and guide us towards progress.

Europe is bordered by the Atlantic, Asia and Africa, its history and geography inextricably entwined, and its past comprehensible only within the context of the world at large. The territory retains the name given it by the ancient Greeks, and the roots of its heritage may be traced far into prehistory. It is on this foundation – rich and creative, united yet diverse – that Europe's future will be built.

The Making of Europe is the joint initiative of five publishers of different languages and nationalities: Beck in Munich; Blackwell in Oxford; Critica in Barcelona; Laterza in Rome; and le Seuil in Paris. Its aim is to describe the evolution of Europe, presenting the triumphs but not concealing the difficulties. In their efforts to achieve accord and unity the nations of Europe have faced discord, division and conflict. It is no purpose of this series to conceal these problems: those committed to the European enterprise will not succeed if their view of the future is unencumbered by an understanding of the past.

The title of the series is thus an active one: the time is yet to come when a synthetic history of Europe will be possible. The books we shall publish will be the work of leading historians, by no means all European. They will address crucial aspects of European history in every field – political, economic, social, religious and cultural. They will draw on that long historiographical tradition which stretches back to Herodotus, as well as on those conceptions and ideas which have transformed historical enquiry in the recent decades of the twentieth century. They will write readably for a wide public.

Our aim is to consider the key questions confronting those involved in Europe's making, and at the same time to satisfy the curiosity of the world at large: in short, who are the Europeans? where have they come from? whither are they bound?

Jacques Le Goff

Foreword

What was, what is, and what will be the role of the sea in the European adventure: Europe is a continent, but most of its inhabitants have misunderstood, or have been unaware of, the sea beyond the fashion for windsurfing or ocean cruises. Yet the sea, or rather, seas, surround that continent. Borders of fear or shores of hope, the European seas have seen the arrival and departure of merchandise, ideas and men. History has been aware of the relationship between the centre and the periphery. On three of its sides the European periphery is maritime. To the south there is the Mediterranean and its ancient civilizations, the horizons of the Greek and Arab worlds, of the Middle East and North Africa, of Islam and oil. To the north is the world of the Vikings, sagas, herring, salmon and whales, the world of the North Pole and oil from the North Sea. To the west is the immense expanse – quite shrunken today – of the Atlantic Ocean with its American and African horizons, and beyond, the once fabled Indies, both West and East, the lands of the black, red and brown men – a vast world ignored by most, whose surface had just been scratched until the end of the Middle Ages, but which has since become essential for Europe. The sea isolates and connects at the same time. In spite of aeroplanes it has been and still is one of the fundamental givens which geography has offered – both an obstacle and an opportunity – to the history of Europe. Thus the necessity in this series of devoting a volume to the historical relationships between Europe and the sea. In time as in space, the further one looks, the more significant what one sees becomes. To go very far back into the past would be to evoke the global time when the seas and the

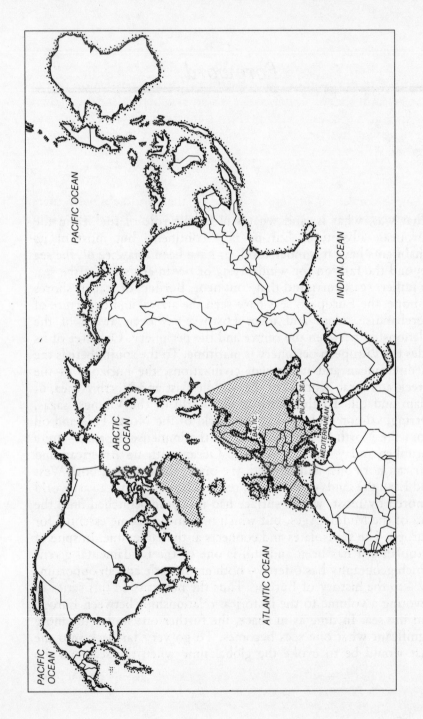

Europe, almost a little island

European continent were tightly enmeshed. It would above all be to examine the historical time that brought peoples to settle on ocean shores, to organize their lives, to cause rivalries, conflicts and at best, competition between them for the possession of the waters and the exploitation of their resources. In their own fashion, all Europeans have perceived the expanse, the colours and the voice of the sea; it has then invited them to see and to go beyond its horizons.

The image Europeans have had of their part of the world has varied throughout time. At first Europeocentrist in the way the Chinese conceived of their Empire of the 'Middle', Westerners have represented the universe as centred around their little world and their culture. Then, without relinquishing the conviction of their primacy, they organized the map of the Earth as emanating from their Europe. Geographical maps are the expressions of a

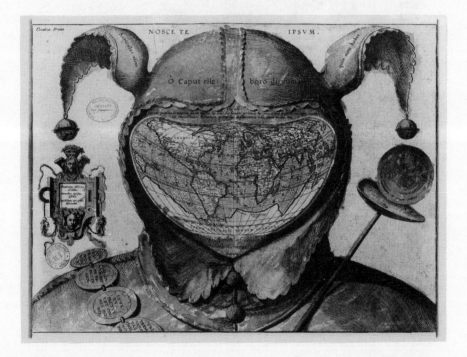

The world in the head of a jester, hand-coloured engraving of *c.* 1590 attributed to Oronce Finé (*Bibliothèque Nationale, Paris, cartes et plans, Réserve Ge D 7895).*

A humorous map of Europe in 1870, by Hadol (Paris, Bibliothèque Nationale)

civilization. They are not, however, incapable of linking a search for exactitute of proportions with a certain humour.

Examples of such humour make one wonder. In the fourteenth century (around 1337) a certain visionary, a genius in some ways, Opicinus de Canistris, took advantage of the time he had to spend in prison in Avignon for his theological deviance (he called himself the Antichrist) to sketch a unique map, one having anthropomorphic traits, accompanied by legends. Two human heads face each other on either side of Gibraltar, a woman with long hair and a man with a semitic nose wearing a burnous; they are Eve (Europe) and Adam (Africa) at the moment of their sin. The strait, source of all evil, expresses the fear of the ocean; the Mediterranean (*Diabolicum mare*) is like a demoniacal octopus ensnaring the European peninsulas with its tentacles. The entire map is embellished with ironical or critical commentaries.

A second example dating two centuries later is attributed to a great scholar of the Renaissance, Oronce Finé. Using an uncommon projection in the shape of a heart, he uses scientific techniques and places Europe with its modest proportions in a world portrayed by a cap o'bells with its attributes, along with his various formulae commenting on the proverb *Vanitas vanitatum et omnia vanitas* ('Vanity of vanities and all is vanity'): an audacious mockery of the European claims of universal domination at the time of the Great Discoveries.

A third example which conveys European competition is a satirical map of Europe of 1870. States are represented in the form of caricature figures or animals corresponding to their temperaments, ambitions or antagonisms. The division within it is striking.

Without presenting more examples it is clear that time, while modifying the political disposition of Europe, has not changed the presence or the fundamental role of the seas. They thus appear as a permanent component of the European personality, whose stability conditions the future as it did the past. A long-term given, the action of the seas on Europe has, however, changed and will continue to change following the vicissitudes of history, whose waves, however permanent they may be, are continually transformed like the waves of the sea.

Part I

Europe and the Sea in Time and Space

1

Like a Puzzle

European maritime ancestry lost in legend

Europe's ties to the sea go back to the beginning of time. The legendary figure who gave Europe its name was born on the shores of the Mediterranean. Europa was gathering flowers on the coast when Zeus, whose brother Poseidon ruled over the sea, took her and carried her through marine space on the back of a bull whose form he had assumed. Myth and legend do not necessarily conflict with geography and history. Herodotus admitted his ignorance of the way in which the name 'Europe' was given to the western continent. The tradition passed on by Ovid and taken up by Dante has come down to us today. The son of Europa's union with Zeus, Minos, the ruler of Crete and its surrounding waters, was unable to prevent Icarus, the son of Daedalus, from escaping from the labyrinth by flying through the air. Before burning his wings like a butterfly with the heat of the sun, Icarus perhaps caught a glimpse of the panorama of the 'Peloponnesus and the islands surrounded by waves', to which a *Hymn to Apollo* from the eighth century BC already applied the name of Europe, meaning the land of the setting sun. Thus transposed on a geographical level, the term, later extended from the part to the whole, symbolically corresponds to the image which our own age receives from a satellite: the pieces of a sort of puzzle whose elements man's imagination and observation over the course of centuries have striven to assemble. Horace, including the myth of Europa in one of his *Odes* (III, 27), has Venus say, as a way of consoling the nymph in tears on the edge of the sea: 'Learn well to maintain your high condition. Half of the world will owe its name to you.'

3

Intimacy with the sea

Regardless of the way the Earth is represented, either by a map or a globe, or of the mode of cartographic projection or the angle of photographic vision, Europe's silhouette conveys its intimacy with the marine element: it is a small, very small, peninsula surrounded by the seas which assail it. Joined in the east to the expanse of Asia, it ends in the west in delicate articulations and is broken up into archipelagos in both the south and the north.

Where does Asia end and Europe begin? When geography hesitates, history offers its hypotheses. Herodotus, without giving his reasons, considered the Tanais River (the Don) to be a border; men of the Middle Ages, loyal to their 'authorities', followed that opinion – for example, in the thirteenth century, men such as the Flemish Franciscan Willem Van Ruysbrouck, the precursor of Marco Polo among the Mongols. Later, others limited their sights to the Volga. In our time, General de Gaulle saw the limits of Europe at the Urals. Geography remains both less precise and more concrete. For geography, the contrast between Asia and Europe goes beyond continentality. It involuntarily justifies the opinion brought back from the Far East by Paul Claudel: 'The West looks to the sea and the East to the mountains' (*L'Oiseau noir dans le Soleil Levant*).

The contrast is clear. To go swimming in the sea no Western European travels more than 350 kilometres; the distance is doubled for an inhabitant of Central Europe; it reaches 11,000 kilometres for a kulak of the Russian plains; and as for the nomads of Central Asia, their endless travels over the steppes and deserts do not lead them to marine water, which they never see. There is nothing surprising in this, given the ratio of the length of the coasts to the continental area in Europe and in Asia: 4 km per 1000 square km for the former, and 1.7 km for the latter.

Climate emphasizes the maritime character of Europe

No region is as dry as the endoreic basins of Central Asia, which are enclosed by enormous mountain chains; their intermittent rivers do not open into any sea and often dwindle into the sand. Even the Hungarian *puszta* did not offer its immigrants on

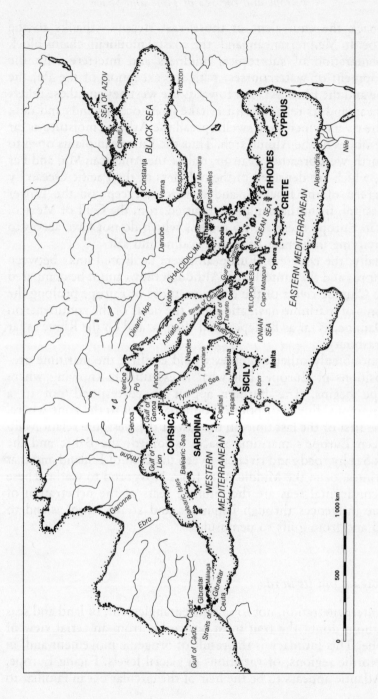

Figure 1.1 The Mediterranean seas

horseback the equivalent of those vast steppes – thanks to the Danube. In Mediterranean lands the coastal mountain chains block the penetration of subtropical mildness and interfere with the development of watercourses, with the exception of the Po, the Rhône and the Ebro. At least towards the west beyond these reliefs the ocean and its related features take over; ocean winds and rain, and the rivers which they swell, spread the Atlantic moisture as far as the slopes of the Alpine arch. Thus the European plains open to the north-west breathe ocean air, unlike the American Mid and Far West, which are deprived of the mildness of the Pacific Ocean by the screen of the Rockies, and distanced, except on the Lower Mississippi, from the dampness emitted from the Gulf of Mexico. Thus in Europe there are no regions which do not have access to the vivifying influences of marine iodine and salt.

Finally, the course of European rivers facilitated links between the shores and the hinterlands. Although they cannot be compared to the Chinese rivers or the Amazon, those of Europe prolong the rhythms of maritime navigation into the heart of the continent: on the Danube, as far as Budapest and Vienna, and on the Rhine as far as Strasbourg.

Undoubtedly other examples would confirm the maritime pre-dispositions of Europe. But what is essential is knowing where Europe begins. The borders appear to correspond not to a mountainous, fluvial or political boundary, but to the zone where, for the first or the last time, in the east or the west, the relationship between Europe's maritime spaces is joined: the Baltic and the Black Sea by roads and rivers between the Gulf of Finland and that of Crimea, or in the Middle Ages from Novgorod to Caffa. These two continental seas are the intimate seats of the penetration of marine influences through isthmuses and straits, from island to island and from gulfs to peninsulas.

The ocean and its borders

The interpenetration, not to say the entanglement, of land and seas is without doubt the trait most noticeable from an aerial view of Europe. This intimacy is the result of orogenic movement and, in the Nordic regions, of variations in glacial levels. Facing Europe, the Atlantic appears to be the heir of the circular ocean familiar to

the Ancients and the men of the Middle Ages. From its Arctic
continuation into the Barents Sea it extends a continuous sheet as
far as the subtropical confines of the 'Mediterranean Ocean'
encountered by Fernand Braudel off the shore of Gibraltar.
However, this mass is not uniform; it has different personalities
depending upon its particular sectors, whose limits are continental
shelves, and it communicates between them in varying ways. The
Gulf of Gascony – or the Bay of Biscay – then the Celtic Sea,
between the French Cournouailles and English Cornwall on the
one side and Ireland on the other, beckon their dwellers to the high
seas, urging them to go north through the 'channels'. The Irish Sea,
reduced to 23 kilometres at its narrowest passage, opens into the
Norwegian Sea, to the east of a passage from Scotland to Iceland.
The English Channel itself deserves its name, since, only 34
kilometres wide between Calais and Dover, it leads to the North
Sea, a Nordic Mediterranean analogous to the Mediterranean
Ocean mentioned above, functioning as an antechamber to the
Baltic Sea. Over this ensemble of annexes to the ocean, islands of
differing size play the role of an advance guard, for their conti-
nental bases attest to their connection to Europe; this is true of
Great Britain and Ireland, as well as of the adjacent archipelagos
(Man, Shetland, Orkney, the Hebrides, and further to the north in
the arctic region, Lofoten and Svalbard) and of Iceland and even,
all the way to the south, the Azores.

Routes to the inland seas: the Sound and Gibraltar

At the heart of continental Europe, the Baltic and the Mediterranean seas reflect each other in conditions whose differences
balance out any similarities. Certainly, the massive quadrilateral of
the Iberian peninsula is in no way comparable to the frayed
silhouette of Jutland, and if, beginning in the Middle Ages, the
Frisian navigators transferred cargo in order to pass from the
North Sea into the Baltic at the narrowest point of the Danish
peninsula, on the contrary the Aquitanian isthmus, in so far as it
can be called such, was crossed only in the seventeenth century by
the Canal du Midi, 'a promise not kept' (P. Wolff). Access to the

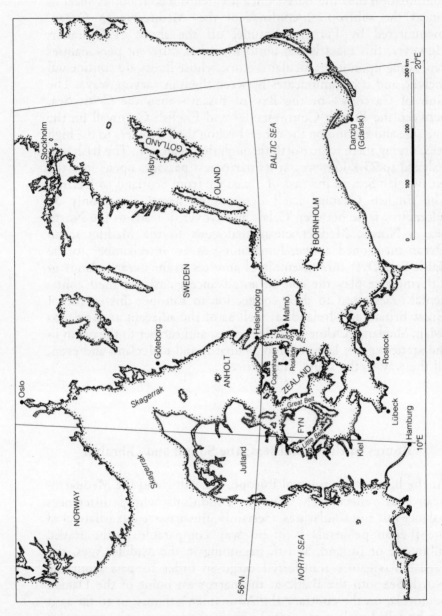

Figure 1.2 The Baltic and the Danish straits

two European Mediterranean seas, that of the north and the south, experienced vicissitudes on physical, economic and geostrategic levels.

Navigating in the Danish straits, crossing the Straits of Gibraltar or flying over them in a plane enable us to grasp their importance and roles. Similarities and differences are immediately apparent. For the passenger coming from the west, the Skagerrak appears as a channel before it tapers into the funnel of the Kattegat. There is nothing similar about the approach to Gibraltar, which is largely open between the Gulf of Cádiz and Morocco. However, the openings of the straits into each of the inland seas is rather impressive. To the north, if the path were not traced by the procession of ships gliding at reduced speed, an inattentive eye might hesitate on the route to follow between the countless islands (Denmark has 474), the largest of which, Sjaelland or Zealand, gives access to Roskilde Fjord; and the captain of a ship of even slight draught would risk running aground on the shallows of the Great and the Small Belt. But the path is safe by way of the Sound, despite a maximum depth of 8 metres and the narrowness (around 5 kilometres) of the passage between Helsingborg on the Swedish side of Scania and Helsingor on the Danish side. The name Elsinore and the memory of Hamlet are in all our minds; and although since 1857 there is no longer the toll instituted in 1429, a moment of reflection is needed when one ventures into another marine realm. True, one could certainly shorten one's trip by taking the Kiel Canal, which cuts the Danish isthmus across its base, but the time thus saved deprives the traveller of trying out the passage from the North Sea to the Baltic.

There is a clear contrast between the monotony of the shores of the Sound and the grandeur of the relief of Gibraltar. The height of the Island of Zealand does not exceed 172 metres and Scania is scarcely higher; in razing the land the Quaternary glaciers prepared it to receive the invasion of the sea. It is different at Gibraltar. On the port side the channel shows us the low banks of Andalusia, overlooked in the distance by stripped sierras, makes us double round the Punta Marroqui, which bears Tarifa, the point closest to Morocco (at a distance of 7.7 kilometres), then, in the very pleasant bay of Algeciras, we come upon the face of the Rock of Gibraltar, a sheer drop of 425 metres into the sea: a sort of 'sphinx of granite, enormous, huge' (Théophile Gautier). The

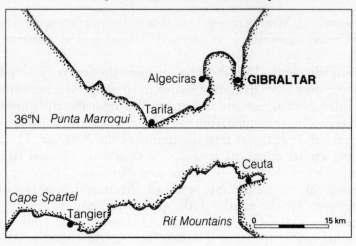

Figure 1.3   The Straits of Gibraltar

harshness of the landscape contrasts with the greenery on the banks of the Sound, and the intense southern light is in sharp contrast to the skies of the Baltic, half-coloured even in clear weather.

From a plane the visual impressions are even sharper; they offer extended panoramas, and a single look grasps the configuration of the straits. At the moment when the plane descends into the quasi-amphibious airport of Copenhagen, the landscape seems indefinite and infinite at the same time: Danish islands, sea arms, the Swedish plain make up a complex and limitless universe. On the contrary, the sharpness of the reliefs and the crudity of the light distinguish in a wide panorama the Iberian mountain chains, the Rock of Gibraltar, the summits overlooking Ceuta, and, in the distance, the crests of the Rif. The confrontation and connection between the two African and European sisters are violently asserted. The sea at least softens the harshness of the image with the charm of its colours. At a low altitude, the gamut of nuances between the Mediterranean and Atlantic waters allow us to perceive, if not the bathymetric levels, at least the differences in depth and the quality of the intermingled waters. What a crossroads! Europe/Africa, the Inland Sea/the Ocean. This site is unique for an understanding of the role of the marine element in the destinies of Europe. The Pillars of Hercules are a fraction of a nautical mile from Trafalgar, just as the castle of Elsinore recalls better than the 'rotten' kingdom haunted by Shakespeare the greatness of the Hanseatic League, the ambitions of Gustavus Adolphus and of Peter the Great and the Anglo-Germanic naval rivalries. History has maintained concrete symbols on both sites. For it was not unintentional that the kingdoms of Denmark on the one hand and England on the other established fiscal control, one over the Sound which lasted half a millennium, and the other a naval surveillance over Gibraltar which has continued for close to three centuries.

If geographical situations through the results they bring about justify a comparison bearing analogies, the conditions for navigation in turn deserve examination. Let us first look at the surface currents. At Gibraltar, on the approximately 32 nautical miles which make up its crossing, the Atlantic waters flow from west to east at a speed of 2 to 3 knots while passing over a current flowing in the opposite direction – a more salty, warmer and heavier one – at a depth of about 100 metres. On the contrary, in the Danish straits the surface current is established from east to west. The explanation for this comes from the contrast in the water balances of the two seas, that of the Mediterranean being deficient because its content of fresh water is less than evaporation, whereas in the Baltic rivers are of considerable importance. However, the rhythm of navigation is regulated by other influences; first, in both cases there is a variation in wind, although Gibraltar sometimes suffers from a lack of wind from the Mediterranean; in the waters of Málaga ships sometimes remained becalmed for days or weeks; in the eighteenth century even large ships were held up for four months. More often, at Gibraltar as well as in the Danish straits, the frequency of fog is particularly dangerous. The danger is thus double: running aground and colliding with other vessels. Navigating in the winter is difficult, sometimes impossible, for several weeks both between the Mediterranean and the Atlantic as well as between the Baltic and the North Sea. However, the winter freeze in the Danish straits is not always an annual occurrence, and its duration is variable. In these conditions security takes on increasing importance, with a rise in the number of ships. This problem is most acute in the Straits of Dover, one of the trouble-spots of world maritime traffic. Recent statistics show the number of ships in transit on that strait from west to east or between the French and English shores to be 91,000, almost double the traffic (57,000) at Gibraltar. In the English Channel the conditions are neither more nor less dangerous than elsewhere; the risks result from the intensity of the traffic, which had to be regulated in the Channel as has been done on the coasts of Brittany with the 'RAIL' system. But between Dover and Cap Gris-Nez the narrowness of the channel, in a passage less than 34 kilometres wide, is aggravated by the presence of shallows around Calais and Dunkirk and often by the violence of the storm waves from the North Sea. A memorable example of the perils thus incurred is that of the Invincible Armada in 1588, but one might also cite many others, such as the famous catastrophes of 1421 and 1953. Thus the rewards have to be high for Europeans to exploit at that very risky level the opportunities offered by the maritime routes joining Gibraltar to the Sound, and England to France.

The full value of a strait is obtained when such passages develop their role as crossroads. But 'crossroads' can also mean a junction or lock. A strait commands a passage. Historically, that which has been said of Denmark, 'the gate-keeper of the Baltic', has also been applied to the English claim to control over Gibraltar, and to Constantinople, 'the entrance to the Black Sea'.

Peninsulas and islands: the first historical figures

For Fernand Braudel, the Mediterranean peninsulas are 'the first historical figures'. They cut the major pieces of the puzzle mentioned above, following a capricious pattern in which bays, deep gulfs and adjacent seas are cast together. Arranged in the directions of the meridians, they act as 'causeways to Africa' (R. Blanchard), opening the way to the high seas, just as they facilitate the penetration of the seas into the heart of the European continent. This is the case with Italy, framed by the Gulf of Genoa and the Adriatic, where the sea creeps into the canals (*canali*) of the Dalmatian archipelago.

A meridian placement offers many opportunities for the sea to advance, for example at the end of the Italian 'boot' between its legendary foot and heel. Elsewhere articulations resembling the human hand predominate, in true grandeur in the Peloponnesus, on a lesser scale in Chalcidicum (three points, five gulfs), and as a simple sketch in the Crimea. Added to this is the multiplication of islands of all sizes, gifts given to the sea or conquered by it following seismic convulsions, volcanic effusions and sometimes coastal silting. The western Mediterranean counts its islands by the unit, but they are generally bigger (the Balearics, Corsica, Sardinia, Sicily); its eastern sister can scarcely count the islands of the Adriatic coast and in the Aegean Sea. Interpenetration thus appears more ordered and rational in the west, and more whimsical in the east.

Having entered less precociously into history, the Atlantic peninsulas play a somewhat analogous role, with an equivalent north–south orientation in the principal cases. The Iberian mass, largely situated from north to south, assures Mediterranean individuality, just as the median position of Jutland and the location of Scandinavia over 16 degrees of latitude preserve the individuality of the Baltic. These 'figures' are not unique. In the heart of the English Channel the Cotentin peninsula alternately imposes its advances and its threats on England. Facing the oceanic high seas, the three Celtic capes – Land's End in Cornwall, the Breton points of French Finistère and Cape Finisterre in Galicia – assert their role as end-points for the procession of peoples towards the setting sun; Alphonse Dupront understood this and described it remarkably in connection with St James of Compostella. But inversely, these promontories, with the islands that precede them – Sein, Ouessant, and Scilly – signal to the navigator coming from the west the approach to a world where the sea makes common cause with the continent.

The Mediterranean seas

The sectoring of European seas is particularly accentuated in the Mediterranean, where the distinction of two basins, the result of the play of continental plates, is obvious. Sicily and its neighbouring islands, occupying its junction, are seated on a deep substratum of only some 100 metres between Trapani and Cap Bon, a mere 20 metres near Malta. To the west of this shelf a distinct zone begins at the exit from Gibraltar with, according to Braudel, the 'Mediter-

ranean Ocean'; in turn the 'Balearic Sea' extends toward Corsica at
a depth of 3420 metres. Shallows join Sardinia to Tunisia, bord-
ering the Tyrrhenian Sea, 3730 metres deep towards the Ponziane
Islands. Areas and distances are, however, not great, since from a
plane flying at high altitude above southern Sardinia you can
simultaneously see the Gulf of Cagliari, make out Sicily and in the
distance follow the mountain chain, snow-capped from the
beginning of autumn, of Calabria, creating a link between Europe
and Africa.

In his *Meteorology*, Aristotle was already surprised at the depths
of the Mediterranean, which were scarcely suspected in his time.
He was unaware of the abysses of more than 4000 metres to the
south of Cape Taínaron; but he was no more insensitive than the
others of his age to the difficulty of the passage between the two
Mediterraneans. Homer had described it; Virgil turned it into
legend: 'To fall from Scylla into Charybdis' can no longer either
shock or frighten us. Seas said to have no tides hold some surprises.
Indeed, a distance of six hours between the Ionian and the
Tyrrhenian Seas for a weak tidal range (20 to 40 centimetres) is
enough to cause every six hours a current of 5 knots, accentuated
by the narrowness of the Strait of Messina (less than 3 kilometres);
the encounter of this current with the coastal counter-currents
causes violent eddies on the rocks of Scylla to the north of Messina.
Although other regions in the world experience phenomena of this
kind, this reminder transmitted through classical culture attests to
the importance of European peoples' ties with the sea.

Beyond this lies the marine environment of the gods and ancient
heroes. Plato put it like this: 'We are gathered around the
Mediterranean like frogs around a swamp.' These words are harsh,
because the philosopher's countrymen were not content simply
with croaking on the shores. The Adriatic, named the Gulf of
Venice in the Middle Ages, not without reason, is indeed as much a
gulf as it is an adjacent sea, and is even more a long sea corridor
(740 km), leading to the foot of the Alpine arch, near the mountain
access to central Europe. The contrast is sharp between the western
banks, quite inhospitable with the exception of Ancona, and the
eastern banks where the sea, behind the many islands arranged like
ramparts, advances into the heart of the Dinaric Alps, sometimes
deeply, at the mouths of Kotor, for example. Improperly called a
canal, Otranto is actually a strait only 65 kilometres wide and 740

metres deep; it commands both access to the Adriatic and the coastal route off the shores of Albania and Greece. A true crossroads, the Strait of Otranto witnesses the confrontation of East and West. On the eastern banks there begins an ancient natural route towards Constantinople, the Via Aegnatia; and it was in these waters that the fate of Europe was decided on several occasions at the battles of Actium (31 BC), Lepanto (1571) and Navarino (1827). Here the sea asserted its role in the destiny of the continent.

Whoever commands the Strait of Otranto has an open path towards the eastern Mediterranean. The canal of Corfu, crossed by a current, offers a sheltered, though longer, route than crossing the Ionian Sea. This route is undoubtedly the most favourable to an advance into western Greece, but whoever feared passing around the Peloponnesus had to wait for the opening of the 6 kilometres of the canal of Corinth, running between high cliffs of white limestone, not completed until between 1882 and 1892, although it had been started in the year 67 under Nero.

Straits

From the Ancients to our time, everything possible has been said about the continental and maritime ambivalence of the Hellenic peninsula. Seen from Europe, with the exception of the inner navigation of the Aegean archipelagos, traffic is dominated by two poles of attraction. One escapes Europe, without leaving it indifferent, for its relationships with the Middle East and beyond Suez are part of its horizons. The other belongs uniquely to Europe, for with two other adjoining seas, Marmara and the Black Sea, it involves certain historical trouble-spots, the Dardanelles and the Bosporus, 'straits' *par excellence*. The convergence of maritime routes towards Istanbul involved all of the Greek islands and caused ships to advance into the countless irregularities of its shores. Today a panorama cannot neglect the Anatolian coasts; without belonging geographically to Europe, they are linked to it by many memories and are currently are under the sovereignty of an associate of Europe. Our work of synthesis has everything to gain there.

'Straits' pose a political and military problem which will be discussed at length below. At present let us focus on geographical givens on a maritime level. Whether they originate in Alexandria, Beirut, Rhodes and Izmir, Thessalonica and Athens after the Strait of Corinth, or directly in the ports of the western Mediterranean, ships travelling to Istanbul pass by Bozca Ada before advancing into the Dardanelles. To the east the entrance to the Bosporus collects ships coming from the European ports of Varna, Constanţa, Odessa, the Crimea and the Sea of Azov, as well as Trabzon in Asia. All of this traffic rushes to both ends of the straits, and the diversity of the flags flown constitutes a complex element of the issue.

To reach the Dardanelles from the Aegean Sea is not without some difficulty, even in our time, and it was even more difficult in the time of sailing ships. In the Aegean Sea the winds are unstable in bad weather. The passage through the 70 kilometres of the Dardanelles carries the risk of the narrowness of the passage (4 kilometres at the entrance and 1,800 metres at the narrowest point); it is dangerous to wander from the channel, which has signals in peacetime (though naturally not in March 1915!), and has an unfavourable current in the direction of the Bosporus, favourable in the opposite direction; in bad weather there are violent squalls (35 to 50 knots) from a northern glacial wind. This is in sharp contrast to the good season, when etesian winds from the Aegean Sea are favourable to navigation.

Conditions are identical on the Sea of Marmara and the sea is sometimes choppy. The difficulty comes from the surface currents, which are, however, less rapid near the Bosporus, and the coastal fog which, even in the summer, presents the risk of running aground. In addition, the navigator must take into account the difference in signal systems between the Dardanelles and the Bosporus: in the Dardanelles Europe is portside, and in the Bosporus it is starboard, for international maritime law, recognizing the legal equality of the Mediterranean and the Black Sea, grants the same status to the European and Asian shores due to their both having fallen for close to five and a half centuries under Ottoman sovereignty. All the same, this principle is limited by the international use of the passage by all nations, notably those living on the Black Sea. There opens up one of the important chapters of Europe's relationship with the sea.

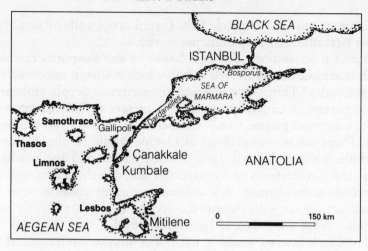

Figure 1.4   The Straits

Moorings in the Sea of Marmara do not offer absolute security, for example near the Asian shores in front of Dolma Balce (the tower of Leander), where ships drag their anchors; the sea floor, covered with wreckage, preserves a wealth of history. Throughout time it has been better to let one's ship be carried by the flow, with the help of a pilot, towards the shelter of the Golden Horn, 7 kilometres deep, for its calm waters offer excellent possibilities of anchoring, in contrast to the two shores. However, the Golden Horn is not an idyllic place to stay all year round. The Ancients testify to this: the expedition of the Argonauts was not a luxury cruise, and more recently Pierre Loti in *Les Désenchantées* denounces the illusion of an eternal springtime and prophesies for winter 'the sinister corridor where there are engulfed, under a leaden sky, all the icy squalls of Russia and all the dangerous currents by which the two seas are joined'. In this crossroads of contrasts the warm season, on the contrary, offers the seductions of luminous seas. There are few visions more beautiful than the spectacle seen from the air during a radiant sunset: the wind blows from the west, and in order to land, the aeroplane has taken up position at the opening of the Bosporus on to the Black Sea. The minarets of Istanbul stand out on the azure sky, framed by the Sea of Marmara and the Thracian hills. Here Europe ends on one of the most beautiful marine panoramas in the world.

But is it an ending? The two banks of the Bosporus resemble each other like the slopes of a valley, which is what it once was. But what a valley! Thirty-two winding kilometres so deeply embanked as to become a canyon from 2.5 kilometers to 550 metres wide before increasing again to 4.7 kilometres as it opens into the Black Sea. There the maritime limits of Europe would be almost imperceptible without the wild grandeur of nature and the works of men, the fortifications of the past, and that of a short time ago, the intercontinental bridge. The discharge current coming from the Black Sea carries with its impetuosity the cold of its slightly salty waters – what a contrast to the Dardanelles!

The Black Sea is a world in itself. The southern terminus of the marine belt of Europe, it seemed quite far away to the Ancients. The melancholy of Ovid, in exile on its shores, joins the sombre evocations of the Pontic cold for Herodotus; though it is true that the enthusiasm of Xenophon's soldiers at the comforting sight of the familiar sea somewhat balances those pessimistic impressions. The opening of the Bosporus into the Black Sea demands no less caution than does its opposite end, even using contemporary nautical instructions, and the European shores are rarely welcoming, except in the estuaries. The European seas end to the north-east of the harbour of Crimea, in an annexe whose hydrological balance is even more positive; the Sea of Azov, abundantly fed by the Don, has a minimum depth of 14.5 metres at its centre, and its communication with the Black Sea, the Strait of Kerch (the Cimmerian Bosporus), is only a gully 130 metres wide and 7.3 metres deep at most. Thus closes the long maritime belt which runs from Gibraltar to the first slopes of the Caucasus.

Northern seas and southern seas

In the South as in the North, Europe is thus surrounded by roughly symmetrical seas arranged in a circular arc. The Mediterranean arc runs from 6.5° W to 41° E (including the Black Sea) and spreads from 31° N to 47° N (the Sea of Azov). The Baltic arc climbs in latitude to 54° N, not far from the polar circle, and covers 19° in longitude (from 11° to 30° E). In the eleventh century Adam

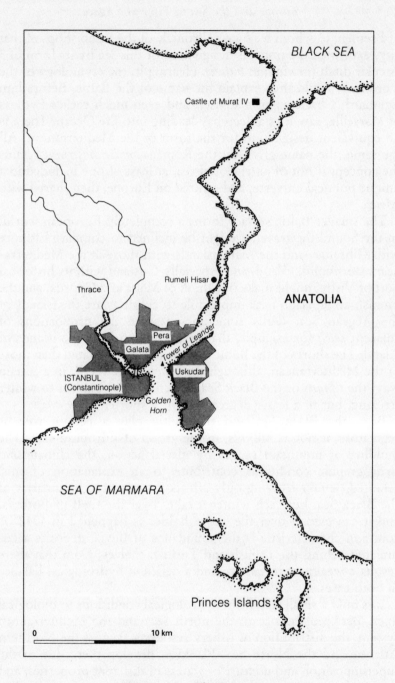

Figure 1.5　The Bosporus

of Bremen, to whom we owe a chronicle of the archbishops of that
city, explained the popular designation of this sea by its form of a
circular ditch (*in modum baltei*). Hearing it, the etymology of the
word *belt* would thus explain the name of the Baltic. Before him
Eginhard, Charlemagne's adviser, and even much earlier Pytheas
of Marseille, saw it as a deep bay leading into the Ocean. There is
no equivalent designation for the form of the Mediterranean. All
the same, the name given by the Romans, *mare nostrum*, retains
the concept if not of an enclosed sea, at least of one included in a
unique political universe, and centred on Europe, then shared with
Africa.

The smaller Baltic surface forms a completely European world.
In the Sound the traveller might be inclined to compare Elsinore
with Gibraltar, and the Baltic islands with those in the Mediterranean. Bornholm, Öland, and especially Gotland with its historical
port of Visby, might make one think of Malta and Cyprus; and the
Finnish archipelago is as impossible to count as are the islands of
the Aegean Sea. Gulfs sometimes assume the proportions of
adjacent seas: for example, that of Bothnia, behind the islands of
Aland. The shores of the Baltic are much less articulated than those
of the Mediterranean, although the *hafen* there recall, in a certain
way, the *limans* of the Black Sea, which are also subject to winter
freezing, but to a lesser degree and for a shorter time.

Both the Black Sea and the Baltic play a certain role as
regulators, if not as killjoys, in the group of European seas. The
building of mountain ranges by glacial action, the climate and
hydrographic conditions contribute to an explanation of this.
Granted, winter freezing only affects the northern boundaries of
the Black Sea, but each winter it takes over the Gulf of Bothnia,
and it can extend over the entire Baltic, as happened in 1942. A
common characteristic is the abundance of fluvial deposits accu-
mulated behind the Danish and Turkish shelves; from that there
results a weakness in salinity and a deficient hydrological balance
in both cases.

It is only a small step from hydrological conditions to biological
ones. Between the ocean, the north seas and the Mediterranean
system, the distribution of fishery resources favours the Northern
Atlantic and the North Sea. Plankton develop there due to the
superimposition and mixture of waters of different properties, and
follow the upstream course of the North Atlantic Current. The

diversity of species is great and their migrations encourage fishing from the Danish straits as far as the Irish Sea. In the Mediterranean, although there are fewer fish, fishing is most successful where the continental shelf is not so deep.

There are other resources, less equally offered by the European waters, that is, mineral products. First there is salt, indispensable to human beings and animals, as well as for preserving food, and in our time for chemical industries, which is available in proportion to its content in sea water. The need for it has encouraged all types of processes for exploiting it: solar evaporation in the summer wherever it is in abundance (the Mediterranean and Atlantic shores), treatment through boiling sea water on the northern shores. Present everywhere, sea salt is one of the elements of Europe's relationship with the sea. Unlike salt, which has been exploited since the most ancient of times, oil has been found and drilled from the sedimentary depths of the North Sea between England and Norway within only the last few decades.

Thus the marine inheritance of Europe, however unequally distributed it may be, exists and demands a concerted exploitation on the part of its European and non-European beneficiaries.

The unequal distribution of maritime resources according to the arrangement of the ocean floor and the outline of coasts illustrates natural complementarity and solidarity, which the comparative lengths of the shores of European countries brings to light. There are close on 68,000 kilometres of European coastline, to which are added 10,000 kilometres on the arctic shores of Russia. In the forefront are Norway (20,000 km), Greece (13,575 km), Sweden (7624 km), Italy (7458 km), Denmark (7438 km), France (5400 km), and Spain and Portugal (4359 km). Even from this partial list we see a slight predominance in northern Europe. We must also take into account the importance of the peninsulas, especially for Scandinavia, Italy, the western part of the Balkan peninsula and Greece; the sometimes profound indentations of the rocky coasts, particularly on the Atlantic face; and the considerable number of islands of all sizes born of orogenic movements and shaped through erosion. As for the coastal topography, it contributes to the placement of ports and to their development. Finally, the outline of the shores has a considerable influence on the interpenetration of marine waters and land masses, of maritime societies and terrestrial milieux.

Returning to the statement that in Europe few regions of the continent are very far from a coast, we observe that between the two large maritime sectors of the North and the South, the peripherical link assured by the ocean is seconded by isthmic connections arranged by man with unequal facility. Early on he dreamed of creating such links, either by using natural passages, or by constructing junctions. Certain projects which were conceived in Antiquity (the Isthmus of Suez and Corinth) and the Middle Ages (Kiel) were not accomplished until more recent times. There exists a double French isthmus, one in Aquitaine and the other between the estuary of the Seine and the delta of the Rhône; similarly an isthmus connects the North Sea to the Adriatic or to the Black Sea through central Europe by the Danube; and plans have been made for a highway from the Baltic to the Black Sea. A map representing the initiatives accomplished or planned would express better than long exposés the solidarity of the maritime sectors of a continental Europe, which in reality is rather small. Let us widen our perspective. The progress of contemporary technology is joining ancient experiences. Suez, Corinth and Kiel are not just the realizations of ancient projects. A junction between the Gulf of Finland and the estuaries of the Black Sea is being planned. The Russian isthmus thus ceasing to be a pipe dream, the Varangian boatmen of the High Middle Ages will appear as unique precursors.

Thus between the North Sea and those in the South, the silhouette of Europe has been refined throughout the centuries and its maritime environment seems more significant. The positioning of the puzzle pieces becomes delicate, but necessary. To say this is not to plead in favour of a particular European maritime imperialism. But we can hope that in organizing the puzzle the presence and the influence of the sea will not be forgotten, nor even minimized. It is true that history, with some exceptions, appears to have neglected the seas and has been more interested in the sedentary working of the fields and in the victorious clanging of boots. Its view has favoured the frayed territory where peoples have flowed and scurried. Of the many explanations for this one of the most plausible is the mutual misunderstanding experienced over centuries by the two maritime faces of Europe. Two words sum up the ancientness and the depth of this double image: the

Levant and the Ponant; their consonance is particularly vivid in the speech of the Latin countries, French and Spanish, endowed with both a Mediterranean side and an opening into the Atlantic.

2

Mediterranean Primacy – from Athens to the Italian Towns

Avatars of an image: two distinct universes

Until the High Middle Ages, that is, towards the end of the thirteenth century, the two maritime regions of Europe often turned their backs on each other. The people lived their own lives within a rather closed circle, and the men of the sea, speaking different languages, conceiving the world in their own fashion, were unaware of each other. The image of Europe as seen from the sea thus resembles a cracked, though not broken, mirror.

The birth of Europa on the Phoenician shores before her flight to Crete on the back of a winged bull is symbolic. Another symbol is the awakening of the continent to maritime life thanks to the fleets of her heir, King Minos, whom, according to Thucydides, the Hellenes regarded as their model. The European role of the Mediterranean since antiquity has been discussed at length by Victor Bérard and Albert Thibaudet. Jacqueline de Romilly has taken up the theme as it relates to Thucydides. Maurice Lombard has formulated rich hypotheses on the mediating role of the inland sea. Hélène Ahrweiler, Jean Rougé and Michel Reddé have devoted now classic works to ancient Mediterranean navies. And Fernand Braudel has left definitive writings on the Mediterranean. Let us limit ourselves to looking alternatively at the southern shores of Europe and out to sea in an attempt, while limiting our ambitions, to discern a few historical areas of interest in the relationship between Europe and the Mediterranean.

The attraction of the sun

The attraction of the sun-bathed shores for the peoples of the
North reaches back for many centuries. The contemporary fashion
for Mediterranean cruises is a distant heir to the voyages of
northerners towards the sun. Among the many reasons for this, we
can cite the successive movements of peoples. Having come in
successive waves, the Hellenes did not all adopt a maritime life, but
piracy and the raids of the 'peoples of the sea' left sinister
memories. The long, streamlined and decked ships of the Myce-
naeans replaced the large, heavy boats of the Cretans and enabled a
rapid expansion on the one hand as far as the Tyrrhenian Sea and
on the other as far as the Black Sea: in this we recognize Ulysses'
Odyssey and the expedition of the Argonauts, the first European
maritime epics. The great invasions of the end of the Roman world
were followed by the successive waves of Germanic peoples in
quest of the sea. Although they did not all reach it (the Franks did
not), some, such as the Goths, settled around the western Mediterranean, whereas a third group, the Vandals, succeeded in circling it
and settling in Africa.

Thus a movement towards the South took place concurrently
with one to the west, through an orientation born of circumstances
and the welcoming reputation of the Mediterranean civilizations.
The Black Sea was equally attractive: remember the descent of the
Varangians on the Russian rivers as far as Constantinople, where
the *basileus* took advantage of their vigour by recruiting a guard
from among them. In the ninth century, too, the western Mediterranean received a visit from the Vikings. These episodes resemble
the flights of birds, precursors of migrations. Those occurred later
under the same impulse, exercised by an attraction of living better
and of becoming rich. There was the descent of the Normans of
Cotentin, companions of Tancred of Hauteville and of the Guis-
cards, the founders of the kingdom of Sicily at the time when their
countryman William was conquering England. Heirs of the Normans of Sicily, the Hohenstaufens led those Germans who were
attracted to the warmth of the Mediterranean sky to the southern-
most end of Italy. The name of Emperor Frederick II in the
thirteenth century in itself sums up the acclimatization of Germanic peoples to the seductions of the south. Most of the newcomers
never sought to return to the cold and damp regions they had come

from. In fact, won over by the Mediterranean environment, they dreamed of pushing their conquests beyond the sea in the direction of Byzantium. Moreover, added to the attraction of the Mediterranean was the participation of northern Europeans in the Crusades at the cost of a long crossing, in the twelfth century, for example.

The town is born and grows on the Mediterranean shores

The settlements on the Mediterranean shores established a number of future points of contact between Europe and the inland sea. Ports were established on it and between them there developed ties of dependency or other relationships at the same time as urban life began to grow. One must risk some anachronisms in making connections that defy distances and centuries. A map of ports swarming with Greek towns on the European coastal fringe can be compared to other maps showing Genoese and Venetian dependencies in the fourteenth century. The coincidence of many places is verified by archaeology and historical texts. Ancient toponymy sometimes survives in current names; the case is clear for the coasts of the Peloponnesus, in Corfu, in Magna Graecia, in Sicily and in the island ports on the route to the Bosporus, for example at Thasos and on the shores of the Euxeinos Pontos. The Genoese and the Venetians occupied sites once chosen by the Greeks on the western coasts of the Black Sea and Crimea; on the way, Byzantium preceded Constantinople. The Adriatic, long neglected due to the preferred direct route through the Strait of Otranto, later saw the same animation awaken Ragusa and the Illyrian ports before reaching Aquileia, and found Venice at the deepest point of the sea's advancement into the continent, at the opening of the Alpine valleys. Similarly, way back on the Tyrrhenian Sea, Genoa sprang up at the foot of the mountain wall, at the junction of the continent and the peninsula. To the west the banner had come directly to meet Gaul on the sites of Marseille and Arles, as it met Iberia on the banks of the future Catalonia and the Spanish Levant. There is no need to insist in order to recognize continuities.

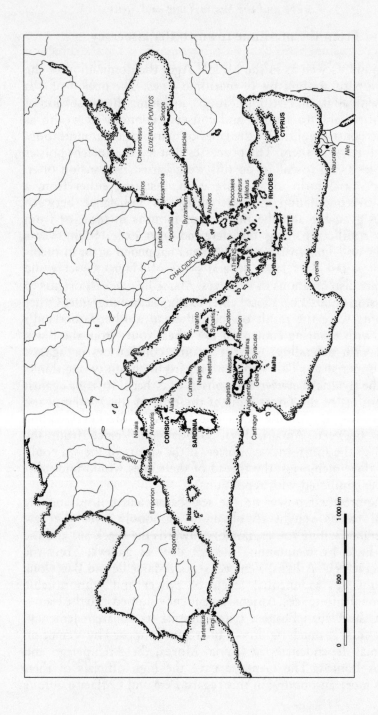

Figure 2.1 The Mediterranean in Hellenic times

From the maritime town to thalassocracy

In Antiquity as well as in the Middle Ages the domination of the
sea was a natural objective of maritime cities. The notion of 'sea
power' with all its diverse implications, including the possession of
a naval force able to acquire and conserve commercial wealth as
well as to control politically the lanes of maritime communication,
was not foreign to them. The processes that led the ancient polises
and the medieval towns to do this were varied. Expansion often
took the initial form of an emigration, resulting either from a
relative overpopulation engendered by an imbalance between
resources available and the number of mouths to feed, or from
partisan conflicts forcing the defeated into exile. Such events
involving well-known figures in Athens happened again in medieval Genoa and Barcelona. Several ports of Magna Graecia and
Sicily were also creations of fugitives. Marseille owes its origins to
a concession granted by a local chief to Phocaean emigrants. Other
settlements were the result of the Athenian mother/fatherland's
concern with ensuring control of the wheat route from the Black
Sea and with defending it either against competitors or against
Persian imperialism. This said, with regard to antiquity one thinks
first of the rivalries between the polises, of Athens' struggle against
the ambitions of the Great King at the time of the Median wars.
Similarly, for the Middle Ages one thinks of the never-ending
conflicts between Amalfi, Pisa, Genoa and Venice from the
eleventh to the fourteenth centuries. If the spirits of the sea could
recount their memories, the thread of their tales would undoubtedly be encumbered with repetitions.

To acquire their power on the sea the ancient polises and the
medieval towns sought to obtain a monopoly over the few
long-distance sailing routes, notably towards the Black Sea and the
Middle East, by maintaining a large fleet of galleys. Thus the
thalassocracies of Athens, Venice, Genoa, Marseille and Barcelona
were built up, at unequal levels of power and with notable
institutional differences. Athens' ascendency slipped into the framework of the Delian League. Later, despite its apparent leniency,
there was just as much rigidity in the regime imposed by Venice on
its colonial dependencies in Illyria, Morea, the Archipelago and
Euxeinos Pontos. The Genoese gave the high officials of their
agencies more autonomy; in this regard Péra and Caffa are unique

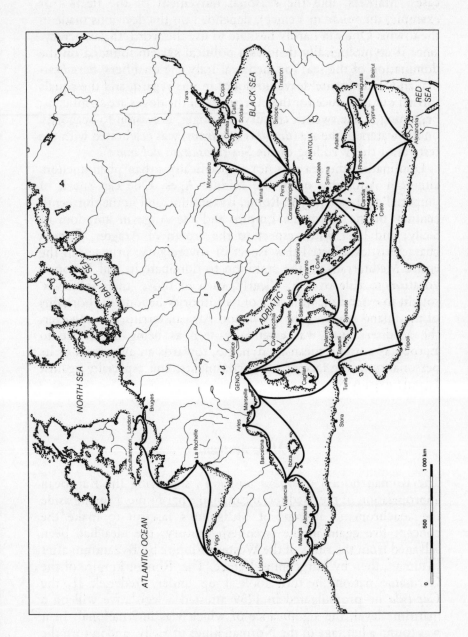

Figure 2.2 Genoese maritime expansion

cases. Markets, like the seasonal movement of the fleets (for example, the *mude* in Venice), depended on the decisions made in the towns. One can hardly hesitate to use the word 'thalassocracy' since it etymologically denotes a political system founded on the domination of the sea; for medieval Italy the qualifiers 'Serenissima' and 'Dominante' leave no doubt in this regard, and the rituals carried out in Venice for the investiture of the doges are significant: beginning in the twelfth century the doges' accession to authority on the waters of the sea (*dignitas aquarum*) was celebrated with the festival of the Wedding of the Sea (*sposalizio del mare*).

Dominating the sea was not a specifically urban phenomenon, either in Antiquity or in the Middle Ages. One can speak of 'imperial' thalassocracy in Rome, Byzantium, and in the thirteenth century in the Germanic Empire and the Angevin kingdom of Sicily, and later with respect to the crown of Aragon. Certain characteristics affected this aspect of sovereignty: primacy in the entire Mediterranean, the ambition to dominate it, and Europe's vocation to rule over it. Clearly, each of those 'thalassocracies' sought to extend the influence of its authority beyond the horizons of the inland sea over the Asian and African territories; however, the Mediterranean was essentially seen as being of service to Europe as a useful means, a dynamo, towards an awareness of its personality in the face of other continents, and especially against Islamic expansion.

'Mare nostrum'

The Roman notion of *'mare nostrum'*, signifying the European appropriation of the Mediterranean, had a hard time. Leaving aside the anachronistic attempt of Mussolini's fascism to make the concept live again in the twentieth century, the idea had been salvaged from the ruins of the Western Empire by Byzantium after Justinian, then by burgeoning Venice. The 'Roman Empire of the Germanic nation' in turn took it up under Frederick II; the *Capitula* he promulgated in 1239 attested a legislative will on a maritime level, the significance of which was international. In it was found a heritage of the Norman kings of Sicily; and in turn the Mediterranean ambitions of Charles of Anjou in the thirteenth century and of the Aragonese Alfonso the Magnanimous in the fifteenth century were similarly inspired by such precedents.

'*Mare nostrum*': that arrogant, but legitimate, formula which we attribute to the Romans finds its original justification in their victory over Carthage. The ruin of the Punic capital resulted in placing the Mediterranean under European rule. The maritime power of any polis or kingdom of Africa or Asia was finished as one by one Carthage and Syria were defeated. And yet the Romans, not being a nation of mariners, had to improvise their naval forces through borrowings and imitations and had to be apprenticed in navigation. The example of the fleets of the Hellenes, their allies, gave them experience; the struggle against the endemic scourge of piracy was a hard school in which Pompey had the opportunity to comb the eastern Mediterranean and put Roman naval superiority to the test. From this came the double commercial and military aspect of Roman 'sea power', based first on the disposition, studied by Michel Reddé, of a military navy divided into regional fleets, then on the organization of commercial transports, described by Jean Rougé, which advanced convoys of *annona* from Alexandria and Carthage towards Ostia, Aquileia and Thessalonica. Europe was thus the principal opening for this traffic. This European supremacy contributed to the engendering of a maritime imbalance at the time of the invasions.

Byzantium recovered its sea power in the Mediterranean with the help of the Justinian reconquest, but it was incomplete and temporary. The organization of 'themes' enabled it to arrange its naval forces in sectors and thus to confront piracy. It could not, however, prevent the nibbling away of its bases on the one hand by the Normans in southern Italy and Sicily, and on the other by the Arabs in the Aegean Sea, any more than it could stand up to the competition of the Italian towns. Venice was the great beneficiary of the fall of Constantinople in 1204, but sixty years later Michael VIII Palaeologus was able, by recovering his crown, to inaugurate the final naval efforts of the Byzantine Empire before the Turkish conquest in 1453.

The Mediterranean, lungs and breast of ancient and medieval Europe

The Europe/Mediterranean dialogue continued until the end of the Middle Ages, and perhaps even beyond, under conditions which were rather similar to those in ancient times. As in a human organism, the inland sea played the regulating role of a lung; the air from the Orient brought the breath of the mind and maritime activity sustained the nutritional function of circulation.

Almost all intellectual and spiritual movements originated in the Mediterranean. Jacqueline de Romilly has shown what the ideal of public and individual freedom owes to Greece and how, in particular, the victory at Salamis over the Persians preserves a symbolic value. This work is the most recent example of the philosophical and scientific enrichment received by Europe from its Mediterranean margins. Without them, what would our classical culture be?

It was thanks to its maritime relationships that Roman society was initiated into oriental cults and mysteries. It was at the cost of torturing sea voyages that Paul brought Christianity into Italy. Following his example, oriental monasticism came by sea to the shores of Provence, and the name of St Honoratus given to a monastery on the Island of Lérins preserves the memory of it. In the opposite direction, the practice of pilgrimage to the Holy Land of Palestine was established in the West as a return to origins, at first on an individual level which lasted for more than half a millennium: the voyage of the Spanish nun Etheria in the fourth century is one of the most ancient examples. The Crusades themselves were initially an extraordinary collective pilgrimage of piety and penitence, which, despite deviations, remained such for a large number of people. The expression 'overseas journey' by which it remained known was full of meaning: heavy with devotion, of course, heavy with renunciation, heavy also with all the anxiety inspired by the difficulties and the length of the voyage on a feared element – the sea; who could be assured of his return? And yet the Mediterranean was a means to salvation.

It was not so only for Christians, who, granted, were in the majority in Europe, for the dispute of 1054 became a break only in 1204, when the Latin races laid hands on Constantinople. Western Jews, who were numerous in Spain, Provence and central Europe, did not forget their native Palestine beyond the sea. Islam too achieved much of its expansion through the maritime route to Sicily, the Balearic Islands, as well as that from Morocco towards Andalusia, thanks to the shortness of the passage.

As for the material interdependence of Europe and the Mediterranean in the realm of trade, in order to describe it, it would be necessary to recall the entire history of the ports, to consider its nature, volume and procedures, and to follow the distribution of products. One book would be hardly sufficient to do this. The important thing is less to calculate the amount of traffic (impossible to evaluate with exactitude) than to estimate its frequency, and above all to determine the nature of the exchanges and the points where the sea and the continent met up.

The Mediterranean shores expected to receive their sustenance primarily from the sea. First and foremost, beginning in antiquity, was the grain which the Greek ships, principally Athenian, loaded in the ports of Euxeinos Pontos; it is known that Hellenic survival and freedom depended upon maintaining that line of communication. The Romans likewise knew the same imperative. They were naturally forced into it through the demographic growth of their city, and out of necessity; but not through atavism. While explaining the origins of the port, Ostia, destined to become the most important in Roman Italy, Jöel Le Gall notes that the descendants of Aeneas having lost their ancestors' desire to travel, maritime life came rather to seek them out by way of the Tiber, in the form of the Greeks in the fourth century. The students surpassed their masters, and maritime wheat traffic became an institution supported by Africa. Along with wheat traffic that of wine, described by A. Tchernia, was quite active in all the ports of the European coast. There were also oil and salt, harvested wherever the mountains gave way to coastal swamps. The rare, and as such, expensive, commodities which came from the Orient should not be forgotten: 'spices', and especially perfumes. As well as a geographer like Strabo, the anonymous fourth-century author of the *Expositio totius mundi et gentium* made a list of the articles that Europe received from the Mediterranean. However, in it the intense activity of earlier times is not apparent.

Muslim expansion, despite what Henri Pirenne says about it, did not cause much change. It did not, whatever Pirenne thinks, prevent every 'plank' from sailing on the Mediterranean. Arles'

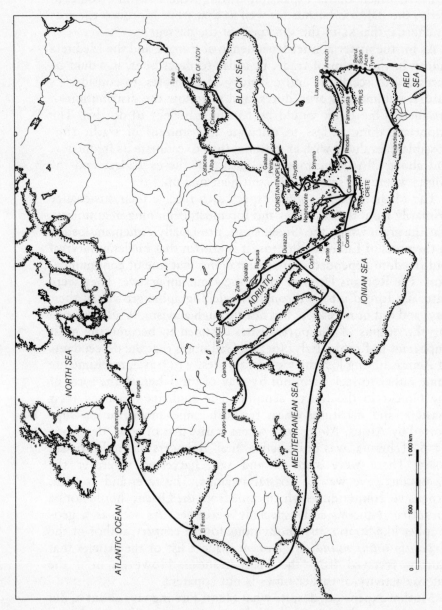

Figure 2.3 Venetian ports of call

function as a harbour in the ninth century merited a glowing description by Theodulf, the archbishop of Lyon. At the beginning of its rise, Venice enjoyed an even greater range of influence than did Arles. The latter supplied the regions of the Rhône, particularly Lyon. But Venice's relationships already extended as far as southern Germany through the alpine valleys, as well as on the shores of Illyria. Maurice Lombard has shown that the Mediterranean ports received the range of wood indispensable to naval construction from the interior, as well as metal, ferrous or not, and wool and linen cloth to exchange in the Orient for silk. The interdependence of the continent and the sea early on set the stage for a promising development.

By the end of the thirteenth century this development of Mediterranean exchanges within a European framework reached beyond the limits of the Mediterranean. It was a political, military and economic necessity, as much as the fruit of intellectual and religious influences and the manifestation of a geographical curiosity. In the distance the horizons beyond Alexandria surrounded the extra-European relationships of Antiquity with a mysterious halo. The shimmering of gold and gemstones blended there with the liturgical perfume of incense. The Hellenistic world transmitted these memories, and the gifts of the caliph Haroun al Rashid to the Frankish emperor sustained and prolonged such dreams.

As to dreams, the mists of the North were in no way inferior to the emanations of the Red Sea and the Indian Ocean. In fact, certainties are few. By land routes from time to time there arrived in Constantinople, Venice or Arles an organic fossil material, a sort of resin, amber, collected on the beaches and commercialized by barbarian merchants who had transported it from the shores of the Baltic through Poland, Bohemia and Styria. This was the continental route taken by amber, which a Roman knight was ordered by Nero to explore. Amber was not the only import received by the Mediterraneans via continental Europe; there were also honey and wax, furs, notably from beavers, and there was also a quite active slave trade. Coins, pottery and bronzes of Roman manufacture attest to such trafficking in the archaeological sites of Central Europe.

Herodotus was already writing that, like amber, tin 'came from the end of the world'. The technique of making bronze from an alloy of copper and tin resulted in tin-mining in ancient lands. It was found in the Celtic lands of Galicia and Armorica and in Cornwall. The Romans learned of it from the Phoenicians and, following in their tracks, pursued it by the land routes and also by sea as far as the Scilly Islands (the mythological Cassiterides) and to the tip of the Vilaine, aptly named Penestin. Such was, most probably, along with obtaining amber and tin, the object of the mission Alexander was believed to have given to Pytheas of Marseille. This exploration went as far as the British coasts and the North Sea, perhaps as far as the latitude of Bergen. This episode, before its time and without an immediate future, constituted a precedent. We know how Caesar waged a campaign on the coasts of Armorica against the Veneti, and crossed the English Channel; that Drusus, around 4–6 AD, led a squadron as far as Jutland (the promontory of the Cimbri); and that the Empire maintained a fleet on the English Channel. These were the most ancient northern undertakings of Mediterraneans beyond their familiar southern waters. The example was not to be unique, nor the experience lost. Before 700, bishop Arculf, returning from the Orient, embarked from Sicily for England and Ireland. Another landmark occurred at the beginning of the twelfth century, when archbishop Gelmirez of Santiago summoned a Genoese and a Pisan to Galicia to construct two boats to be used in the fight against the Saracens.

However, in customary fashion, the Mediterraneans preferred to stay near their inland sea and left to the mariners of the ocean and the Nordic seas the task of sailing on their own. But in the second half of the thirteenth century the distribution of tasks between the two sectors began to evolve, as initiatives corresponded to a significant change in the image of the world.

A Mediterranean invention and invitation: the portolan chart

Abruptly, at the end of the thirteenth century, the cartographic image changed and an innovation appeared in the western Mediterranean, in Italy, on the shores of the Gulf of Genoa. Until then cartographic tradition had been a global representation reflecting a conceptual, even a theological, notion of the terrestrial universe. The Mediterranean held a central place on those maps, corresponding to its role as the source of the diffusion of the Gospels. Europe was favoured, although represented rather awkwardly, with improbable disproportions. The most perfect of these *mappae mundi*, dating from around 1240, was preserved at Ebstorf in Germany before its destruction in an air raid; luckily excellent reproductions of it have survived. The cartographer had done his best in an attempt to reconcile the traditional schema with a concern with curiosity and a faithfulness to concrete detail. The different parts of Europe are in their approximate places, but their forms are somewhat whimsical.

Everything changed in just half a century. The famous *carta Pisana*, conserved in the Bibliothèque Nationale in Paris, is based on a completely different schema. It was the work of a Genoese cartographer of around 1296–1300; its name comes from the fact that it was bought by an old family from Pisa. Drawn by quill pen on vellum, it represents, despite its bad state of conservation, the Mediterranean basin from the Black Sea to the Atlantic, and Western Europe. Its originality lies in its mode of construction: it is based on a precise knowledge of the shores. The Mediterranean people had acquired such knowledge in determining the position of ports, with the help of the results of calculations obtained through Arab-Judeo-Christian science, perfected since the twelfth century and particularly in the thirteenth century in the *Tablas Alfonsíes* (planetary tables) which took their name from Alfonso X, 'the Wise', king of Castile. Moreover, there was the use of the magnetic needle, noted in the twelfth century and widespread in the thirteenth thanks to the invention (attributed to Gioia d' Amalfi) of the little box (*bossola*) destined to contain it; thus the compass made it possible to specify and verify the position of ports. Indeed, Italian navigators commonly used books indicating the location and the description of ports, which for that reason were called *portolani*, portolano books. This information was represented graphically on portolan charts, more simply called portolanos.

The technique, which seems to have been invented in Italian maritime milieux, consisted of inscribing the names of ports in red and black depending on their importance, taking into account their known distances and directions, on a parchment on which a grid of lines was drawn, forming stars according to the direction of the winds and the cardinal points, in tangential circles and divided into compass points.

Such as it is, the *Pisana* gives proof of Mediterranean advancement. Give or take a few years, its date corresponds to the first Genoese and Venetian convoys in Flanders. This 'first' cartography is thus contemporary with the 'first' nautical sea charts. The indications it contains are symptomatic. Without any doubt, they come from first-hand information, exact for the Mediterranean, less precise from Gibraltar to Bruges, and hazy for the southern English coast, which is scarcely recognizable. But that was of little importance, for a step forward had been taken.

The progress of cartographic techniques was filled with as yet unimagined, but real, possibilities. Granted, the portolano contained neither a system of projection nor geographical coordinates. But the *Pisana* was oriented towards magnetic north, and, on first glance it seems that the extension of the Mediterranean in longitude is rectified to almost 1° of its true dimensions. Above all, the hope for the future was that the system of compass cards, inscribed in a group of tangential circles (two for the two Mediterranean sectors), would lend itself to an indefinite possibility of step-by-step representations.

To conclude: the Mediterranean mariners first set an example, then proposed an encounter with their colleagues in the North; then the gift of new cartographic techniques which could be extended to the entire earth could appear as a premonition of European mastery of the universe of the sea.

3

The Ocean Enters the Stage
(Eleventh to Fourteenth Centuries)

The curtain slowly rises

The 'obscure mist of the icy Ocean where the eye could scarcely see anything': this statement by Adam of Bremen in the eleventh century introduces the account of a voyage on the North Atlantic. A cultivated man (he was a canon), the author blended remembrance of the dark and the wind which ruled over the primitive waters (Genesis I:2) with the Virgilian reminiscences of the *Aeneid*. But this man was one of the rare informed and credible travellers of his time; his history of the archbishops of his town appears as an account of their apostolic efforts among the Nordic peoples. At that moment, Venice, the heir of Byzantium, Rome and Greece, was beginning its expansion by competing with Genoa and Amalfi. A lag in their relationships with continental Europe continued to contrast the Mediterranean and the northern seas, the light of subtropical latitudes with the subarctic mists.

Those mists dissipated only slowly. Until the eleventh century the successive waves of peoples coming from the east contributed to hiding the horizons of a disturbing world. Legends and myths were to survive until the age of the Great Discoveries and even in the dreams of Romanticism. It is enough to believe that Europe at first only touched the ocean with the tips of its fingers: a concept more apparent than real of a hand touching the South on one side, and on the other stroking the North, resting its palm on the shores of the West.

In Adam of Bremen's time mysteries were no longer as thick as they had been in earlier centuries, or at least what they hid was progressively unveiled. A few routes went across the ocean. Where did they lead? Who travelled them? Whom did they connect, and whom did they separate? The universe of the Atlantic Ocean has successively and cumulatively presented a field of dreams, of confrontations, a realm open to profit and power. Through these stages Europe became aware of its Nordic seas and took possession of them.

A field of dreams

In the beginning was the dream. But for those living at the beginning of time, what later was regarded as dream might well have appeared as reality. In the concrete human and mental representations of the medieval imaginary of Nordic worlds, the sea holds an important place. Maritime references to Celtic, Scandinavian and Germanic mythologies reflect a close connection with the sea, which in subject matter was in no way inferior to their Mediterranean equivalents, though perhaps with a harsher note. Thus among the Scandinavians, Njord, the god of the seas, did not like the howling of the wolves in the mountains; but his wife, Skadi, the giant of the hills, could not bear the cries of the sea birds and could not sleep on the water; as a result of this conflict the couple broke up. Is there any better example of the internal conflicts of a society where an instinctive loathing of the dangers of the sea clash with the attraction of adventure? Another legend, this time in the Icelandic *Edda*, evokes the origin of life through the giant Ymir; the earth is his body, but his blood is the sea; however, as a child Ymir was nursed by the cow, Audhumla. The response to the passage from the parsimonious earth to the sea full of promise was a return to the generative soil, symbolized in traditional pottery on the Isle of Man and in the Shetlands. There, during the twelfth night of each year a viking ship is solemnly burned. Such remnants of tradition prove the deep-rootedness of certain notions more profoundly than their fashionable resurgence in the nineteenth and twentieth centuries among writers, artists and politicians, in the quest for the deep sources of the Germanic soul. In 1799 the University of Copenhagen held a competition on the theme of the advantages of Scandinavian mythology over the classics. The sentimental yearning for the past honoured once more the legend of Ossian.

The fashion for Germanic and Scandinavian traditions for a long time supplanted the memory of Celtic folklore, whose personality is vigorous, at least in a maritime context. The most famous example is the legend of St Brendan. In the sixth century the Irish hermit was believed to have sailed on the ocean from island to island – for three months according to some, and for seven years according to others – with seventeen mariners on a circular boat made out of skins stretched over a frame of light wood, without a rudder. In the course of their quest for the 'Promised Land of the Saints', they experienced extraordinary adventures, such as running aground on Easter morning on the back of a whale they thought was an island, and which began to move during the celebration of mass. The legend, enriched from one generation to the next, survived to the Age of Discoveries, to the point of being portrayed in the cartography of the Turk Piri Re'is, who was inspired by a Genoese model. The elements of a European maritime tradition were blended here: a primitive embarkation, a hazardous sea journey, the quest for a new and ideal world: a pagan thread Christianized.

At the heart of the legend lay the universal myth of the island, 'the great figure of human fancy' (Jacques Le Goff) – a closed, mysterious world where fiction engendered the projection of an ideal existence. The concept of the island invokes distant shores, earlier than the inhabited earth (*extra orbem*), new worlds (*alterae orbes*) beyond the mists of the immense sea. In the course of its first millennium Western Christendom transposed from the shores of Anatolia towards those of the Great North the cave of the Seven Sleepers of Ephesus, old men whose bodies and clothes were not, for time immemorial, subject to the corruption of the tomb. This transfer from East to West expresses the myth of a Nordic hibernation, the reflection of eternity; elsewhere, and later, beyond the silence of the peninsular extremities, the island myth projected onto the Islands of the Blessed and the 'Island of Brazil' the yearning for a new terrestrial paradise. Patrick Gautier-Dalché bases upon ancient Anglo-Saxon and Carolingian texts the hypothesis that the unknown of the *ultimae fines* was, in the beginning, indispensable to the psychology of the inhabitants of Europe. He is undoubtedly right to raise the issue, for some men were already wondering about the connection of the lands 'lost' in the 'immense mists' to their own world. Later, in the court of Charlemagne, Alcuin, himself an Anglo-Saxon Christian, sensed the difference between the pagan heritage of the island-dwellers from the North and the Romano-Christian culture of those living on the continent: 'What connection', he wrote, 'can Ingeld [the hero of a Germanic tribe] have with Christ?' However, the greatest Anglo-Saxon poem, *Beowulf*, shows up no differences between them and their continental cousins, the Danes and the Saxons. As for them, Dicuil and Johannes Scotus Erigena did not consider the distant islands of the West as being outside their world. It is true that Dicuil had come from Ireland with Charlemagne, that having travelled as far as the Faeroe Islands he mentions the land of the midnight sun, Thule, and that he left us his *De mensura orbis terrae*. As for Johannes Scotus Erigena, who was also Irish, he sang the praises of the sea; in his eyes, far from being a perfidious element, it attracted him: 'It is there', he said, 'that reason can show all that it is capable of.' This attitude was unique, inspired perhaps by some cliché. The Celtic tradition, passed on through Ireland, contaminated by the Anglo-Saxons, must have exercised some influence. Talking with his tutor Alcuin, Pepin, the son of Charlemagne, admitted his fear of and curiosity about going to sea; Alcuin reassured him: 'A vessel is a floating house, a ubiquitous inn, a traveller who leaves no tracks.' A quarter of a century later those words would no longer be the same. From being a field of dreams the ocean and its Nordic outliers had become, in the minds of the inhabitants of the coastal regions, a field of repeated confrontations. Curiosity gave way to fear.

A field of confrontations

Even the aggression of the peoples pejoratively called Vikings contributed to the personality of primitive Europe. For several centuries their dialogue with the sea was tempestuous and full of conflict. The tale of those domestic quarrels is less important here than it is to note how that inseparable couple remained marked by them, for in the end the Viking contribution to the maritime image of Europe appears in some respects truly positive.

While the stony land of the Norwegian mountains gave little to an over-numerous population, the sea brought compensation through fishing, and the dreams evoked by the infinite horizons suggested the hope of distant settlements or, at least, of lucrative spoils. The sea was responsible for the adventure of the islands of the Great North, the descents to the rich estuaries of the continent, the pillaging of walled cities and monasteries, the capture of slaves destined for lucrative markets. The Viking expeditions must be considered from the open sea and not just from the shores they visited.

Granted, the devastations of the eighth and ninth centuries put the western coasts to fire and sword and provoked the panic noted in the annals and chronicles. For Hariulf, the abbot of Saint-Riquier, the sea was the antechamber of hell, if not hell itself: 'The Sea', he wrote, 'vomits upon its shores monsters which it feeds with its fish . . . The Danes, those barbarians, from the middle of their raised masts appear to us as wild beasts in the forests.' As they approached the inhabitants fled towards the interior, while the monks, like those of Noirmoutier, moved the relics of their saints, which were both their treasure and their protection, from one place to another. *A furore Normannorum, libera nos, Domine*, sang the litanies. Carolingian legislation organized three defensive 'steps' between the Scheldt and Armorica; but such efforts were in vain. The coast, already largely uninhabited, was deserted even by the hermits, and even in the twelfth century the poet Wace, himself a Norman of young 'Normandy', deplored the fact that 'no man dared live on the shores'. It would appear that around the year 1000 continental Europe was turning away from the sea. Was this more general? Was it definitive?

While in France the ancestors of the Capetians were defending the land in the absence of any action on the sea, the English king Alfred, rightly called the Great (871–899), cut his losses on land by temporarily abandoning the regions in the north to the 'law of the Danes' (the Danelaw), but the construction of a fleet enabled him to bar their access to the south-western coasts while waiting for his successors to achieve a binational, Anglo-Saxon and Scandinavian, kingdom.

One might wonder whether it is not just as excessive to take the complaints, however legitimate, of the victims of Viking raids and piracy literally, as it is to celebrate unreservedly the exploits of the 'kings of the sea'. Everyone knows that sagas are literary texts written several generations after the events by authors who embroidered on a real theme. It is therefore not paradoxical to grant the Vikings a stimulating role in the maritime history of a burgeoning Europe. It was a negative stimulation: against them England experienced its first defensive reaction in the naval realm, and in the following generation the Bretons of Count Alain Barbetorte threw into the sea the Scandinavians who had conquered Nantes. Their inferior numbers, too, prevented the Vikings from founding several 'Normandies'. On the other hand, their settling in Neustria was a positive stimulus, for their dynamism enabled them to choose the right estuary sites: they succeeded better on the Seine than on the Loire. This perspicacity, joined with a spirit of enterprise, endurance, and a consummate skill in naval construction and navigation, enabled them to supplant their predecessors and competitors in their own activities and with their own methods. To the spoils of piracy the Viking added the profits of trade. The seas of North-Western and Northern Europe rediscovered their vocation as realms of profit and power, a vocation which they had never truly lost.

A realm open for profit

The Scandinavians, like their Anglo-Saxon and Celtic predecessors, did not ignore the potential profit from the traffic coming out of the North: tin, amber, precious stones, wood, salt, wine, grain, weapons, cloth and furs. In this realm the most characteristic example is that of the Frisians, the object of an important study by Stéphane Lebecq. Frisia, in the wider sense, covered the coasts of the North Sea between Jutland and the Scheldt. This location gave those living on these shores the role of intermediaries in long-distance exchanges between the Baltic and the English Channel, where the Frisians did not fail to penetrate. In addition, the topography of their amphibious region hardly left them any choice other than to make use of the sea; their environment found its sole anchorage points to the continent on the protuberances built by man, the *terpen*. From the sea water around them they drew the salt necessary for their survival and for that of their livestock, and for the conservation of fish, another resource derived from the sea. Rivers such as the Rhine, whose course was still uncertain, opened the interior markets of Europe to a quite well-developed inland water transport system. Thus the Frisians are representative of Europe's relationship with the sea on a scale enlarged in all directions. The Frisians were merchants above all, and less war-loving than the Vikings from whom they had to suffer, and they developed a supremacy which at its apogee in the ninth century benefited the peoples of the vast Carolingian hinterland.

At the 'tortuous' (in our time) confluence of the Lek and the Rhine archaeologists have found the vestiges of the principal Frisian port, Dorestad (modern Wijk-Bij, Duurstede); over almost a kilometre wharves were built on piles, perpendicular to the river, where boats came in to tie up. Pottery and coins uncovered during excavations confirm the textual accounts of an economic influence which made Dorestad the ancestor of Rotterdam.

On a map the Frisian communications are inscribed on the same routes as those of the Scandinavians, on the one hand towards England, and on the other towards the Baltic through Jutland. The destinations were London, where in 678 the Venerable Bede encountered a slave trafficker, the first Frisian merchant in history; York, where Alcuin booked passage in 780 for Dorestad; Hamwih (modern Southampton), where people embarked to cross the Channel to join the coastal route coming from the north in the estuary of the Seine. The passage to the east followed the Saxon coast by Heligoland as far as Jutland; from there to reach the Baltic there was a choice of two routes: one cut the Danish isthmus not far from the present-day Kiel canal, by following the course of the Treene, then, having unloaded cargo, taking a land route of 18 kilometres opening into the port of Haithabu (Hedeby): the other route, further north, cut Jutland at Riba to reach the Danish archipelago. Virtually alone, the Norwegian route from the Great Arctic North descended through the Danish straits. But almost all the traffic ending in the Baltic converged at Haithabu.

Under Frisian control in the eighth century, then under Danish control, the crossroads of Haithabu 'dispatched', via the island of Rügen, traffic between the Polish and Swedish coasts through the Danish archipelago and through the islands of Öland and Gotland, the latter on the eve of its development. The Frisian convoys completed their voyage first in Birka, then at the end of the tenth century in Sigtuna, a bit further north. In their distant agencies on the banks of the Baltic and in the English ports, the Frisians, like their Scandinavian and Slavic emulators, established colonies. The

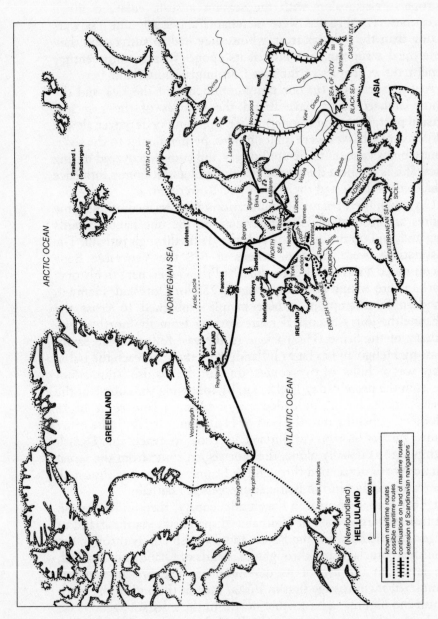

Figure 3.1 Nordic seas and navigations of the tenth to twelfth centuries

life of St Ansgar cites the very curious example of the lady Frideburg, a rich Christian from Birka who, in the middle of the ninth century, requested of her daughter Carla before she died that she would distribute alms to the poor of Dorestad – where, she said, they were numerous, whereas there were none in Birka. Rightly or wrongly, there comes to mind a connection between these Germanic merchant colonies from lake Mälaren and their Italian equivalents in the Crimea and the Sea of Azov, a few centuries later.

This analogy, keeping in mind the chronological distance and maintaining a sense of proportion, at least has a foundation in the extension of traffic through the Russian expanse. In the eleventh century the link between the ports of Lake Mälaren and Novgorod through Lake Ladoga took two weeks; then by using rivers you could join the Black Sea. Just as the Italian merchants established the link between the Black Sea and deep Russia, their agents on the Sea of Azov and in Tana were open to Asian perspectives. Travellers who spoke Arabic, Ya'qub for example, describing Haithabu in the tenth century, attested to these eastern extensions, and archaeologists have discovered proof of them in monetary finds on the shores of the Baltic. Northern Europe was therefore not lagging behind the South in opening up maritime life, even if the arctic regions remained mysterious.

An occasion for power

Nordic trade could only prosper with the blessing of the territorial princes. This was so for Frisia, dependent upon the Anglo-Saxon kingdoms and the Germanic ecclesiastical seigniories, and for the Danish kingdom and the Slavic principalities of the Baltic. Such being the case, the source of power offered by control of the sea did not escape the political authorities. That power took various forms: the wealth derived from trade and from the fiscal system which taxed it; the possession of shores and their resources; and superiority at sea. It is tempting to say that some Nordic potentates of the eighth to twelfth centuries conceived of 'sea power' in almost modern terms.

However, the rulers living on the coasts did not have such a clear notion of the importance of their prerogatives and of their coastal interests before the end of the Middle Ages. A precocious maritime ambition is, however, apparent among some rulers. It was vigorous in the Anglo-Saxons, as in Alfred the Great, and short-lived in the Norwegian expeditions and the Danish ambitions. The former were still in around 1100 seeking to extend an authentically Viking hold over the neighbouring archipelagos of England: the Hebrides, the Orkneys, Ireland, the Isle of Man and Wales; but the descendants of Harald Fairhair were unable to repeat his successes. The Danish achievement of Canute the Great had a completely different significance: his empire encompassed the greater part of Norway, southern Sweden and all of England, and extended from the Baltic to the Irish Sea. Centred on the North Sea and the Danish straits, supported by an organized naval force, Canute's empire was a prototype of a maritime state, but it did not survive the centrifugal forces born out of its very expansion.

However, even weakened Danish power preserved its prestige and a significant naval potential; that enabled it once again at the end of the twelfth century to impose its law on pirates and to dominate the Baltic. This explains why the Capetian royalty, now waking up to affairs of the sea, sought Nordic alliances against its English adversaries: initially against John Lackland, when Philip Augustus contracted a marriage with Ingeborg of Denmark; and a second time, a hundred years later, when Philip the Fair negotiated a naval collaboration with the king of Norway in 1295 against Edward I. At a distance of a century, these two episodes mark the continuation of rivalries among European rulers for domination of the sea.

The Norman conquest of England in 1066 had a significance which went beyond the stifling of Danish maritime superiority; in the end it was to engender another, rather different dominance. William the Conqueror's expedition, according to Lucien Musset, had no connection with Scandinavia, despite the Viking appearance of the fleet portrayed on the Bayeux Tapestry. Moreover, his goal was not at that time the exploitation of the sea for itself, but its use in the union of the two continental realms. This function, destined first to link England to conquering Normandy, took on an entirely new meaning when the dowry of Eleanor of Aquitaine gave the Plantagenet king Henry II south-western France. Yves Renouard was right to situate the centre of gravity of the Plantagenet kingdom in the Atlantic, somewhere off the Breton coasts. The

Plantagenets, who had come from Maine, much like the Conqueror, himself born in Normandy, persisted, however, in setting their sights beyond and above the sea before the continental setbacks of the Hundred Years' War forced their successors to become clearly aware of England's insular position. Until then the 'Navy' had a limited core of naval forces, furnished by the Cinque Ports, just as the kings of France were slowly organizing a permanent navy. The western European states thus did not begin to take possession of the sea until the second half of the Middle Ages. What is true for both Plantagenet England and Capetian France was equally true for the Iberian kingdoms and Brittany. Brittany rather rapidly perceived the advantages of its peninsular location, and its dukes did not hesitate, as Jean Kerhervé has shown, to use the sea in the political, military, commercial and fiscal arenas.

The Hanseatic League

For its part, beginning in the middle of the twelfth century, Northern Europe experienced the start of an hegemony of which the sea was the principal base. The founding of Lübeck in 1158–9 and the associations of merchants, and soon of towns, served as a prelude to the domination of the Hanse towns on the North Sea and the Baltic, then to the expansion of its trade as far as southern Europe. The term 'thalassocracy' seems appropriate here. The Hanseatic League, of which Philippe Dollinger has presented a brilliant historical synthesis, progressively grouped together close to 200 merchant towns, from the Zuiderzee to the Gulf of Finland, the largest of which were located on the sea: Stralsund, Danzig (Gdańsk), Visby, Riga, Hamburg and Bremen. Outer branches served as bases for the usual lines of traffic, among them Bruges, London, Bergen and Novgorod were the pillars of the League. The sea dictated this distribution, which did not exclude a number of smaller ports. We can recognize the distant heritage of Frisian trade in a vigorous structure extending as far as the Mediterranean. From commercial superiority to political hegemony, the link was logical and the maritime imperatives determinative; we can see this in the decisions of the Diet, and especially in those of the Council of Lübeck. That city played a guiding role. An organization, born of the opportunity derived from position, combined flexibility and

Figure 3.2   The Hanseatic League in the fifteenth century

initiative. Autonomous in their management, the four large branches were simultaneously the instigators of communal or local activity and relays for collective decisions. Such empiricism, baffling for the Latin mind, was of fearsome efficacy against its competitors. The Hanseatic League repressed, or used, piracy (the *Vitalienbruder*), which was endemic and sometimes encouraged by some of its members. Rather than resorting to force, used for example in Visby against Denmark or against England, the Hanse often preferred sure economic constraints over the expense and risks of war; blockades, closures or temporary transfers of branches and foreign trading posts and overtaxing competitors could result in diplomatic solutions. Thanks to the judicious use of those means, the Hanse worked its way into Scandinavia, settled in the Low Countries and in England, took over Denmark, expelled the English from Bergen, and took over the route from the Straits of Dover towards the Atlantic saltworks of Brittany, Poitou and Portugal, where they brought their wood and grain.

The achievement of that vast expansion and its apogee at the end of the fourteenth century were due to the enterprising spirit of the merchants, to the intrepidity of the sailors, as well as to the amount and quality of their means of sea transport. The ocean was a source of wealth and power which demanded comparison with those of the great Mediterranean ports. Out of their connection was to be born the maritime personality of modern Europe; at the end, it is true, of a long journey.

A source of knowledge

However, the development of maritime life in Northern Europe was unequal, for the original fog dissipated slowly. For a very long time legends and folklore were intermixed with the classical knowledge received from Greco-Latin Europe. The Venerable Bede made judicious observations on the tides. To his translation of Orosius, Alfred the Great added the tale of a probably true voyage, in 890, beyond the North Cape. Adam of Bremen told of the tragedy, apparently actually experienced, of sailors who had escaped tempests only to be confronted with cyclopes, of a size conforming exactly to the adversaries of Aeneas. As for the cartographers, they dared to locate on *mappae mundi* of theological inspiration quasi-infernal places inhabited by dragons; true kingdoms of sin. Akin to that conception, but much more orthodox, there appeared Honorius' *Imago mundi*, illustrated by Henry of Mainz, and a cartographic project by Hugh of Saint-Victor. This was in the twelfth century, and knowledge was becoming more exact: Saxo Grammaticus perfected Adam of Bremen's notions on the incurvation of the Norwegian coast in the direction of the White Sea, which he seemed to make specific. The thirteenth-century manuscript of a *History of Norway* discovered in Scotland in the nineteenth century combines traditional book-learned theories with concrete information on the Orkneys, the Faeroes and Iceland; however, along with Laplanders 'skiing' on ice faster than birds with the help of smooth planks of wood under their feet, were found cyclopes and amazons!

These images, at least until the fourteenth century, had taken on the characteristics of accepted facts which 'scientific' literature had gathered. The *Otia Imperalia* composed by Gervais of Tilbury for the use of Otto IV are a collection of folklore. The encylopaedists of the thirteenth century, such as Vincent of Beauvais, accepted the knowledge, well-founded or not, of their time; but they did not neglect, as with Roger Bacon, to pass it through the sieve of criticism and the primacy of experience. They also enriched it with first-hand observations; for example, Bartholomew Anglicus described the 'slow or frozen sea' in Iceland and interpreted the 'Isles of Cristal' in the *Navigation of Saint Brendan* as an evocation of ice-floes and icebergs. The 'marvellous geographics' fused the contributions of the West and the East. The latter was favoured by the public, which in the fourteenth century ensured the success of writers such as Sir John Mandeville and the Spanish Franciscan author of the *Libro del conoscimiento*, which makes no mention at all of sea journeys to the North.

However, a change came about from those living in the second half of the fourteenth century; they began to show an interest in the coasts of the Baltic and in Scandinavia, which was no longer just culled from books and which transformed the image held among Europeans at that time. The development of the Hanseatic League contributed to this, as did the opening of the Sound to international navigation, and the development of fishing in the North Sea and in Scania. But beyond economic explanations, human relationships on an intellectual, religious and social level were decisive. From now on there were many visitors from the northern lands and from the East to the West: there were Swedish, Norwegian and Danish students in the young German universities, or in the colleges which had been established for them alongside the Italian and French faculties, such as Skara in Paris; there were collectors and papal nuncios, bishops coming *ad limina sancti Petri*, representatives of Scandinavian churches to the councils at the time of the Schism; and in the opposite direction knights in quest of feats of valour joined the 'Prussian crusades'. All of these travellers brought an exceptional body of information to a public thirsting for adventure.

Any criticism must take into account errors of observation and exaggerations, sometimes bragging about the Prussian crusades, sometimes the optimistic exaggerations of vain 'tourists', and sometimes the deprecatory exaggerations of the disappointed. Some travellers, though, made an effort to be objective. Cartography profited from them; Giovanni da Carignano correctly represented the Baltic, as well as the Norwegian coasts, and drew in polar bears to fill in the blanks. His successors were more precise, especially those who brought to the church fathers of the Council of Florence information about the Church of Iceland. A literature of Nordic voyages flourished. Along with Gaston Phoebus and Jacques de Lalaing, the most prolific was Philippe de Mézières. A veteran of the Oriental crusades, driven back from those of Prussia, in the *Songe d'un vieil pèlerin* he set forth edifying reflections on remarkable knowledge, from the geographical and nautical points of view. In the Nordic seas that habitué of the Mediterranean appeared at a loss. According to him, for every two shipwrecks occurring in the Inland Sea, there were forty in the 'land of the Teutons', whom he believed 'very backward in their profession'. In the Nordic seas, he specified, one had to navigate by soundings, without a compass; one saw only 'a low coastline and mountains in fog', and this not without 'shaking in your shoes'; to reach them, he relied upon an old pilot, Jean, whom he compared to a just man avoiding sin. Out of one hundred sailors who left for the Great North, scarcely a third returned. According to Mézières it took three years to return from Norway and '*en route* one found marvels, ghosts and devilry'. Antoine de La Sale, another hero of the Nordic crusades, noted the seasonal extension of the ice-floe, 'forty cubits thick, spanning forty leagues in the sea,

which melts only in June'. In the course of that new awareness of
the arctic borders, the humanist Enea Silvio Piccolomini, the future
Pope Pius II, had a quite precise vision of the Baltic and corrected
the opinion of the Ancients, who were ignorant of its unique
western link to the Ocean. The Roman Church communicated
with its Nordic antennae: with Iceland, beginning in the twelfth
century, and with Greenland, until the catastrophe which in the
fifteenth century buried its bishop and his flock, whose bodies
were found frozen in the twentieth century. And on another front,
to the north-east, in 1512–26 an imperial ambassador, Sigismund of
Herberstein, soon reached the White Sea, towards the estuary of
the Dvina.

The uniqueness of Nordic seas

In an elongated area from the north of the Baltic to the Portuguese
coast and westward towards infinity, Northern and North-
Western Europe asserted the uniqueness of its maritime identity.
The tides stupefied the Mediterraneans. Despite notable differences in height, for example between the coasts of the Isle of
Wight where they are highest, and the lowest, observed in the Gulf
of Bothnia, their diurnal alternation determined navigation conditions and rhythms of social life unknown to the Mediterraneans.

Northern and North-Western Europe provided for the needs of
naval construction in an abundance unknown on Mediterranean
shores: oak wood for hulls, Scandinavian pines for masts, pitch,
their substitute needed for caulking, hemp and linen for sails and
ropes.

The development of naval archaeology and the study of illustrated documents such as the eighth-century stelae of Gotland and
the eleventh-century Bayeux Tapestry enable a technical approach.
Without confusing the Celtic and Anglo-Saxon types, dating to
earlier than the Viking ships, the latter, through the effect of
invasions, contributed to the diffusion of models adapted for
military or commercial purposes. The earliest prototype, studied
by Eric Rieth, had a flat bottom; it was a long, clinker-built ship
whose planking overlapped, and it was for a long time amphidro-
mic, propelled by both oars and sails, with a square rigging, steered
by two lateral oars; later a hollower ship was used, one with a more

elevated hull, more practical for transporting cargo. This relationship gave birth to the cog, then to the hulk, adapted, according to
Jacques Bernard, to the large cargoes of a conquering economy,
without eliminating the small local cruising vessels. At the end of
the thirteenth century, Oceanic Europe was equipped to face
Mediterranean competition. To these technical aspects were joined
the components of a maritime culture unique to Northern and
North-Western Europe. The sea was, if one may put it thus, a
geometric location, contrasting or connecting ethnically different
but analogous populations through the conditions of their
existence. The life of the fishermen of the North Sea is an example
of this, as is the case of the Baltic: Teutons, Slavs, Scandinavians
and Finns all dipped their feet in it at the same time; their
representatives cohabited in Visby, which was nevertheless quite
troubled in the fourteenth century. The sea was always a link,
sometimes a factor of unity, even at long distances. During the
Christianization of the Celtic and Scandinavian countries the
frequent role of the sea as carrier has been forgotten; thus, starting
in Bergen, Norway took the Gospel 'to the ends of the earth', then
only recently discovered, that is to Iceland and Greenland.

Other signs, moreover, attest to the connection of the maritime
peoples of the North, in the material framework of their daily
lives, their towns, their houses. Similarly, mariner societies shared
certain rhythms of professional, familial and social life, for example
the departure and the return of ships to port following the rhythm
of the tide and the whim of the winds, at Bergen just as at Dieppe,
Penmarc'h, Pasajes and so on; the timing of weddings and births
was dictated by that of campaigns at sea; the liturgy of those lost at
sea followed the caprices of tempests. In as convincing a way as the
sharing of the same problems, seamen used similar customs within
the vast sector of the North-West: the *Rules of Oleron*, customs of
Damme and laws of Visby – their possible connection, beginning
in the twelfth century, and their mutual borrowings leave many
questions unanswered, but there is no doubt of their relationship.
Indeed, seamen, by dint of dealing with each other, invented a
solution to the problem of communication: not without an
analogy to the Mediterranean *lingua franca*, the language of the
mariners of the Ponant (the Atlantic region) ultimately formed,
from one people and language to another, an ensemble to which
each group contributed. Around 1520 in France a captain of the

royal navy, Antoine de Conflans, wrote: 'It is understandable that in the Mediterranean seas the language is mixed and it seems that Normans and Provençaux can understand each other.' Indeed, for more than two centuries the Ponant and the Levant had been in close contact.

4

Convergences

Mediterranean advances in the late thirteenth century

Towards the end of the thirteenth and the beginning of the fourteenth century Europeans came to realize the advantage of a direct link between their two maritime areas. Certainly, one circumstance that favoured such a link was the progress of the *Reconquista*. Its completion in Portugal restored control over Cape Saint-Vincent; Aragon, master of Valencia (1238), and the Castile of Cartagena (1245), of Seville and of Cádiz (1248) were able to watch the approaches to the strait and offer ports of call and refuge to ships in distress and those pursued by pirates. Moreover, a rather precarious *modus vivendi* between the Christian and Muslim inhabitants of the strait reduced the hazards of the passage from one sea to the other.

Passages to the North

Between 1275 and 1300 the development of three series of events is noteworthy. The first is the progressive establishment of routes of commercial navigation between Genoa and Venice on the one hand and between Genoa and Flanders on the other. In 1277 a member of an important Genoese family, Nicolozzo Spinola, set sail from that port *en route* to Sluys; the following year two of his countrymen, Nicolino Zaccaria and Uguetto Embriaco, did the same, voyaging to Southampton, Sandwich and London. In 1287 and in 1293 Genoese galleys were sighted at La Rochelle and in Brittany; in the interval other ships transported alum from Asia Minor to Flanders in 1289 and in 1292. This was the prelude to an

57

annual passage beginning in 1298, documented at least until the middle of the fourteenth century. Genoa maintained its superiority, but in turn Venetian galleys travelled to Flanders via Gibraltar from 1314 onwards.

At the same time as these commercial relationships were being developed, the link between the Mediterranean and the North Sea also saw military activity. Simultaneously the kings of France and of England, at war, but lacking naval forces, acquired the habit of resorting to cooperation with Mediterranean merchants. On the French side, Philip the Fair placed an order for thirty Genoese galleys in 1292; those ships, leaving Marseille on 1 April, 1295, reached the estuary of the Seine in two months and joined up with the Genoese and Provençal specialists who had come by land to lend their assistance to the royal arsenal in Rouen.

Nautical commodities

A third development, connected to the previous ones, was of a technical nature and concerned ships and navigation. The arrival of galleys on the ocean was not the result of a transformation of those ships, nor of a change in habits. Mediterranean ships continued to spend the winter during bad weather in their ports of origin. On the other hand, the well-known Florentine historian, Giovanni Villani, points out the adoption in 1304 by the Genoese, the Venetians and the Catalonians of a type of boat, the *coca* or cog, borrowed from the Bay of Biscay. It was larger, decked, and more economical. The Mediterranean shipyards in Genoa built such vessels in the following decades and increased their proportions to the point where they reached the dimensions of huge ships. The security of these ships came in part from the stern rudder, fixed on the stern post, the 'Bayonne tiller', which, at first in conjunction with and then instead of steering oars, governed the performance of a ship's course.

The progress of Italian trade on the ocean route is reflected in the portolan charts. The first generation of maps that followed the *Pisana* used a nomenclature constantly enriched by harbour sites. The European coast was initially represented by a simple oblique line oriented south-west–north-east from Lisbon to Denmark. However, less than twenty years later the work of the Genoese

Petrus Vesconte, the only cartographer who left a portrait of himself in his work, gives proof of greater knowledge. The western coasts are represented in a truer fashion, around a few junction points of navigation – Cape Saint-Vincent, Cape Finisterre, the Point of Brittany, Land's End and the Cotentin peninsula. This precision is particularly noticeable in the portolanos in the Bibliothèque Nationale in Paris (1313), and in the library of the city of Lyon (around 1321). The Baltic countries benefited, particularly in the middle of the fourteenth century, from this increasing knowledge. The *Libro del conoscimiento* shows that in Spain the location of ports was well known and the toponymy was more recognizable than was previously believed; if 'Litefame' designates the Lithuanian coast and 'Vçibandt' precedes the name of Courland, we have no difficulty in understanding Dançicha for Danzig, Rivalia for Reval and Ungradia for Novgorod. From voyage to voyage, from portolano to portolano, the Mediterraneans' knowledge of the Atlantic coastline improved from the end of the thirteenth century onwards.

Routes and ports of call

The choice of port of call was naturally not incompatible with the non-stop navigations of lengthier journeys. However, it does not seem reasonable to make generalizations from the performance of a few Genoese ships transporting alum directly from Chios to Sluys. The length of the trips (three months from Genoa to England), the risks, the necessity of getting fresh water and of obtaining news about the political situation in certain maritime and continental zones where peace was precarious, all implied calls into port for technical reasons and stops in a few ports of order. It is difficult to imagine a non-stop sailing from Galicia to Brittany, without a landing somewhere at the approaches to Cape Finisterre on the one hand and at those to Point Saint-Mathieu on the other. The Mediterraneans were used to sailing close to shore. Further, the opening of new routes was preceded, often well in advance, by the positioning of a logistic system. Since the Genoese had been pioneers west of Gibraltar, in Seville (1251) and thirty-eight years later with the Vivaldis on the high seas of the Atlantic Ocean, their presence still seemed natural in Galicia at the beginning of the twelfth century, and in Lisbon in 1147. As mentioned earlier, the archbishop of Santiago, Diego Gelmirez (1100–1140), had called upon two shipbuilders, a Pisan and a Genoese. Two centuries later the first galleys *en route* to Flanders put in to port in that area. There is evidence that the Genoese assumed the customs of Corunna, beginning in 1321, whereas, in order to avoid them, the Venetians, on their return journey from Flanders, stopped at El Ferrol. Elisa Ferreira Priegue's work *Galicia en el comercio maritimo medieval* sheds the light one would expect from Galician archives upon these facts.

Once the cliffs of Cape Finisterre had been lost from sight, ships had a choice between two routes. At La Rochelle a small colony of Genoese welcomed them. The first members had perhaps arrived there through the land route by way of the Aquitaine isthmus from Montpellier or Narbonne, a short and safe route. Others had already chanced a route via the sea. At the time of the city's attachment to the Capetian realm in 1224, two Italian businessmen were found on the list of inhabitants residing there for at least one year; one of them was named Tommaso da Genova. Although we do not know how he came, we do know that eight years later one of his countrymen, Gherardo Pessagno, escaped a tempest in the Bay of Biscay by taking the sheltered corridors near the Ile d'Oléron and escaped just in time from the island dwellers, who were betting on his being shipwrecked so they could plunder the wreckage. La Rochelle was so well known by the Italians that Marco Polo called the Poitou and Saintonge waters the 'sea of Rocelle'. At La Rochelle at the end of the thirteenth century the presence of agents of Italian commercial and banking companies, from Pistoia in particular, in business with the Galician ports, proves the frequency of their relationships.

As the Italians welcomed their countrymen in Saintonge, so they did likewise at the other stops on the way to Flanders. Renée Doehaerd has pointed out the presence in Brittany – that is, in Nantes, Quimperlé, Quimper and Dinan – of Genoese galleys in 1293. A survey taken in the duchy in 1296 reflects the activity of the Lombard bankers and, among other businesses, mentions the shipwreck on the Point Saint-Mathieu of a ship from Morlaix chartered by a merchant from Florence to transport wine from La Rochelle to Flanders. The precision of the portolanos from the beginning of the fourteenth century attests to a knowledge of the Breton shores.

The route followed by the Italians deviated from the Brittany coasts in the direction of England at approximately the level of Saint-Brieuc. In Southampton the Italians met up with their countrymen and gathered news of their associates who had settled in the city they were making for, Bruges. Thus the maritime route was dotted with Italian colonies, many of which had been established for decades.

The sea/land alternatives

A sort of shock-wave seems to have been felt from the Aegean to the North Sea. It united the Italian and Flemish economic poles into a sort of 'world economy', according to the Braudelian formula, around a centre occupied first by Genoa. That city, victorious from Pisa to Meloria on the Ligurian coasts (1284), then from Venice in the Adriatic to Curzola (Korcula) in 1296, appeared at that time to be the leader of the European maritime impetus. The causes of this development are very complex. The setting up of maritime exchanges was not an innovation, for the continental routes had for a long time assured North–South relationships through the fairs of Champagne; we should rather see the sea route as a complement to and an adaptation of commercial traffic to new economic, political, technical and even intellectual circumstances.

According to the evidence we have, the establishment of the Atlantic route coincided with the decline of business in Champagne more than it provoked it. Although it has been discussed for a long time, there does not appear to have been a definite or absolute relationship of cause and effect. Mariners did not aim to put the travellers by land out of business. Of the latter, some transferred their meeting-place to Paris, at least for a time; others preferred the Alpine and Rhenish route favoured by the opening of the St Gotthard pass in 1237. In any event, the fairs of Champagne survived the opening of the Straits of Gibraltar until at the latest around 1320, and the land routes preserved an active role, although less substantial than Jan Van Houtte believes. The debate is situated, as stated above, in more complementary than competitive terms. The advantages of the maritime route were cheaper travel, though at a slower pace, the possibility of large loads, and the savings on transhipment and on a multiplicity of tolls and bureaucratic annoyances. Indeed, between the two, the risks were balanced out, whether they came from nature or from other men; high altitudes, storms and avalanches were no less treacherous than tempests and the substitution of pirates for brigands. The most convincing argument is the adaptation of modes of transport to the nature, the weight and the volume of the cargo. So at the end of the thirteenth century, from one pole to the other of the maritime axis, traffic of heavy cargo began to prevail, beginning with that of alum in Genoese hands.

There then came into play the merchants' business sense and their spirit of enterprise; among them at that time the most representative was Benedetto Zaccaria, whose career Roberto S. Lopez has carefully followed. Along with his brother, he was a concessionaire of alum exploitation and trade from the Black Sea and Asia Minor. With the help of the eviction of the Venetians after the restoration of the Byzantine Empire, he practically held the monopoly of that product, so necessary to the textile dyeing and leather treatment industries. This exceptional business tycoon was also a politician and a man of war. His personal fleet was at the forefront of all of Genoa's commercial and militiary operations. Having settled at Puerto Santa Maria, near Cádiz, through the favour of the king of Castile, he controlled access to the Atlantic, as could be seen when in 1292 his galleys loaded with alum from Phocaea went through the strait *en route* to Bruges. Zaccaria's reputation earned him the business of Philip the Fair. The king did not stop at hiring naval construction specialists in Genoa; he rented some boats there and granted Zaccaria command of his fleet under the title of admiral. In around 1300, this was an indication of an effective symbiosis of the Mediterranean and the Atlantic Ocean.

The ocean is accommodating

In the dialogue between the North and the South, the Italians often both made requests and supplied answers. Requests? Answers? These terms were at first inadequate; indeed, the Genoese, Venetian and soon Florentine ships, while returning from Flanders or England, were often in ballast, and the Genoese, particularly in the fifteenth century, found only in the saltworks of Ibiza a heavy and abundant cargo destined for their city and its clients.

Little by little

The situation gradually evolved as maritime societies grasped their opportunities, acquired their autonomy, formed their own units and made efforts to reduce the obstacles that divided up their activity by obtaining the decompartmentalization of the Sound and better security off the coasts of Brittany. In the south the horizon grew clearer towards the promising waters of sun and profit; little by little the lighthouses lit up between the Baltic and Gibraltar.

The Nordic region was organized under the control of the Germanic Hanseatic League, then, going beyond that framework, reached the Hispanic limits at the threshold of the Mediterranean in under two centuries. The Dutch and the Flemish embarked on the same sea lanes. In turn, the English, all the while sustaining tough competition with the Hanse in the North Sea and the Baltic, asserted their presence on the southern route, which the possession of Aquitaine in the twelfth century and the Portuguese alliance at the end of the fourteenth rendered familiar to them. Concurrently the Bretons and the Basques introduced their contingents into the floating cohorts of the European West. Finally, in the fifteenth century the people of the Atlantic had enlarged their region so much that after having knocked at the door of the Straits they ultimately went through it and advanced *en masse* into the inland sea from west to east.

The progress of the Hanse (between the Gulf of Finland and the 'Bay' of Bourgneuf)

The progress of the Hanseatic League first to the west, then to the south was based on the conquest – an initial and necessary step – of Germanic, Slavic and Scandinavian sea regions. Lübeck, Bergen, London, Bruges, and Novgorod were the four bases of the League, but it was in Bruges, even more than in London, that the appetite for access to the south was whetted through contact with the Italians at the end of the thirteenth century. Another circumstance favourable to an advance into the English Channel and the Atlantic Ocean resulted from the extraordinary development of fishing in the North Sea around 1300. The fish-salting industry – principally herring – could not obtain enough good-quality salt through the technique of water evaporation, since the water from the Nordic seas was in any case not very salty; in addition, the production of rock salt from Lüneburg, which nevertheless had a high content of sodium chloride, was insufficient – hence the habit of resorting to the highly concentrated marine salt of the Atlantic and the Mediterranean. It appears that already around 1300 the Hanse brought salt back from Ibiza; that fact remains isolated and unique, for the Hanse habitually sent an annual convoy to the saltworks of southern Brittany and Poitou in the Bay of Bourgneuf, to the south of the Loire; the salt convoy (*Baienfahrt*) sometimes included a considerable number of ships belonging to the merchants of the principal Hanseatic towns as well as to the Teutonic Order; in 1449 the English captured no fewer than fifty ships in the Channel, on the salt route. The Hanseatic hulks were familiar with the Atlantic moorings in the Bay and, until the end of the fifteenth century, few went beyond it. In 1418 and 1421 some of the forty ships of the *Baienfahrt* went as far as Lisbon. The Portuguese capital held a certain number of Hanse members, quite well regarded, who participated in the first acts of Portuguese expansion. A German ship contributed in taking Ceuta in 1415. The advance into the Mediterranean awaited only the opportunity. Visits to the Ibiza saltworks were renewed in 1404. In the course of the fifteenth century the German presence in the south of the peninsula became increasingly active, notably in Lisbon, at the beginning of the Age of Discoveries; in this connection one must mention Valentin Fernandes, Peter Reinerl and the Behaims. The route between the ports of the Baltic, Reval and Gdańsk in particular, held almost no secrets for the sailors armed with instructions from the *Seebuch* – a true route chart in the German language, which described the most minute aspects of the shores. The number of ships crossing the Sound had not ceased to increase ever since the Hanseatic League had imposed its will on the king of Denmark in 1432; the accounts for the toll, preserved from 1497 until the middle of the nineteenth century, testify to this. Thus in 1464 forty-four Prussian ships were sighted returning from Lisbon. In that city the Hanseatic hulks transhipped the Nordic grains destined for Andalusia, North Africa, Catalonia, and Italy onto Portuguese *nefs*. Indeed, the composition of the traffic reflected the balance of the exchanges between North and

South: going south were grain, wax, wood and tar, which were traded for fruit, oil, wine, cork and especially salt, alum and woad for the North. Portuguese salt, of high quality, was better able than its French competitor, which was less white and less dry, to endure treatment in the northern factories; despite its higher price and being located further away it was a fearsome competitor for the 'salt of the Bay'. Setúbal became the meeting place of mariners from the North and from the Mediterranean at the time when salt (as Virginia Rau writes) was asserting itself as 'one of the unifying elements of the western economy'. The mass traffic of heavy products, such as salt and grain, and of cumbersome products, such as wood, also corresponded to a certain division of tasks between the sea and land routes. The difference in freight costs favoured the sea and was heightened with the development in the fifteenth century of alum and woad traffic to the North, products whose use became widespread in the industrial centres of North-Western Europe.

To what can the late development of the Hanse advancement into the Mediterranean be attributed? The episodes noted in the fourteenth century were occasional, like the flight of a single swallow which does not indicate spring. Sicily has served as an observatory for Henri Bresc, who found only a single German ship there during the first half of the fifteenth century; and Jacques Heers makes a similar remark regarding Genoa. There are various explanations for this. As the Hanseatic League's immediate object-ive was the economic domination of the Baltic and the North Sea, it had enough to do to impose itself in Bergen and to hold steady in face of the English advance into the Baltic. To the west of Calais, only the *Baienfahrt* was vital, and it did not require a trip beyond Portugal. Moreover, contacts with the southerners remained the business of the agencies in Bruges and London until the moment when Antwerp replaced Bruges and then was in turn replaced by Amsterdam – that is, late in the sixteenth century and at the beginning of the seventeenth. The Dutch then took over from the Germans and accompanied the English, notably at Leghorn (Livorno) and Venice; at that last destination Pierre Jeannin has found that there were twice as many Dutch as Hanse members at the end of the sixteenth century.

Burgundian initiatives

Completely separate and isolated, the efforts of the duke of
Burgundy, Philip the Good, appear in the middle of the fifteenth
century in his attempt to make a place for himself in the Mediterranean. Like many of the princes of his time, he was aware of the
profit to be made from trade; it was not by chance that he was the
ruler of Bruges and Antwerp in his early years, and the husband of
a Portuguese princess, Isabella. In addition, Philip was of French
stock and had inherited the Valois ambitions and their dreams of
the Crusades. Portuguese engineers were summoned to Flanders to
construct a fleet for him. At great cost he purchased the use of a
Mediterranean port, Villefranche, from the duke of Savoy. Thus
for a few years the banner of the 'great duke of the West' flew over
the inland sea as far as the Orient. Was that not the moment when
Jacques Coeur reminded the kingdom of France of its Mediterranean destiny and when the fall of Constantinople awakened a
Christendom which was dozing despite the Ottoman threat?

The growth of Bristol: Robert Sturmy in the Mediterranean

In the midst of Atlantic attempts to dispute the Mediterraneans'
claims of control over European maritime interests, English participation is of special interest. The initiative did not come from
London nor from Southampton, where the Italian presence
assured profit without risks. In the middle of the fifteenth century
England, barely disengaged from the quagmire of its continental
wars, was bogged down in the interminable rivalry of the Wars of
the Roses, of York and Lancaster. The spark, on the contrary,
came from a port whose inhabitants were neither linked to the
Hanseatic League nor concerned with Italian financial connections, and who were free to look far away, towards the south and,
soon, towards the west – Bristol.

The repercussions of the Sturmy affair have symbolic value. E.
M. Carus-Wilson has shed light of the full details of it. Sturmy was
an enterprising and shrewd merchant; like his contemporary
Jacques Coeur, he seized the chances offered him in the middle of
the fifteenth century. Like Coeur, he profited from the end of the

Hundred Years' War, but on the English side, by transporting supplies to the troops stationed in Normandy. Also like Coeur, he sought to break the Italian monopoly over Mediterranean traffic, the English beneficiary of which was Bristol's competitor, Southampton. In 1446, under the cover of a licence to export wool and tin to Pisa and with a cargo of 160 pilgrims going to the Holy Land, one of his ships, the *Cog Anne*, sailed from Bristol to Seville, crossed the 'Straits of Morocco' and landed its passengers at Jaffa. Whereas the pilgrims preferred to return by way of land, the *Cog Anne*, like Jacques Coeur's ships at the same time, profited from the difficulties the Venetians were having with the sultan of Cairo and loaded spices in Alexandria. Unfortunately, the ship sank with all hands on the Greek coasts, opposite Methóni.

In no way affected in his fortunes, or in the regard of his fellow-citizens (he was elected mayor), Sturmy renewed his attempts. In 1457 he fitted three ships for the Levant, of which the archives of the kingdom of Aragon in Barcelona preserve the memory; but the Genoese, having sworn to see him fail, captured two ships near Malta. Although Sturmy's attempts did not have any immediate result other than a momentary upset in Anglo-Genoese relationships, it was nevertheless true that the entrance of the British into the Mediterranean compensated for the interruption of their trading in Aquitaine and announced their new initiative, by and for themselves, in maritime interests on a European scale.

Obliging transporters: Basques and Bretons

As noteworthy as certain voyages of Hanseatic and English ships into the Mediterranian had been before the sixteenth century, they did not have the regular and definitive character of the part played among the Portuguese and Andalusians by the Basques and Bretons. Both groups, especially after the end of the fourteenth century, possessed a considerable number of boats, generally of slight tonnage, extremely seaworthy, and manned by crews trained to navigate in any weather and knowing perfectly the passes and markers which enabled them to locate their position. As of the fourteenth century, Castilian wool was supplied to Flanders; iron from Biscay was exported to the Mediterranean, to Valencia or

Barcelona, as well as to the North; on the other hand, both northern and southern shippers used Basque boats for other heavy cargoes, sometimes over long distances. Jean Delumeau places the golden age of the Basque navy at around 1500, a navy which made sure of the major part of the alum shipments from Tolfa departing from Civitavecchia for Rouen in particular.

The Bretons were better placed on the maritime routes than were the Basques: their location put them in contact with all the fleets circulating between the Channel and the Bay of Biscay, and ensured them more than just control and a possible seizure of their wreckage; they provided a security service. Beginning in the second half of the Middle Ages, the ducal institution of 'briefs' ensured foreigners the protection of a system of convoys along the coasts, with the possibility of finding refuge and restocking there. From that more passive role to following the example of its clients and renting them their services, the Breton navy quickly took the next active step. Brittany did not leave the distribution of its salt entirely to foreigners. Its numerous small sailing vessels, quickly loaded, leaving quickly, not very costly, had an advantage as far as the Mediterranean. There they carried wheat, cloth and the most diverse merchandise to be traded for alum and wine. They were seen among the ships which Fernand Braudel describes 'in close ranks' passing Gibraltar from west to east around 1530. However, a few decades earlier, even before the adventures of the Englishman Sturmy, the Bretons had frequented Mediterranean ports; thus Jacqueline Guiral-Hadjiossif notes the arrival in Valencia of a ship from Groix in 1413; similarly, the archives of Genoa report two Breton ships present in 1439. The descent of the Bretons into the Mediterranean increased, especially after 1480; the same is true of the Normans who, for example, were in Barcelona as of 1420.

The Ponant during the Italian wars

The activities of Bretons and Normans in the Mediterranean were not limited to the commercial realm. The necessities of the Italian wars determined the unification of Atlantic naval resources. The joining of Brittany with the crown of France through the marriage of the duchess Anne with Charles VIII facilitated the union of the ocean and the inland sea. Let us take two examples. At the same

moment, thirty Breton *nefs* were off Alicante on 14 July 1494, and
thirteen others from Normandy and La Rochelle joined them to
form an assembly and a naval review, which was taken in Genoa by
the duke of Orleans (the future Louis XII). Less than seven years
later, at the dawn of the sixteenth century, a wide-ranging operation was carried out in the eastern Mediterranean against Mytilini
by a primarily Atlantic squadron which included the *Cordelière*
from Morlaix, celebrated up until our own time in a popular
French song. But, as had to be, in the course of the international
quarrel of which the Mediterranean was only one of the theatres,
the French were not the only ones to come from the Atlantic.
English, Castilians and Portuguese were also present.

Indeed, at that time one could hardly distinguish warships from
merchant ships by the artillery found on board; merchant ships
were all more or less armed for their defence or for privateering,
but at a greater cost on the Mediterranean than on the ocean. In the
end, whether it was to encourage peace or for the risks of war,
around 1500 Europe mobilized all its shores, to the north, the west
and the south.

5

Encounters and Sharing: the Genesis of a Europe of Merchants (Fifteenth to Sixteenth Centuries)

The sea belongs to all

Let us imagine for a moment the presence, around 1450, of observers posted simultaneously on the banks of the Bosporus, on the Strait of Otranto, on the Straits of Messina and Gibraltar, at Penmarc'h on the Point of Brittany, at Calais or Dover, and finally on the coasts of the Sound. They would have been able, we may imagine, to determine the status of maritime traffic, in much the same way as Lloyd's Registers and the Bureau Veritas. Despite many imperfections and gaps, the image thus created would reflect the almost incessant movement of ships coming from all over Europe. Granted, a natural regional distribution prevailed wherever coastal traffic predominated; however, the small Flemish, English, Breton, Basque, Portuguese and Mediterranean sailboats sailed alongside the *galere de mercato*, the huge carracks, the galleys and naves, the weighty hulks that they met at sea and whose cargo they redistributed after having lightened their loads. At that same moment, the Genoese ships would pass through the Bosporus in the direction of Caffa; and they could have encountered the flotilla of Duke Philip of Burgundy, recently built in Bruges, as we have seen, by Portuguese specialists, whose unsuccessful goal was to aid the Varna crusaders. Venice remained concerned about controlling its Adriatic 'gulf' as if it were a game preserve; however, the Ragusans intended to enlarge their influence there and extend their business into Sicily, Naples, Aigues-Mortes and Barcelona.

At Gibraltar there were more Portuguese, Basques, Bretons and English. At sea they might have crossed with Mediterraneans *en route* towards Southampton, London and Sluys, as they might also

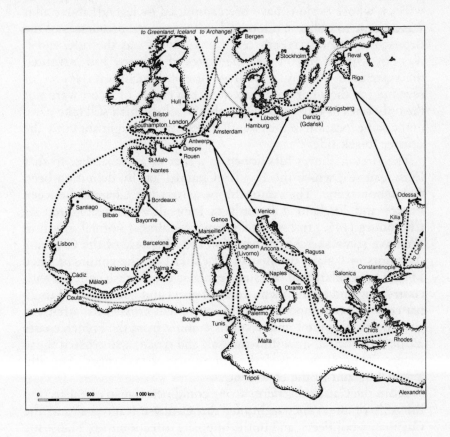

Labels visible on the map:

to Greenland, Iceland to Archangel Bergen
Stockholm Reval
Riga
Hull
Bristol Königsberg
Southampton London Lübeck Danzig
Amsterdam Hamburg (Gdańsk)
Antwerp
Dieppe
St-Malo Rouen
Nantes Odessa
Bordeaux Venice Kilia
Santiago Genoa
Bilbao to Caffa
Bayonne Marseille
Lisbon Barcelona Leghorn Ancona Ragusa
(Livorno) Constantinople
Cádiz Valencia Palma Naples Salonica
Málaga Otranto
Ceuta Chios
Bougie Palermo Rhodes
Tunis Syracuse
Malta
Tripoli Alexandria

0   500   1 000 km

•••••••• 15th–17th century

••••••••• 18th-century extensions

◂——— land links

Figure 5.1   European maritime routes in the modern age: north-south convergences

have done at the Point of Brittany. The port of Le Conquet in particular was not just the haunt of corsairs and pillagers of wrecks, whose exploits have been amplified by legend; above all it was a home to obliging pilots and cartographers, precursors of the Brouscons in the sixteenth century. Caution was the rule, and it was not without reason that the dukes of Brittany had instituted the system of 'convoy and safety briefs', a significant source of revenue for their coffers. Moreover, the coasts of Léon were not the only ones in Europe to cause shipwrecks, which still take place in the same location in the twentieth century, brought about by the sinister 'black tides'.

The Breton shores functioned as a sort of antechamber to that European sea, which the English Channel has by definition been throughout time. The relationships across the Channel between France and England did not take long after the reconquest of Cherbourg (1450) to resume a normal, or almost normal, rhythm. We have some sketchy information only because of the Customs Accounts of Calais, the British beachhead on the continent since 1347. The regularity of crossings explains the English concern with controlling and taxing them. In both good and bad years, 20 to 25 per cent of wool imports onto the continent crossed the straits. A good portion of the London traffic coming from the French coasts of the Atlantic (along with wine, salt and woad) also crossed those waters. Thus, it was as if the continuity of exchanges viscerally linked England to the continent.

From the Calais observatory one could perceive in one direction the sails of the Venetian *mude*, the Genoese 'caravans' and the Castilian wool fleets, and in the opposite direction huge Hanseatic transports *en route* to the Atlantic saltworks and vineyards, from which they hauled off on their return, well loaded, in groups of ten or more, towards Flemish, Dutch and German ports.

In the Sound, where the Danish crown had instituted a toll in 1429, the diversity of flags increased in the fifteenth century. Members of the Hanse fought bitterly to preserve their primacy. They had succeeded in repelling the activity of the Norwegians north of Bergen, but the Teutonic Order, their confederate, was beaten by the Polish at Tannenberg (1410) and had to retreat to Königsberg in 1466. As for the English and the Dutch, they benefited from the internal conflicts of the Hanseatic League and the difficulties of the Novgorod agency (ultimately taken over by Ivan III in 1478) to move into the Baltic, notably into Gdańsk.

The violence of competition in the North had no reason to envy the relentlessness of Mediterranean rivalries. They were true family quarrels! All the disputes of that sort centred around the sharing of similar rights to a common inheritance.

Harbour types inherited from the Middle Ages

As the sea belonged to everyone, Europeans encountered each other not only on the open sea, but in a few places designated by nature and fixed by circumstances. As if to assert the character of family property, ports were set up, equipped and maintained with the same concerns in mind, which any diversity did not preclude. Differences came from the hydrological conditions of the ocean and the Mediterranean; but men were able to take advantange of, or break free from, the imperatives of geographic locations and topographical sites.

Counting the ports would amount to describing the western economy at the end of the Middle Ages and at the beginning of the so-called Modern Age – a superfluous task. The secondary cross-roads which dotted the maritime paths of Europe were so many stepping stones and stopovers; to grasp the cohesion of the whole, attention has to focus simultaneously on the two poles of European maritime traffic, which had a decisive impact on the fifteenth and sixteenth centuries: the Low Countries to the north, and the great southern ports. Such an overview makes it possible to discern certain traits and behaviours of a unique personality – Europe.

Earlier, we observed the sites of Istanbul/Constantinople and Gibraltar as from an aeroplane. This contemporary view is not incompatible with that which could have been seen in the past from the top of a mountain or a man-made monument at the end of the Middle Ages: for example, Genoa seen from its mountains, Venice from its campanile, Marseille from the hill of Notre-Dame de la Garde, Lisbon from its castle, Rouen from the heights of Notre-Dame-de-bon-Secours, or even Barcelona from the towers of its cathedral or Seville from the summit of the Sé; the tower of

Notre-Dame in Bruges, 122 metres high, and that of the cathedral in Antwerp were landmarks visible from afar.

The rich variety of harbours in Europe can be classified according to their sites and functions. The rhythm of the tides, or the absence of them, has since Antiquity conditioned the placement of ports, through the development of appropriate techniques; the principal one was the construction of holding basins and locks, notably in the North Sea and the English Channel. The layout of the continent played a different role in the Mediterranean and on the ocean coasts. In the first case deep creeks or open bays offered sites that were quite easy to protect (Athens, Ragusa, Naples, Marseille, Collioure) with their old ports, Barcelona and Valencia with their wide 'plains'. On the Atlantic coast, the sites exploited since the Middle Ages were the estuaries benefiting from a wide expanse of deep water at a distance from maritime threats: Seville, Lisbon, Bordeaux, Nantes, Rouen, Southampton, Bristol, London, Antwerp, Hamburg and Lübeck. Coastal ports often used a ria (in Galicia, Guipuzcoa, Brittany, Norway) protected by a narrows, or they exploited their situation either on the traffic routes (La Rochelle, Brest, St-Malo, Calais) or at the opening of developed agricultural and industrial regions. Medieval Europe has bequeathed to us a range of ports adapted to the naval materials of its time; their number, greater than the possibilities for a healthy profitability, nevertheless corresponded to a general awareness of an important maritime potential.

Although different, the types of harbours showed aspects which corresponded more or less faithfully to a model that has become commonplace: a natural access narrowed or restricted through human work, between towers linked at night by a chain: we know the fate of the chain of the port of Marseille, taken as a trophy to Valencia by Aragon in 1423. At the far end of protective harbours, one or several 'home fires' or lighthouses guarded the entrance, for example in Genoa, Dieppe and Calais. As to coastal fortifications, there was the Fort St-Jean in Marseille, the Tower of Belém in Lisbon, the defences of Brest, the Tour d'Ordre in Boulogne, the Tower of London, the Steen of Antwerp, the Schloss of Danzig and the Burg of Lübeck. The port itself, in addition to moorings in open water necessitating handling and transferring of cargo by barge, included quays made first of earth, then of stone, slanted landings, then slipways that were at right angles to the shore, served by carts and porters, and equipped with stores. For hoisting operations there were loading masts on ships and, on certain quays, cranes moved by a man-powered wheel; illustrations have given us images of this in Damme and Antwerp, and there are still a few specimens of them in existence (Gdańsk, Lübeck . . .). These installations were needed for heavy cargo (wine, salt, grain, wood, minerals, wool), for which there were specialized harbours. Thus from one end of Europe to the other, the harbour landscape showed similarities and differences which were the result of the specific functions of ports and the practices of the time.

In connection with harbour functions, let us focus on the role of the users. Fishing ports were innumerable, as were the little coastal ports, ports for putting-in for technical reasons, or for revictualling, to get fresh water or to open letters containing instructions from their partner(s) as to the final destination of the voyage. There were also 'sanitary' stops, harbours equipped since the last quarter of the fourteenth century along the lines of the Ragusa institution of quarantine. A special category included the outports, which enabled boats which were only in passage to avoid going up an estuary, such as the Guadalqivir, the Gironde, the Seine, the

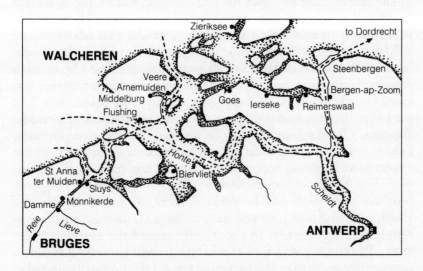

Figure 5.2 The approaches to Bruges and Antwerp

Thames or the Scheldt, with deeper waters than in the inland ports. The case of Bruges is typical with its two outports of Damme and Sluys, which gradually silted up with mud from the mouth of the Reie. The typology also included two other categories: military ports specialized in the distribution of loaded artillery; and naval concentrations for security, for example the Venetian *mudes* assembled in Venice, the Castilian wool fleets, the *Baienflotte*, the 'convoys' protected by the Breton navy between St-Malo and La Rochelle, and the Italian fleets regrouped in front of Rye (*Chamber* or *La Chambre*), before their return to the peninsula. Following a similar principle, zones such as the roadstead of Winchelsea or the Netherlands waters were used as winter docking; on the Atlantic coast the Mediterraneans maintained the habit of suspending shipping between October and March; and the Hanse ships waited in the Low Countries for the breaking up of drift-ice in the Baltic before hauling into their ports of origin.

Personal contacts

On board ship and in port human contacts reflected the melting-pot role played by maritime life on an international level.

The recruitment of crews for small fishing and sailing boats was in general of local or even familial origin, as Jacques Bernard has presented it in relation to Bordeaux, a model that has remained valid for the entire West almost until the present time. Those men, however, were not deprived of all contact with seamen from other regions: sometimes, however, the violence of such encounters was eased by an awareness of belonging to the same profession. In a time that did not know division by 'quotas', Normans, Bretons, Basques, Castilians and Portuguese already fought over the same fishing areas, and their quarrels degenerated into the war between France and England, for example, during the reign of Philip the Fair. The North Sea experienced conflicts from boat to boat, from port to port, between Norman, Picard, Flemish, Dutch and English herring boats; or yet, despite the war, they got together in clandestine agreements. In the Mediterranean the encounters between Provençaux and Sardinians during coral harvesting could be cooperative or hostile, but everyone felt at least implicitly united in the same task.

In the realm of trade mixed recruitment and wide-ranging traffic posed some problems. Among the seamen concentric solidarities went from being related, from friendship and a common origin, to the simple fact of sharing the same life on board.

Often that solidarity did not go beyond the limits of those familiar groups; it could exclude, depending on whether one was Breton, Norman, Picard, Flemish, Poitevin, Saintongeais, Gascon, Basque, Catalan, Languedocian or Provençal, sailors who were not; disputes were settled in a bloody manner in some tavern during a call into port, especially if a foreigner – English, French or otherwise – were involved. At such moments, shipboard disputes were forgotten; the members of a crew closed ranks together; sometimes mariners from other ships, even from different countries, lent them a hand. In La Rochelle in 1483 a ruffian named La Rousse exchanged punches with some mariners. These fleeting solidarities were solidarities of place and nation more than an expression of 'European' solidarity; their manifestations were reactions inspired by common values, seen in investigations and acts of justice – as in France, in the letters of remission granted by the king; on the contrary, the sentences of the Water Bailiff of Sluys in the second half of the fifteenth century, in the diversity of those sentenced, men from different countries, leaves the impression of a European aspect.

It was not just a matter of occasional encounters. Merchants and businessmen, in a few economic centres of international importance, formed groups organized according to their geographical origins and endowed, as foreigners, with a legal status and with privileges granted by the public powers. The relationships these groups maintained with their country and town of origin, like the relationships they maintained among themselves, were harbingers of the elements – embryonic, it is true – of a European merchant community.

Southern 'nations' at the Bruges crossroads

When Erasmus, the 'father of Europe', was born in Rotterdam in 1467, in the former Low Countries, under the duke of Burgundy, Charles the Bold, Bruges exercised fully its function as a crossroads, before ceding its position to Antwerp, then to Amsterdam.

A grandiose manifestion of this was the procession, the following year, during the lavish wedding celebration of the new 'Grand Duke of the West', when Charles, the son of Isabella of Portugal, sister of Henry the Navigator, married Margaret of York, the daughter of the king of England, Edward IV. Taking place in a setting conceived by the painter Hugo Van der Goes, no one missed the celebration, the pomp of which is related in Olivier de La Marche's *Mémoires*. The occasion brought together representatives from the merchant milieu, marching behind ambassadors and prelates, in the following order:

> The Venetians came first: ten merchants on horseback, wearing red, each one carrying a torch, followed by six servants on horseback. Next came the Florentines: first sixty men on foot wearing blue, carrying torches, then four pages wearing silver cloth with short mantles of crimson velours, on horses covered with white satin; there followed eleven merchants led by Tommaso Portinari, their chief and the advisor of Mgr the Duke, wearing crimson satin; after them came eleven porters wearing simple crimson satin; finally came twenty-four servants wearing blue, all on horseback. There were twenty-four Spanish merchants on horseback, wearing purple damask, having twenty-four pages on foot wearing black satin; in front of them went sixty torchbearers wearing purple and green cloth.
>
> The Genoese had riding before them a beautiful girl who represented Joan of Arc, whom St George protected from the dragon, then St George armed with all his weapons; next, there followed three pages, and one hundred and eight merchants on horseback wearing white damask, with as many valets wearing white cloths.
>
> The Osterlins had seventy-two torches carried in front of them; following six pages wearing purple came one hundred and eight merchants on horseback, all wearing purple cloth.

This highly colourful description conveys the importance of the groups of merchants and the consideration they enjoyed. The author mentions neither the English, who were naturally concerned with the ceremony, nor the French, who were not considered foreigners in Bruges, since Flanders was under the crown of France until the reign of Charles V.

Only a small number of English resided there, for it was through Calais that wool imports travelled. As for the French, there were enough of them to have a common house, the 'Halle de Paris'; their influence also stemmed from the fact that their language served as the means of communication with those from the North and the South. The issue of interpreters in the international arena has not been studied as much as its importance might warrant: in Bruges, there was a great variety of spoken languages.

The example of Bruges does not just show the diversity of nations through their geographic origins and languages. The 'nation' there was a social and legal entity as live as it was in the universities or had been, a few decades earlier, in the conciliar assemblies at the time of the Schism. A numerous national group, coherent and influential, could obtain from the public authority the status of 'nation', juridically different from a simple 'colony'. In Bruges or any other port there was a convergence of interests between a group which formed into a sort of defensive syndicate and the local powers concerned with controlling the activity of foreigners.

The eminent place held by the Italians in the procession described by Olivier de La Marche corresponds to the importance of their 'nations' in Bruges, in accordance with the length and importance of their presence there. That presence went back further than the opening of direct maritime relationships with Genoa and Venice at the end of the thirteenth century; but the organization into nations was ratified only in the fifteenth century through ducal charters. Their structure in Bruges was of the same type as in other towns. The 'nation' forced its nationals into a group; their annual assembly elected a consul and counsellors; the consul exercised a disciplinary and juridical power over the members of the nation, and he also had to assist them in times of need, before local authorities. The nation had its own building. The brotherhood which generally accompanied it benefited from the hospitality of a religious order of its choice.

The true importance of the nations in Bruges corresponded to Olivier de La Marche's account, beginning with the Florentines. The consideration and credit Tommaso Portinari enjoyed reflected on his 'nation'. After around twenty years in Bruges, the director of the Medici's offshoot had become adviser to Prince Charles before the prince became a duke; Portinari shared Charles's taste for and the temptations of grandeur, leading a lavish lifestyle in one of the most beautiful residences in the city, purchased at a high price, the Hôtel Bladelin, truly a palace. Speaking French fluently, Tommaso enjoyed exceptional influence and prestige. This is not to say that the other Italian groups were poorly represented. Olivier de La Marche might have mentioned the Lucchese and named Dino Rapondi and Giovanni Arnolfini; likewise, he might have mentioned their activity in the financial transactions which occurred in the Van de Beurse residence, the name which gave the European 'Bourse' its name.

The other southern 'nations' did not carry the same weight on a financial level, but their commercial role was important. There were initially four: Biscayans, Castilians, Catalans and Aragonese; then the Navarrois at the beginning of the sixteenth century. Their organization was similar to that of the Italian nations, each one having its consul and its house; the Bruges toponymy preserves their memory, for example in the street of the Spanish, the square of the Biscayens. A few patronyms emerge in documentation, often the same as in other ports, as we shall see later in the Iberian diaspora.

Northern Hanseatic agencies and the Fondaco dei Tedeschi in Venice

The 'Osterlins' described by Olivier de La Marche brought up the rear of the nuptial procession of Charles the Bold in Bruges. In this city as in others, the 'Hanseatics' had the unique status of forming a closed nation, with its own particular organization and customs. The building which it still owned in the twentieth century preserves its austere appearance of a barracks and a warehouse. However, in Bruges more than elsewhere, the Hanseatics mixed with the population and had contacts with other nations. This was the result of Bruges' status as a junction between the northern sector of European trade and the western and southern sectors. Transport activity involved transhipping and taking on new cargo; often added to this was the winter docking of ships until better weather arrived. There was nothing unusual about the fact that in 1457 an assembly in the Bruges agency had brought together more than 600 German merchants.

Elsewhere, Hanseatic agencies had a tendency to reduce their contacts with other nations and to keep to themselves. In London, the Steelyard, on the banks of the Thames, kept to itself. Above all, in Bergen the German quarter was a group of buildings even more closed than a European concession in China at the end of the nineteenth century. There was no question of living elsewhere or of having personal relationships beyond the quarter. This might be explained by the youth of most of the German residents, whom the authorities in Lübeck wanted to keep from having contact with the native population. In Novgorod, as a security measure, the wooden barracks were grouped around a stone church dedicated to the chief of the Apostles, which was used as a store as well as a place of worship and of refuge, the Peterhof; all the buildings were enclosed by a fence.

In Venice, in the parish of San Bartolomeo, in a more complex environment, the Fondaco dei Tedeschi was a 'fiercely guarded' building (Philippe Braunstein). Merchants from the other side of the Alps had to lodge there, and life was so segregated that the monk Felix Faber, *en route* to Jerusalem, noted in 1483 the presence of a dog who jumped up and down and wagged its tail around people speaking German and who growled when Italians, French, Greeks or Slavs arrived. Without specializing solely in maritime activity, the Fondaco was a link between east and west, between the Mediterranean and the cities of Upper Germany, who showed a growing interest in maritime affairs. For example, the Imhofs of Nuremberg had a room in the Fondaco whose name translated the quality of its owner, the 'Paradise'. The name of Imhof, among others, evoked the opening of familial merchant networks from Upper Germany. It was not the only one. The Hirschvogels were no less important, for linked through blood and common interests with the Behaims, they found each other on the verge of discoveries in the Portuguese capital; similarly, the Iberian ports, notably Barcelona and Valencia, seats of branches administered on behalf of the Humpis, welcomed the middlemen of the 'Great Society of Ravensburg'. Jerome Munzer, alias Hieronymus Monetarius, at the time of his European journey of 1494, was able to note the diaspora of important German merchants from the Low Countries to Hispanic ports and describe their dynamism.

Although it has been believed, not without argument, that Upper Germany's interest in the sea was awakened by the influence of Venice, one cannot neglect the contribution of the German networks, recently underlined by Philippe Braunstein, to an awakening of a collective awareness of the importance of the sea. From Venice the vision of the businessmen from Upper Germany very quickly appreciated its chances as far as the Atlantic, compared to a relative slowness on the part of the Hanse merchants. On the other hand, for the Italians and Spanish the extension of familial and economic networks on an international scale was little concerned with the constraints of 'nations'.

Italian networks

Given the amount of material written on the subject, it is not necessary to recall at length what Fernand Braudel has termed the 'scattering' of the Italian colonies in Europe: 'Merchants', he added, 'and more merchants'. To illustrate that view one can cite, after R.S. Lopez, himself Genoese, an anonymous versifier from the thirteenth century:

> There are so many Genoese dispersed in the world,
> That everywhere they go new Genoas have unfurled.

The description of such an obvious diaspora would be useless, it is so commonplace. It is more important to stress, once again, its European character and to recall the simultaneous presence of Italian merchants in different countries, some of which were hostile, like France and England during the Hundred Years' War, carrying out financial and commercial business on the maritime level as on others, without regard for conflicts or competition.

A celebrated account was written around 1340 by Francesco di Balduccio Pegolotti. Born of a notable family of Florentine merchants, he was one of the some 330 assistants in the company of the Bardis, carrying out business in their branches, which extended from the Mediterranean (Constantinople, Ayas, Rhodes and Majorca) to the North Sea (Bruges, Antwerp, London), not forgetting Avignon and Paris. Pegolotti, in his *Pratica della mercatura* – a type of manual widespread at that time – noted the trade conditions in each of the places where Italians had interests. In this portrait of businesses, maritime Europe held a considerable place. This is confirmed by the operating charts reconstituted by historians (Federigo Melis, Raymond de Roover) of the business of Francesco di Marco Datini and the Medicis, for the end of the fourteenth century and the middle of the fifteenth respectively. The two cases are characteristic examples, without being the only ones, of the importance of the sea in the interests of Italian businessmen and in their geographic hegemony.

Francesco Datini's system, strongly centralized around the personal enterprise of the master in Prato, and his Florentine banking firm, was a cluster of companies articulated in a large number of offshoots which were generally placed along various coasts. Thus a dozen or so branches in ports such as Venice and Ancona were dependent upon Florence. The Pisa company spread out to ten other places including Leghorn (Livorno), Talamone, Gaeta, Naples and Sicily. That of Genoa directed traffic in Portovenere, Sardinia and Corsica. The ports of the lower Rhône (Arles, Tarascon, Beaucaire), Port-de-Bouc, Marseille, Nice and, at a distance, the business carried on in Lyon, Paris, Bruges and London, were dependent on Avignon. Barcelona was at the head of transactions carried out in Narbonne, Collioure, Palamos, San Felíu and Tarragona, and supervised the Majorcan offshoot (Palma), Minorca and Ibiza. Valencia, under the control of Barcelona, oversaw the business negotiated in Cádiz, Seville and Lisbon, and its influence reached Bruges and London. In a similar spider's web circulated an exceptionally abundant correspondence (around 150,000 letters, according to Federigo Melis), which has been carefully conserved. Its yet uncompleted analysis opens an extraordinary perspective on the close ties of land traffic with maritime circulation.

The extension of the offshoots of the 'Medici bank' in the middle of the fifteenth century generally corresponded to that of Datini's business, but with more rigour in the organization of its structures on a European scale. The bank in Florence was the heart of the organism; international trade, maritime for the most part, sustained the offshoots. They were at the nerve centres of the European economy; four were directly linked with the sea. Pisa supplied Florence with English wool; Civitavecchia, near Rome, exported alum from Tolfa; Venice opened the door to the Orient and to southern Germany; Avignon worked in symbiosis with Beaucaire, Port-de-Bouc and Marseille; and in the North, London and Bruges dealt with an enormous volume of business upon which the balance of the whole depended. The place held by Tommaso Portinari in that last city has provided proof of this.

The brilliance of a few Florentine examples does not eclipse the role of other Italian artisans of European maritime dynamism, both in French and Iberian ports of call in the Mediterranean and on the Atlantic, as well as in England, and of course in Sluys and Antwerp. Many were Tuscan, from Florence or Pisa, more or less directly linked to the Medicis, such as Agnolo Tani, Simone Nori, Francesco Strozzi in Bruges and London, Bartolomeo Marmora and Paolo Morelli in Southampton, Marioto de Nerlo and Rinaldo Altoviti in Marseille, the Tacchinis in Perpignan and Barcelona, the Tovaglias in Bordeaux and Rouen, not to mention the Luccheses such as Giovanni Arnolfini in Bruges or Gherardo Galganetti in Southampton. In fact, the entire Tuscan *Almanach de Gotha* could have been mentioned here.

Quite representative of the maritime surge was the presence, no less diffused, of the Genoese in Marseille and Barcelona, as well as in England, but particularly in Portugal, Aragon and Castile. Under the reign of Alfonso the Magnanimous (1416–1458), the Genoese presence imposed itself in all the territories of the crown of Aragon, from Naples to Valencia and from Palermo to Barcelona. The favour granted by the Catholic kings to Christopher Columbus crowned a situation whose origins go back to the end of the thirteenth century.

The beginnings of Genoese implantation present a remarkable simultaneity in Portugal, Castile and France, with the posting of admirals: Benedetto Zaccaria in France, Ambrosio Boccanera and Ugo Vento in Castile, while in Portugal Manuel Pessagno ensured the holding of that office within his family for several generations. In the fifteenth century Bartolomeo I Marchione, along with his associate Jean Forbin from Marseille, was granted the monopoly of coral in 1433; then Bartolomeo II became involved in African trade and in that of sugar from Madeira before participating in Cabral's voyage, that time in the company of a Florentine, Girolamo Sernigi. But let us not anticipate by yet projecting Europe's vision towards the open sea. All the same a Genoese family, the Lomellinis, deserves mention. In Lisbon in 1424 the first of that name, Bartolomeo, drew on a bill of exchange from Leonardo degli Alberti in Rome. After 1440 he went into business with several of his brothers; one of them, Ambrosio, was in business in Nantes with a Breton in 1443 and 1459; two others, Daniel and Marco, shared the monopoly of Portuguese cork exportation in 1456. Eight years later, Marco had a ship built in Lisbon and corresponded with two of his nephews who had settled in London. After a final voyage to his Genoese homeland, he returned to Lisbon for good. In the meantime two other relatives had settled in Madeira to deal in sugar and honey there, and a third, Raffaele, was in business with Benedetto Spinola, one of the last Genoese residing in Southampton after the Sturmy affair. Thus Genoa, Lisbon, Madeira, Nantes, London and Southampton acted as steps in the typical expansion of a merchant family.

The facility with which Italian merchants adapted to their new homes is confirmed in their writings. Simone Nori wrote from London that he was doing very well there. Tommaso Portinari was happy in Bruges. The young men who, according to custom, carried out apprenticeships in the branches of Francesco Datini and the Medicis did not seem to object to an extension of their stays. The letters Francesco Datini received in Prato have a personal tone which does not aim to deceive. A few merchants adapted to the point of definitively becoming citizens here or there. The stages of a career were, after a commercial association with the local merchants, naturalization, marriage within the local society, the exercise of municipal functions, and the acquisition of land. Assimilation, completed as of the second generation, was expressed by the translation of the patronym into the adopted language. Bartolomeo Marmora was naturalized English in 1417 and married a British woman in Southampton. Benedetto Spinola did the same in 1485. Marco Lomellini, married in Lisbon, was naturalized there; his two children were born Portuguese. The same occurred in Marseille with other Genoese, for example the Remesans from Savona, the Ventos, the Cattaneos (whose name was changed to Castagne) and Rinaldo Altoviti, married in Marseille, a citizen and later provost of Marseille; natives of Marseille, like the Forbins, did not hesitate to admit some of those newcomers into their circle.

The notion of generation adding the dimension of time to the spatial reality of family networks must thus be taken into account to understand the formation and the cohesion of a European milieu. The characteristics of that milieu were gradually delineated through the establishment of a balance between the integration of national groups into the centres where they lived on the one hand, and on the other, the international role they exercised in common on the spot or from one port to another. The evolution which was thus under way is perhaps explained by the individualism of the Latin races as against the Nordic, perhaps even Germanic, preference for collective action.

Indeed, and this is another issue, there was sometimes tension, even confrontation, between foreign groups – colonies or 'nations' – and the local political powers. The tendency of the Hanseatics, for example, to refuse contact – especially through marriage – took on a 'colonialist' appearance, accentuated in Bergen and in Novgorod. Sometimes, on the contrary, the local environment maintained a distance from the foreigner; this happened in England and in Lisbon, even though princes in England and in Flanders had often, through self-interest, dealt tactfully with foreign moneylenders.

Whatever the case may have been, in the second half of the fifteenth century the general evolution was oriented towards the assimilation of newcomers into the merchant societies which welcomed them. Besides the examples already noted concerning primarily the Italians, the case of the Iberians illustrates an accentuated stage of assimilation, destined to be asserted at the beginning of the sixteenth century.

Iberian presences

Geographically and numerically the Iberian presence was asserted in western ports. Without being able to analyse the strength of the groups, in each location one notes its weight, and the closeness of familial and professional relationships based on the identity of economic activities. The latter corresponded to the uniqueness of Iberian products in the ensemble of European trade: Portuguese fruit, cork, wine and salt, sugar from Madeira, iron and merino wool from Biscaye, alum from Mazarrón and oil from Andalusia, the production and trade of which benefited from the coordination and control of the consulate of Burgos. The formation of that body in 1494 coincided within about two years with the ordinance to expel the Marranos in 1492, which accelerated a diaspora begun much earlier.

That diaspora took on the appearance of a spider's web spreading from the Iberian peninsula to the river Scheldt on the one hand, and into the Mediterranean on the other. Among the Spanish 'nations' whose representatives appeared in the nuptial procession of Charles the Bold in Bruges in 1468, the Castilian nation marched in front: it was that nation which carried out the greatest part of all transactions in that city. For their part the Biscayans were involved in maritime transports in conjunction with the Catalans. At the end of the century the attraction of Antwerp disturbed the homogeneity of Hispanic representatives in Bruges. The Portuguese did not hesitate in 1502 to transfer their foreign trading headquarters, with its commercial monopoly on spices, to Antwerp.

The Iberians held the links of a chain between the North Sea and Andalusia. But nowhere, except in Bruges and at first in Antwerp, did their settlement take on the institutional form of 'nations', perhaps due to numerical inferiority, though this hardly affected their influence, particularly in France and England as far as the Castilians and the Portuguese were concerned. From one port to another members of a single family gathered, corresponding amongst themselves and with their countrymen who had remained at home.

In France in the middle of the fifteenth century the Castilians had a common consul, Iñigo Darceo, who defended the interests of those of his countrymen who had settled in Rouen, Nantes, Bordeaux and Toulouse. They were greeted by their countrymen and relatives who had already settled, arranged to have their wives and children sent over, and in turn settled down. Around 1500 the same names were found in Burgos, Bilbao, Toulouse, Bordeaux, Nantes and Rouen, and in London. Where in fact did they come from? In 1499 Fernando de Bernuy was described as follows in an English document: 'merchant of Spain, alias of London, alias of Cales, alias of Brugges'. There were also Bernuys in Toulouse involved in the international woad trade.

Before appearing in Rouen, Nantes, Bordeaux and London, certain families had shown up in the consulate of Bruges: the Gomiels, the Saldañas, the Sevillas, the Medinas, the Quintana-dueñas, the Astudillos and the Pardos. Relatives and friends did favours for each other through an exchange of procurations, transactions, bank transfers and legal representations. Archives

testify to the unity of the Spanish merchant milieu, where ties of
commercial interest doubled those ever-important ties of blood.
This was the case with the Pardos. Around 1500, Juan managed the
affairs of several of his countrymen in London; his brother
Silvestro was the consul to the Castilians in Bruges; a third, Pedro,
living in Rouen, became a French citizen there. A few years later
another Pardo, Alvaro, living in Rouen, went into business with
his two brothers, Jeronimo in Bruges and Diego in Seville; their
relationships were assured by a cousin, Escobar, while another
relative, Juan de Miranda, represented their interests in Lisbon.

Such solidarities, before growing with the help of the dispersal
of the Marranos, were the result of already long-standing situations. In Nantes, the St-Nicolas quarter, near la Fosse and its
docks, in the middle of the fifteenth century included the Miran-
das, the Malvendas, the de Lermas and the Ruizes, just as in the
Chartrons of Bordeaux one encountered the Castros, the Gomezes
and Lopez de Villanova, who counted Montaigne among his
nephews. The Gomezes, the Lopezes and the 'Jayents' could also
be found in Marseille.

Beyond groups with familial interests resulting from a common
origin, these solidarities took on an international appearance. On a
legal and economic level Nantes and Bilbao were united after 1530
in the institutional form of the Contratación. More significantly,
the integration of the Spanish into the cities to which they had
emigrated contributed, for example in Bordeaux, Nantes, Rouen,
Southampton, Bristol and London, to the emergence of milieux
open to the outside. Naturalization through royal consent con-
secrated an assimilation instigated through marriage, followed by
the birth in the adopted land of children whose godparents were
chosen from their French in-laws. Thence the fusion became
effective in the second generation, all the more naturally in that the
newcomers had acquired urban buildings and rural fiefs; they
could bear the name of the seigneury while awaiting (for a very few
years) the recognition of their noble titles and their coat of arms.
Thus who, in Corneille's time – that is, hardly more than a century
after these changes – would have recognized as the grandson of the
merchant Juan de Quintadueñas, the father of Brétigny, restorer in
France of the Carmelite Order, authentically Castilian in its
origins. This was, among many other things, one of the unforesee-
able avatars of the maturity of a European milieu engendered by
western maritime relationships.

Technical exchanges

Meetings encouraged the Mediterraneans and the men of the Atlantic and of the Nordic seas to get to know each other and to compare their customs, their technology, their languages and their behaviour. Maritime Europe did not develop with some regions being absorbed by others, for each region preserved its own personality, but rather with mutual exchanges. If a sort of maritime ecumenism ultimately prevailed, it was not due to one sector erasing another. The North remained the North, and the Mediterranean world preserved its personality. Each borrowed from the other, after due observations and experimentation. What was important for everyone and what ruled them all was the sea.

The choice of naval materials was obviously the realm in which the wisdom of mariners was exercised first and foremost. Let us recall the demands which impose themselves, universally, on the choice of a type of ship. Security, speed, capacity; these three conditions, incompatible in absolute terms, were interdependent at all times; victory came to the ship which combined them in a satisfactory balance. To sacrifice the solidity of the hull to speed was to compromise security and capacity. To increase capacity was to give up speed and make the ship vulnerable. The guiding principle of a solution was, in its strict sense, that of profitability. Still, we must be precise with this term. In ancient times when the same ship was used alternatively or simultaneously for commercial and military ends, profitability was synonymous with usefulness and efficiency in financial gain or victory in battle. For one great specialist in naval history, Frederic C. Lane, an index is the ratio between the useful load of a ship (merchandise, weapons, supplies) and the number of men (crew, passengers, soldiers). He has calculated that for a man on board a Venetian bireme around 1300, that ratio would have been one-seventh of a ton, 0.28 tons on a trireme in 1303, and 1.5 tons on a large galley in the sixteenth century. Analogous calculations for ocean vessels in the same period seem to indicate a parallel evolution tending to raise the ratio, while speed tended to be increased.

In fact – and it is here that the Ponant/Levant dialogue achieves a level of eloquence – everything depended on how the ship was to be used. The Scandinavians were not seeking a Blue Riband when they crossed the Atlantic from Bergen to Iceland in the eleventh and twelfth centuries. The Genoese galleys loaded with alum from

Chios *en route* to Sluys were less concerned with achieving a record speed on a straight route than with a safe, though slow, sailing. And members of the Hanseatic League who had come to get salt from 'The Bay' or from Setúbal were concerned to hasten their return in order to reach the Sound before the winter freeze. As for fishermen, before progress was made in the salting of fish – notably herring – on board vessels, they had to hurry to deliver their catch. Likewise, in the Mediterranean, considering the harshness of the competition as well as fluctuating prices and the changes communicated at a surprising speed, there was an advantage in quickly unloading the greatest amount of spices or silk from the Orient, whose quality corresponded to the tastes of a known clientele at a chosen market at the most opportune moment. For combat it was preferable to have vessels combining seaworthiness with an ease of manoeuvring, useful for surprising and retreating.

The pirate vessel of a Jean de Vienne did not have the same needs as the English troop transports of the Hundred Years' War, nor as the fleets of the king of France during his Neapolitan expeditions around 1500. In conclusion, it was the adaptation of the ship to its missions which governed its technical evolution. This was noted on all European coasts when maritime traffic was accelerated.

The meeting of technology on a naval level from the North and the South starting at the end of the thirteenth century was accompanied by a change in the shape of ships, their rigging and their steering. Under different conditions modes of construction evolved towards a similar result, without it being possible to definitively prove a relationship of influences. In any event, there was a prevailing practice of constructing carvel-built keels, that is where the side planks are jointed and duly caulked. Compared to clinker building, where planks overlapped each other, carvel building, thanks to the more economical use of wood, lightened the boat and increased its capacity; the refinement of its lines made it more responsive and gave it a good coefficient of speed.

The Mediterranean shipbuilders having used carvel building before their northern counterparts were credited with having taught it to them. It is true that Philip the Fair, while having his fleet sail from Narbonne to the English Channel, had offered Norman shipbuilders the opportunity to learn how to build like their Mediterranean colleagues; but especially with having access to the services of a Provençal master carpenter and of Genoese caulkers leads one to think, along with Eric Rieth, that southern technology was practised at the Royal Arsenal of Rouen from the end of the fourteenth century. Unfortunately, for lack of proof, we cannot be certain that the experiment passed from the royal shipyards to other workshops. Two facts seem to prove, both in France and in England, an access to Mediterranean practices. The first concerns the construction and repair of royal galleys in Rouen in 1388–9 using the technique of carvel-building; the second, in 1416–17, concerns Henry V's appeal to Venetian, Catalan and Portuguese carpenters and caulkers to repair eight Genoese ships captured in the Channel by the English, because English shipbuilders were disoriented by a technology which was unfamiliar to them.

Another technological change, noticeable in the middle of the fifteenth century, seems to have been expanding into Western Europe around 1500. This expansion concerned a new type of boat called a caravel, from the name of the type of nail (*carvel*) used in assembling the ribs. Of modest tonnage, good for fishing and coastal trading, these boats owed their success to the Bretons, who introduced them and encouraged their imitation from Dieppe in 1451 and Hoorn in 1460 as far as Bordeaux, where they comprised half of all maritime traffic around 1482.

Technical changes thus tended to substitute one construction process for another and to promote its predominance in the long term. Proof of this can be found in the recasting carried out between 1480 and 1530 in France and England of ships of heavy tonnage, which were originally clinker-built and were then recast using carvel construction. In 1509 England transformed the *Sovereign*, which had been clinker-built twenty years earlier; but in 1509 too, the *Mary Rose* was still being clinker-built, and was not transformed into a carvel-built ship until 1536; this also occurred in France with the *Charente* and the *Grande-Louise*.

Nevertheless, the new technology did not become universal overnight. Inventories of naval resources from various countries testify to this, such as those of a ship's captain in the service of Louis XII and Francis I, Antoine de Conflans. Around 1417 the northern coast displayed a large variety of both clinker-built and carvel-built ships. Beyond Calais to the north, tradition remained so strong that in the middle of the sixteenth century the Scandinavian governments attempted in vain to persuade the private builders to change their techniques, so tenacious were old habits.

Indeed, many things happened around 1300. While the Atlantic was receiving visits from Mediterranean ships, the Inland Sea greeted an Atlantic type of boat, the arrival of which is noted by the chronicler Giovanni Villani in a famous page of his *History of Florence*:

> At that time (1304) certain men from Bayonne in Gascony, with their ships which we call *cocche* [cogs], passed through the straits of Seville and came to our sea while practising privateering. Henceforth, Genoese, Venetians and Catalans began to use the *cocche* for their navigations and ceased using huge boats, in order to navigate with more safety and at less cost. Thus this was a great change for our navy.

Few texts can express more clearly the symbiosis between the Mediterranean and the ocean, and the characteristics of the new type of ship: of Atlantic origin, average tonnage, profitability, security, speed and pugnacity. Even if Villani added a personal note to his assessment, it still deserves commentary.

The term *coca* was not new to maritime language. It appears in 1218 regarding a ship belonging to the Templars in southern Italy. But its use here refers to a definite and known genre: a round, rather short ship, high in the water, decked, equipped with a square box on the poop deck and a castle on a triangular platform on the prow, a great rigged mast and a lateen mizzen: of modest tonnage (at most 300 tons), its speed was appropriate for privateering. Such was, it seems, the *coca bayonesa*, a model for the Catalan, Genoese and Sicilian shipyards. Beyond an etymological derivation, it has been thought to have a connection with the Nordic cog. However, as mentioned earlier, an essential innovation, the stern rudder, the Bayonne or Biscayan or Navarre tiller, added to, then substituted for, the two lateral steering oars, then in general use. The name highlights the inventive role of mariners from the Bay of Biscay, and the importance of that region as a seat of technological progress.

The caravel, the cog and many other boats of average tonnage challenged the navigators of the large vessels, hulks and large *nefs* from the North, big Genoese naves and Mediterranean carracks, whose capacity corresponded to the needs of heavy cargoes and earned them success throughout the fifteenth century. That fashion was short-lived, however, since at the beginning of the sixteenth century the little sailing ship was affirmed as a flexible tool, demanding reduced manpower, therefore economically profitable. In an analogous way, at the time of the Italian wars, other new technology appeared along with the embarkation of artillery; a shipbuilder from Brest is attributed with the opening of the first known portholes in the flanks of *la Charente* in 1501. In addition, a sort of prefiguration of the conflict of the 'New School', at a distance of four centuries, saw at the beginning of the sixteenth century the opposition of the partisans of the huge combat vessels and those of the small harassing ships.

Thus the sixteenth century began with a change in the types of ships. For its part the galley had difficulty achieving a balance between its load of men and that new load, artillery; having reached the peak of its performance, it could no longer make progress. It henceforth had to limit its horizons to those of the inland seas, that is, to remain in the Mediterranean and later, in the eighteenth century, be offered an ephemeral compensation in the Baltic. That unexpected and later transformation at least proves its European character.

On the other hand, the destiny of the sailing ship remained in large part open, even though once the essential principles of its construction and rigging had been acquired, its later career was going above all to spread those principles, develop them and perfect their applications. A few situations show how technical progress was extended towards the north of Europe. Just as the Biscayan *coca* had prospered in the western Mediterranean in the fourteenth century, the new Atlantic sailing ship was making its way towards the Baltic. In 1412 the people of Damme attributed an unusual number of shipwrecks to clinker-built ships and called them 'scoundrels'. Even more significant was the adventure of the *Pierre* from La Rochelle. It was rotting in the port of Gdańsk while awaiting repairs which no one dared to undertake since that type of boat was unknown there. The town authorities judged it cumbersome and considered demolishing it, but in 1474 the war against England persuaded them to use it. It proved to have nautical qualities and served as a model. The inventory made at the time contains one of the first descriptions of a three-master. Carvel-built, the *Pierre* rigged a main mast with a mainsail and a studding-sail, a mizzen-mast with a studding-sail and a foremast with a small sail. Lightened, it took full advantage of the wind, and its third sail, the foresail, neutralized the effects of pitching. Handling it required a smaller crew than the huge hulks with their single mainsail. Capacity, security, speed, profitability – this time reconciled, they formed the claims of the newcomer, which set sail for the conquest of the European seas.

The path was open to which Europe, from north to south, was committed, for the exploitation of innovations was everyone's business. Holding course was facilitated by the general use of the stern rudder. Using the fair wind fully was taken care of by the square mainsail; but to go against the wind by tacking it was necessary to reduce the resistance of the hull as much as possible by neutralizing the drift and by accentuating the finesse of the lines of the ship; another very manageable sail was added to the mainsail, the 'lateen', triangular, fixed on the back of the ship. The lateen was considered characteristic of the Portuguese caravel, better conceived for rapid reconnaissance than for long campaigns. The naval equipment of the Discoveries was thus in place even before Christopher Columbus's voyages, and all Europeans had more or less directly taken part in the preparations.

The progress of nautical materials would not have made its full contribution to drawing Europeans closer together without the support of a perfecting of the art of navigation. In that realm as well, the end of the thirteenth century was decisive. Knowing one's position and choosing one's route, to modern eyes, are elementary conditions of maritime traffic. It has been argued that empiricism and experience, even a maritime sense, were enough for the Polynesians and the Scandinavians to cross the Pacific and the Indian Ocean on the one hand, and the Atlantic on the other. But it would be easy to reverse the terms of the objection: in how many deaths did those undertakings end? And what fruits did they bear, compared to the results acquired thanks to scientific methods?

The Mediterraneans, untiring coastal sailors, were cautious enough to prefer diurnal navigation close to the coasts and to practise winter harbouring. This enabled them to do without navigation instruments when they stayed in the Inland Sea. But what happened if they dared to leave it? Thus who can say whether the Vivaldi brothers had a compass to confront the Moroccan fog? The compass: it was, however, the Italians who transmitted its use to the mariners of north-western Europe. And what service it rendered them, on the ocean, in the English Channel and the North Sea, *en route* to Flanders!

Along with the compass, the use of the portolano was another Mediterranean gift for oceanic navigation. That term designates, as we have seen, two indispensable instruments: the map and the book. Practically speaking, the mariner found his route on the portolan chart, using a system of various coloured lines connecting the indicated places. At the same time, the sea books describing the shores indicated seamarks and beacons, passages and accesses to harbours, pointed out reefs as nautical instructions do, but in a direct style, using the familiar form of verbs. This content of the *portolani* found its equivalents in other European languages under the names of *routier* (French), *derrotero* (Spanish), *roteiro* (Portuguese), *rutter* (English), *Seebuch* (German) and *Leeskaart* (Dutch). The best known, published at the end of the fifteenth century, is the *Routier de la mer*, a work written in French by a Portuguese living in Poitou, Garcia Ferrande, which was translated into several languages.

Along with the descriptive content of these texts there were declination tables, calendars of tides illustrated in the manner of the popular genre of shepherds' calendars. Guillaume Brouscon and his heirs were some of those who produced those little commonly used manuals, working in Le Conquet, one of the nerve centres of the Breton coast; one can find relatively numerous copies of the work in libraries in France and England. This common technical baggage enabled navigators to take possession of the seas surrounding Europe.

There are other indications of that possession, harbingers of maritime discoveries. The most significant come, paradoxically, from the heart of continental Europe, specifically from Upper Germany; the Nuremberg School contributed, under conditions to which we shall later return, with its speculations to supporting the concrete effort of the Portuguese. Martin Behaim, through his cartographic work and his presence alongside the first discoverers, brought the message of all of Europe to the little team of great navigators.

Language and culture

Convergences justify no illusions. Europe had a thousand ways of communicating with the sea; so many differences contrasted the North and the South, the Ponant and the Levant. In Spain and in France, because of their two maritime façades, the contrasts are revealing. A French mariner has of course testified to this at the moment when the affirmation of monarchic unity and the overseas projection of the European nations argued in favour of a common identity, hidden by family quarrels.

Antoine de Conflans, a shrewd man, that northerner who went to war in the Mediterranean, wrote a *Livre des faiz de la marine et navigaiges*, and dedicated it to Francis I in 1519, four years after the king's accession to the throne. His reflections are not limited to France, but extend from the Baltic to the Adriatic, going beyond the diversity of naval resources to perceive human and cultural aspects. He noted that men who belonged to the same country and faithfully served the same king did not necessarily speak the same language, Normans and Provençaux, for example; but fighting together in the Aegean Sea, they ended up understanding each other. At the time when Conflans wrote, the languages of mariners in each country of Europe were reaping the rewards of an osmosis through which each group could recognize the contribution it had provided according to its unique genius and the particular orientations of its maritime activities. Augustin Jal, on the eve of the death-throes of the sailing navy in the middle of the nineteenth century, had been rightly inspired to undertake the inventory and the polyglot analysis of that common linguistic patrimony.

Underlying that linguistic diversity, Conflans acutely perceived the psychological diversity of seamen: 'The men', he wrote, 'in the Mediterranean sea are more subtle, at least they trade more subtly than those of the Ocean; those from the North go frankly and freely to work.' There was also a diversity of customs; it is regrettable that Conflans dispensed with commenting on 'the forms and ways of navigations' contained in the *Routier de la mer*, to which he only briefly refers. But he could not avoid a comparison between the customs regulated by the Consulate of the Sea at Barcelona and the *Rules of Oleron*, in use, he says, 'from the strait of Russia [the Sound] as far as the strait of Gebaltal [Gibraltar]'. According to him, the Consulate of the Sea was 'little different from the Rules of Oleron'; both on the commercial as well as on the military level, the Mediterranean, in his opinion, had rights 'similar to the ordinances of the Admiral' of France. Conflans thus seems to play down the differences he stressed earlier.

The coexistence of several juridical areas on the European seas cannot be doubted. Clearly, after the wish formulated by the International Commission of Maritime History at the Stockholm International Congress of Historical Sciences in 1960, there still remains much work to be done for the critical edition and the comparative study of ancient texts relative to the law of the sea. The heirs of Pardessus and Capmany, editors of the best-known juridical maritime texts, in no way discouraged by the abundance of manuscripts of the *Rules of Oleron* and the *Consulate of the Sea*, have specified the points of contact and the most characteristic differences between those two collections of jurisprudence.

The Greco-Latin heritage regarding maritime law had been preserved, in large part, in Mediterranean cities through the intermediary of Justinian legislation and especially with the *Lex Rhodia*. In the thirteenth century the *Partidas* of King Alfonso the Wise were inspired from the *Digeste*; in the following century Bartolomeo da Sassoferrato, using Roman principles, established certain general productive ideas for the later distinction of territorial waters and of the open sea, but which were already useful in his time for case-law concerning catches. At that time Latin tradition continued to be perpetuated in Venetian, Amalfitan, Genoese, Marseillais, and Catalan customs; especially in Barcelona, experts in 'the art and practice of the sea' had compiled the body of law in use at the end of the thirteenth century in the sort of code found in the *Libre del Consolat de Mar*. Mediterranean navigators sailing up to the northern ports disseminated the content of it in relation to commissioning and chartering ships, to the relationships between crews and employers, to the disputes resulting from risks and accidents at sea as well as disagreements between men.

As for those practices in use from the Bay of Biscay to the North Sea, they were not exempt from the classical and Mediterranean influences that came by sea. In some points the *Rules of Oleron* are indebted to the *Digeste* and to the *Basiliques*, and they retain from the Rhodian Sea Law the same arrangements concerning jettisoning as the *Consolat*. Oleron is located in the zone of contact between written and common law; the island was on the path of the crusaders and the *jacquets* travelling on pilgrimage by sea to the Orient and to Compostella, and La Rochelle included Italians among its inhabitants. It was there that the possibility of advancing southern influences could be found.

However, the *Rules of Oleron* having a practical objective, they were filled with daily realities, at least apparently local and diverse, for the regional names of their versions hid real connections and a common origin. The hypothesis attributing the origin of the text to Queen Eleanor of Aquitaine and its place of origin to Oleron Island has reason to stress the connection between the extension of the Plantagenet 'empire' and the influence of the traffic of wine and Aquitaine salt towards northern Europe.

Since the *Rules* were enriched with additions and changes at different dates in the course of their diffusion, the existing versions are of varying length and content; but their partial analogies or similarities are of the same genre as the affiliations of urban charters in the twelfth century. Europe possesses around forty-four such manuscripts, thirteen of which are from the fourteenth century, shortly after they were compiled. The languages into which the *Rules* have been translated or adapted (English, Flemish, Low German, Castilian), as well as the names of various printing houses, reflect the extent of their influence. That influence went from the Customs of Bayonne in Old Gascon to printings for the use of the Flemish (the customs of Damme) and the Hanseatics, from Lübeck, Gdańsk and especially Visby, whose court of justice gave particular fame to the Law of Gotland (*Gotlandisches Vasser-recht*)

The authority of the *Rules of Oleron* extended far and lasted for a long time. It seems hardly possible that in the middle of the twentieth century a court ruling from the United States, dealing with a catastrophe at sea, referred in one of its adduced reasons to an article of the *Rules*.

Gradually the contact between the practices of the North and the South brought about less a reciprocal contamination than complementarities and new developments of a regulatory nature. An example of this is in the practice of maritime insurance. In the middle of the sixteenth century, in part under the influence of the Castilians, notably in Rouen as well as in Antwerp, the perfection of the *Guidon de la mer* prefigured a move towards uniformity in that area of maritime law. At the same time consulary jurisdictions were in general use in the West and institutions of admiralties were strengthened. Indeed, admiralties are a characteristic example of analogies and contrasts, of time lags and complementarities. Thus we note the original contemporaneity of admiralties. The Arab etymology (*emir*) of the word expresses its heritage of caliphates and Byzantium; the institution spread like oil, beginning with the Mediterranean in the thirteenth century (Sicily, 1147; Genoa, 1181; Catalonia, 1230; France, 1248; Castile, 1254; Portugal, 1288; England, 1295), and its extension corresponded to the attention paid to maritime affairs by those states concerned about their authority at sea, over its shores and its men.

In various European countries, in the course of the following centuries, the state had to take those precedents into account, consider the customs and institutions, reject some, confirm others, and begin to construct analogous, sometimes similar, rules. Thus it was through a long development that in France, for example, Colbert's work was prepared: his codes are based upon a secular heritage.

To conclude, let us note that the navigators constantly moving from one port to another, found, despite such inevitable uprooting, a familiar atmosphere wherever they landed. In addition to the welcome and the protection the national groups offered to newcomers, the material framework offered known landscapes. The Mediterraneans, in Venice and Genoa as well as in Palermo, Montpellier, Palma, Barcelona, Valencia, and even on the Atlantic in Lisbon, found in the lodges of the merchants the natural place for the discussions customary where they carried out their business; likewise, the chapels of the fraternities, everywhere, brought them together close to the harbour where their boats were moored. The same thing happened in the North. The Spanish *Lonja* was reflected in the Bourse of Bruges in the fourteenth century. The tall brick house with stepped gables reigned from Artois to the bottom of the Baltic; this aspect of civilization, expressing seriousness and reserve, contains a certain austerity of regular lines emphasized by the red colour of the material and, often, an abundance of flowers. In the tower of the Hôtel de Ville of Gdańsk a Fleming could find a reflection of the belfries of Ypres and Bruges, and through its square towers Notre-Dame reminded him of the churches of

Damme and Malines; for their part, the English could see its connection with the churches of Earl's Barton and Clapham. Finally, they all experienced an impression of familiarity in the Dominican church/halls, for example in Gdańsk, at St Nicolas. There the affinities with the Flemish, English and Aquitaine Gothic are real; they enabled Pierre Francastel to note, through the testimony of art, 'the existence of a world of the sea from the tenth to the thirteenth century'. Further, all those places were decorated with paintings in which Italian and Flemish aesthetics were fused. Two maritime regions, two cultures, but one soul: that of European Christendom.

6

The Framework Bursts Apart:
Europe Present on All the Seas
(Sixteenth Century to the Present)

The initial intention in Europe's taking hold of its surrounding seas was to exploit all shores and to connect the maritime sectors of the North, the West and the South. The maritime element proved to be a source of profit and an arena of power; thus the seamen, who were naturally inclined to voyage ever further afield, then the terrestrial powers, driven to increase their authority, were quick to extend the field of their activity, and in so doing inevitably renewed and increased competition and conflicts inherited from earlier centuries. Whether they were individual or collective initiatives, mercantile and political enterprises encouraged the expansion of influence over neighbouring seas and ultimately extended their hold over all the oceans. It was an age-old process, whose chronological facts are less important here than is an attempt to point out, as precisely as possible, its primary characteristics and certain lines of force.

Initiatives

The opening of the Straits of Gibraltar to relationships with the Mediterranean and the Atlantic Ocean was the beginning of a sort of European conversion towards the West. This movement unfolded before a backdrop whose principal points of reference in the last centuries of the Middle Ages were the end of the Crusades, the withdrawal of the papacy to Avignon, the retreat of the maritime 'empires' of Genoa and Venice, the Ottoman advance – which surged as far as the Strait of Otranto – and the efforts of the Hanseatic League to keep for their own ships the traffic on the Nordic seas and to keep the Westerners as far as possible away

from it, especially the English, who were forced to direct their
navigators to the West.

Artisans and seats of expansion

A remarkable prescience, or rather an innate business sense, made
the Mediterraneans, especially the Italians, active participants in
the promotion of the Ocean. Some chronological coincidences at
the end of the thirteenth century are significant. For example, there
was the audacity of the Vivaldi brothers, lost at sea west of
Gibraltar, the sailing of Genoese and Venetian galleys as far as
Flanders, and the fall of the final Latin 'port' in the Holy Land,
Saint Jean d'Acre – events which occurred at the same time as the
gift of the portolano was given to navigators by the men from the
Inland Sea.

The result was that two centuries later, around 1500, an international chain of merchant groups linked the two poles of maritime
circulation, the Scheldt to the north and the southern extremity of
the Iberian peninsula to the south. The starting points to the north
were (after the decline of Bruges and Sluys) Antwerp, then
Amsterdam and London, and to the south, Lisbon and Seville. The
intermediate centres – Rouen and Nantes, Southampton and
Bristol, the ports of Biscay and Galicia – were not only stops, but
were also points of departure for oceanic expansion. In the western
Mediterranean Malaga, Valencia, Barcelona, Marseille, Genoa and
Leghorn were to serve as rear bases, stimulating business and
reaping the benefits of it.

This distribution of centres of initiative towards oceanic horizons was the direct result of the configuration of European shores.
At the end of the Middle Ages, as at their beginning, those
positions closest to the open sea were the most sought-after
wherever they offered protected sites; this was the case in the
south-west of Britain, in Brittany, in Galicia and Portugal. The
direct location on maritime routes worked in favour of Southampton rather than Rouen and St-Malo, of Nantes and especially of La
Rochelle rather than Bordeaux, and of Valencia rather than
Barcelona. Similarly, the convenience of relations with an extensive
hinterland worked to the advantage of the estuary ports, even

those located deep inside the continent: for example, Seville, Lisbon, Bordeaux, Nantes, Rouen, Antwerp, London and Hamburg.

European maritime expansion favoured this latter type of port because in them were united the factors necessary for development. They formed common ground, and recalling them is opportune, for the interdependence of the sea and the continent was reflected in them. The Oceanic and Nordic ports replicated the Mediterranean models. The Atlantic ports based their commercial role on the twin foundations of a financial function and of evolved business techniques. Without dethroning Genoa, the centres of Seville, Antwerp, Amsterdam and London successively became capital markets, centres of banking and stockholding transactions at home and abroad, headquarters of shipping companies as well as centres of maritime insurance. This last example is particularly significant: whereas Italian businessmen were already using insurance in the fourteenth century, the Atlantic world in the sixteenth century still engaged in the practice of taking out loans for great adventures for distant voyages. Gradually option insurance developed and found a favoured home in London.

The European change of direction from the Mediterranean towards the Atlantic and its northern extensions was subject to technical conditions and social circumstances. For its naval construction Atlantic Europe had abundant supplies of primary materials, which became all the more indispensable as technology became more demanding. The evolution of three-masters, from the caravel to the large vessels, going through the varied gamut of frigates, corvettes, galleons and other types of ships, increased this need. An international European market developed. Whereas local supplies of wood for hulls were sufficient, in many cases it became necessary to import wood from the North for masts. The Hanseatic League came to specialize in such trade, as well as in that of tar and pitch. Cantabrian Spain and Sweden provided iron for anchors; Brittany supplied materials for sails and ropes.

The recruitment of personnel enjoyed almost unlimited opportunities on the banks of the Atlantic and on the Nordic seas. As navigation demanded a lengthy period of familiarization and knowledge acquired through experience, the recruitment of crews depended on two ways of proceeding, though they were compatible. For long voyages it was necessary to resort to international hiring, in particular for pilots. Naturally Magellan recruited primarily in Spain and Portugal, but his expedition also included nine Frenchmen, five Flemings, two Englishmen, a German and several Italians, including Antonio Pigafetta, the narrator of the tale. Thus that crew had a clearly European appearance.

In most cases, though, recruitment was local and was carried out among the fishermen and small boatmen, an abundant and available workforce, particularly on the English, Breton and Hispanic coasts. Inevitably diverse motivations for working varied from the necessity to earn money to an attachment to the sea, curiosity and a taste for adventure.

Europe's first thrust overseas: Newfoundland

Although it was not chronologically the first of the 'Great Discoveries', nor even one of the most important, the discovery of Newfoundland was perhaps the most representative of the way in which Europe's sights were now set beyond the Ocean. Denied access to the Bergen market place by the Hanseatic League towards the end of the fourteenth century, the English from the east coast (Boston, Lynn, Hull) at first turned to the Icelandic waters, where they had found fishermen from Bristol. Those fishermen, when it became necessary in the second half of the fifteenth century to look for other fishing grounds, took the initiative in that exploration and happened on Newfoundland. Then came John Cabot's voyage of 1497. That event, too well-known to be told again here, nevertheless needs comment. The 'banks' of Newfoundland appeared on maps early on as an extension of European fishing grounds. In fact, if the Bristol fishermen recognized this in part of the northern zone, Bretons from the regions of Bréhat and Paimpol exploited the east and south, and led their Norman colleagues there from Fécamp and Agon, then those from Nantes, La Rochelle and Bordeaux. Biscayans and Portuguese also appeared on the 'banks', and locations were named in their languages. The discovery was indeed European. Rights over it were, not without argument, claimed by the English king Henry VII, but like many other such, the discovery could claim Italian parentage, for according to some, John Cabot and his three sons came from the Genoese nation of Valencia in Spain; furthermore, his admitted motive, beyond the quest for fishing grounds, was the search (which had been pursued in Bristol since 1480) for a 'certain island' called 'Brazil', in the tradition of European fancy.

The search for distant islands

Dreams and ambition always play a part in the impulse for discovery. Just as they sustain the desire for profit, they are in turn sustained by tenacity. European ascendency on the seas owes its success to these things.

The dream of islands is not just a literary theme which Europe shares with other cultures. It conceals an extraordinary potential for energy and one of its traits is perenniality. To what degree did European culture invest that dream in its maritime expansion? A technical reason might justify this obsession with islands, discovered by voyagers and represented on maps, up until the eighteenth century – that is, until the moment when, simultaneously in France and in England Berthoud and Harrison invented the marine chronometer, enabling the computation of longitude; before that the location of places was imprecise, especially that of the smaller islands. Stimulated by the help of mirages, the abundance of islands in the Atlantic seemed infinite and encouraged more searching.

Celtic traditions, and especially Europe's cultural inheritance from Antiquity, inspired the cartographers and even the chancelleries of the fourteenth and fifteenth centuries: St Brendan's Island, Antilia and the Seven Cities are destinations mentioned in exploration licences. Europe was seeking extensions and, following its dreams, ended up discovering realities during the two centuries before Christopher Columbus and John Cabot. The Portuguese and the Spanish were in the lead, supported by the Italians. Some Genoese explorers, the Pessagnos, received from the king of Portugal, along with the hereditary office of admiral, a mission to look for the Atlantic archipelagos; it was thus that one of their countrymen, Lanzarotto Malocello, shortly before 1336, discovered the Canaries, a prelude to their conquest by the Norman Jean de Béthencourt and to their attachment to the kingdom of Castile at the beginning of the fifteenth century. The movement then accelerated in more distant western directions: Madeira and

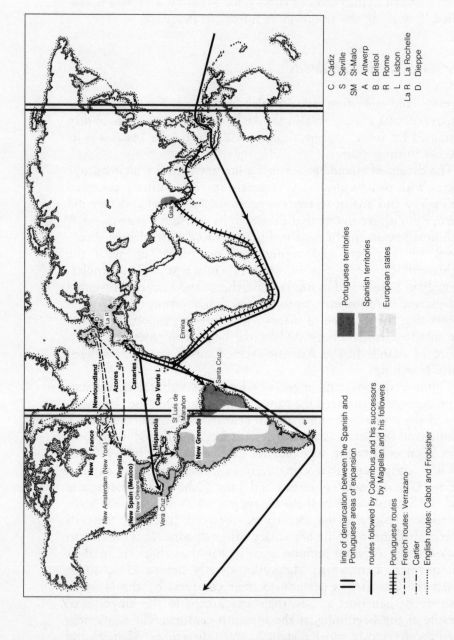

Figure 6.1   The European framework bursts apart: the sixteenth century

Legend labels within figure:

C   Cádiz
S   Seville
SM St-Malo
A   Antwerp
B   Bristol
R   Rome
L   Lisbon
La R La Rochelle
D   Dieppe

line of demarcation between the Spanish and
Portuguese areas of expansion

routes followed by Columbus and his successors
by Magellan and his followers

Portuguese routes
French routes: Verrazano
Cartier
English routes: Cabot and Frobisher

Portuguese territories
Spanish territories
European states

Map labels: New France, Newfoundland, Azores, New Amsterdam (New York), Virginia, New Spain (Mexico), New Orleans, Hispaniola, St Luis de Maranon, Vera Cruz, New Grenada, Santa Cruz, Canaries, Cap Verde I., Elmina, Goa the Azores became Portuguese lands in 1425 and 1427, a few years before Prince Henry the Navigator directed discoveries towards the African coasts. In a few decades maritime expansion north of the 36th parallel opened up for Europe a sector of the ocean covering around two million square kilometres, more than 2200 kilometres wide; this image was immediately drawn on the porto-lanos, not without blending fact and fiction in words that could equally be Latin, Italian or Catalan. The portolano of Dulcert in 1339 mentions only the Canaries, but the situation was already different in the Laurentian Atlas (1351), the map of the Pizziganis (1367), and especially in the 'Catalan' Atlas of Abraham Cresques (1375) and the maps of the fifteenth century (for example, those of Mecia de Viladestes of 1413, and Benincasa of 1467). The Portu-guese *volta* initiative, which pushed the bend of the African coastal route to Lisbon as far out as the Azores in order to avoid the trade winds and to pick up the winds from the west, well illustrates the association of oceanic navigation with that of the European coasts.

All European maritime nations contributed to the immense undertaking, in the nautical realm as well as from a financial point of view. The humble yet decisive role of fishermen, indispensable collaborators, has often been passed over in silence; but although they might have appeared as subordinates, they were not just inert players. Likewise, the importance of Italian financiers, shipowners and captains has sometimes overshadowed the presence of others. Granted, in the Iberian ports we have seen the Genoese, then the Florentines hold the reins due to their numbers, their wealth and their influence. There were, however, others from various nations. Among them was Ferdinand Van Olmen, of Flemish origin, Lusitanianized under the name of Fernão d'Ulmo, the unfortunate precursor of Christopher Columbus; a captain from the Azores, in 1486 he undertook, with the consent of the king of Portugal, an expedition to the west of that archipelago, but his ship sank after he had set sail at the end of the winter of 1487. This is why the famous Genoese came to propose to the king of Castile the same voyage which succeeded in October 1492.

In general official power only intervened secondarily to author-ize, support and, in the best cases, to take advantage of private, individual or collective undertakings. Its active participation, in-deed its initiative, was very slow to assert itself. The antecedence of private initiative resulted, it seems, from the motives of its instigators. To invoke 'gold and spices' is to give priority to economic motives; but although justified, such an interpretation does not exhaust all the motives of maritime expansion at the end of the Middle Ages and the beginning of the modern age. Without those motives all the various conjunctions would not have come together, and above all undertakings would not have been repeated because of the risks and failures. However, the difficulties encountered during voyages were largely compensated for by the seductive attractions of the sun and the light, of escape, of all sorts of opportunities which were offered by the islands, not to mention the profits (sugar from Madeira, the successor to that of Andalusia, of Sicily and of Crete), which spread across the continent from around 1470. All this supported and developed the island myth, in which the 'Islands of America' in the eighteenth century appeared as the promised land: was not 'Antilia', against all odds, to survive in the Antilles islands?

News and propaganda

The ongoing success of the dream owed much to the reputation of its attractions. Twentieth-century advertising for ocean cruises is the great-granddaughter of the spread of news of the sea in earlier times. Various places competed in spreading it. From Seville and Lisbon, rumours were propagated more quickly than one might imagine. The channels they followed were, for example, merchant correspondence destined for Milan, Lyon and Antwerp, announcing the arrivals of ships and the prospect of fruitful transactions. The Roman Curia was the incomparable crossroads of all information, and echoed the addresses of obedience through which the Portuguese sovereign and the Catholic kings let the Head of the Church know of the successes and hopes of the missions that were made possible by European expansion at sea and beyond. Even ordinary folk took part in the explosion of excitement through popular festivals, Portuguese *momos*, Dieppe mummers' entertainments, royal visits to the towns; in them, natives of distant lands, with exotic fauna and flora, were portrayed as active participants. Lisbon, Seville, Antwerp, Rouen, Dieppe, St-Malo, Nantes and London became open doors from Europe into the wide world. As we know, Thomas More set his meeting with Raphael Hythloday in Antwerp, relating Hythloday's ideas concerning an island paradise in *Utopia*; but 'Hythloday' etymologically means 'rumour-monger', and Utopia, 'no place'. It can be seen, therefore, as a dream brought by the distant sea.

The sea – an affair of state: to be king of the sea

With some disagreement between seamen and merchants, those who governed perceived the importance of the sea for the formation, prosperity, independence and defence of their states: hence the role of the sea in the construction of Europe, and subsequently in the awakening of a European personality. Verification of this is relatively easy in the cases of the Italian towns; neither Venice, Genoa, nor even Florence would have reached their preeminent position without the support of the sea. The Iberian peninsula presents a variety of situations: Catalonia and the kingdom of Valencia were inconceivable without the sea; Castile could depend upon the activity of the Cantabrian coast, but it had to await the age of the Catholic kings to acquire the rank of a maritime power, balanced on its three sides – Mediterranean, Andalusian and Basque. Portugal owes everything to the sea, but only became truly aware of this after the war which ended in 1385 on the battlefield of Aljubarrota, and which freed it from its Castilian bonds. The same can be said about England, whose marine destiny only became apparent after it was evicted from the continent at the end of the Hundred Years' War; however, during the hostilities England had already felt the imperatives of its insular position, and all its later history was dominated by that circumstance. At the same time France experienced the demands of its defence and of its commercial interests at the beginning of the thirteenth century under Philip Augustus, who took a series of steps to deal with them, then in the fourteenth century under Charles V and in the sixteenth century from Louis XII to Henry II. Thus the European kingdoms until the sixteenth century gradually, but separately, became aware of their maritime interests. A comparative look at those processes will enable us to discover what they had in common – that is, what was European.

The essential element of that common denominator, even if it engendered competition, rivalries and conflicts, was financial interest, exactly as in inheritance quarrels between close relatives. Gradually, the notion of what the American admiral Mahan called 'sea power' inspired, then guided, the leaders of various states from the end of the Middle Ages. A controversy in the middle of the fifteenth century involved opposing French and English satirists. The final outbursts of the Hundred Years' War encouraged that sort of verbal conflict, underlying the true war: *The Libelle of Englyshe Policye* was written around 1440, and the *Débat des hérauts d'armes de France et d'Angleterre* [translated as 'The Debate Betwene the Heraldes of Englande and Fraunce' by John Coke] was written fifteen to twenty years later. On both sides the authors hurled reproaches and invective at each other, but it is interesting to note in the two principals, both equally devoted to their kings and attached to their homelands, arguments based on common conceptions and proposing analogous, if not similar, solutions. From their writings emerges a quite precise view of Western maritime traffic, the advantages of which are claimed by both pamphleteers. The French author challenges the king of England's mastery over the sea; the French king could, in his opinion, hold it, for he possessed 'good ports' and 'enough merchandise to fill up his ships'. The Englishman, on the contrary, supports the thesis of British sovereignty over the narrow seas which an ardent polemic literature was expressing at that time. 'We be maysters of the narowe see', said the *Libelle*, while another pamphlet proclaimed: 'Anglia! propter tuas naves et lanas omnia regna te salutare deberent'.

Thus in the middle of the fifteenth century a political hypothesis was formulated on the strategic and economic levels, linked to each other in a way which Mahan would not have contradicted. We can extract its broad outlines and perceive its extension beyond France and England, along with the immediate effects and later consequences.

The military aspects of the question are well known. The two adversaries of the Hundred Years' War, as well as the Iberian kingdoms, the Italian towns and the Hanseatic League, and in the fifteenth century the duchies of Burgundy and Brittany, provided themselves with the naval forces which the concept of statehood increasingly implied, with access to the sea to ensure security there

and to protect ships and trade. That became all the more evident as
shipboard artillery and the use of portholes gave warships a
specific appearance and role. The state had its ships, installed its
military ports (for example, Le Havre, Portsmouth), developed
admiralties and maintained a specialized personnel. In the sixteenth
century, from the Italian wars to the adventure of the Invincible
Armada, including the fleets of Lepanto, the European states took
on a naval appearance, separately, but with common traits; when
occasion arose, facing Algiers, Tunis and Djerba as at Lepanto,
concerted naval formations were able to cut a European figure.
Indeed, at that time the Turks served as a catalyst for hostile
energies.

Protectionisms

The common preoccupation of governments with matters of the
sea could be considered egocentric, if not egotistical, and above all
nationalistic down the centuries, but it nevertheless deserves
mention. The satirists mentioned above devoted part of their work
to showing, as the Frenchman said, that 'he who is the strongest at
sea can call himself king of the sea as long as his strength endures'.
Protectionism, starting pretty much everywhere at the end of the
thirteenth century, sought a means through the institution of taxes,
which for lack of another term can be called customs duty.
Collection offices functioned in the English ports to collect
'customs'; in France the term *ports et passages* for the royal
administration of analogous taxes corresponded similarly to a will
to control; the same observation applies to the Catalan and
Castilian *quemas, peatjes, quiatges*, the Portuguese *alfandegas*, and
the Hanse *Pfundzoll*. The duke of Burgundy received half his
revenues from the sea.

Taxation did not constitute the only resource of protectionism,
however. Prohibition of imports and exports was enforced
depending on the moment and even on whim. This often balanced
a system of privileges reserved for a particular port for a particular
item of merchandise. The very name of the regime of the *Etape*,
concerned with enforcing the monopoly of English wool exports
into Calais after its conquest by Edward III in 1347, expresses state
control. There were other analogous cases: the Hanseatic League

reserved fish traffic in Bergen; France favoured the import of spices only through the port of Aigues-Mortes; later there appeared the jealous monopoly of other spices and precious metals in the hands of Portuguese and Spanish kings. The relationship of European countries to the sea was organized through interdicts; although that that did not yet create a Europe, nevertheless through negative paths and a convergence of contradictory interests it prepared one . . . from afar.

Protectionisms went beyond the framework of fiscal administrations and tended first to snugly reserve maritime traffic for 'national' ships. The favour of the flag found its origin in various forms, from over-taxing foreign ships to a preferential fiscal regime for one's own, and to the establishment of a monopoly in favour of the latter. All of this caused other problems; and in the realm of naval construction as well as in the organization of protective convoys, external cooperation sometimes had to be solicited.

Italian towns, having enough ships to be able to rent them out, were concerned with their equipment for that end as much as with reserving the traffic from their external possessions. With Jacques Coeur, France had the experience, short but exemplary, of a monopoly on Oriental traffic reserved to ships flying the flag of the *fleur-de-lys*; but the geographical diversity of its maritime interests sometimes produced contradictory attitudes; thus in 1500 the Saintongeais proposed urging foreigners to use French ships; the Bretons suggested discriminatory measures against the Iberians; and the citizens of Rouen, very bound up with activity in Antwerp, proclaimed that 'nothing is more profitable than freedom'.

Mare clausum or *mare liberum*

However, the cause of free exchange was not won. In France Claude de Seyssel, the bishop of Marseille, advised Francis I not to stop exporting French products in foreign ships. As for Spain, it had chosen the path of a naval monopoly, to which it remained attached until the end of its American empire. It had asserted the favour of the flag in 1491, 1498, 1500, and again in 1523, with an insistence which facts would later contradict. The same was true for Portugal which at the beginning of the sixteenth century launched, to the benefit of its nationals, the notion of *mare clausum*. This phrase was taken up again on behalf of the English navy when John Selden (1584–1664) declared that maritime space was, like that of land, able to be appropriated. However, at that time the partisans of *mare liberum*, open to trade by all, had as their flag-bearer the Dutch juridical school led by Hugo Grotius (1604).

In any case, the two theses proved that Europe was focusing its attention on matters of the sea. Taking a practical position halted competition rather less than it stimulated privateering and piracy. This situation already had long-standing precedents. Indeed, England, to reap the benefit of its insular situation, early on sought to claim the favour of the flag for itself. Its first Navigation Act dates from Richard II in 1381, and the intent, if not the text, which inspired it was reiterated, notably under Henry VII (1489) and Henry VIII (1540). The necessity of these renewals, intended to discourage foreigners, might cause one to doubt the effectiveness of that legislation. It did none the less contribute to the development of the British Merchant Marine, to the extent of its having acquired and conserved the symbolic significance of the mercantilist politics frequently advocated by the House of Commons.

The way in which, from the end of the fifteenth century, England definitively took into account the value and importance of its island location, verifies Fernand Braudel's observation that 'all grandeur assumes a dominated space, more vast than the privileged space which truly belongs to it'; England became, Braudel later says, 'a merchant navy anchored in Europe'. The surrounding maritime space had been perceived by the author of the *Libelle of Englyshe Policye* as a sort of reserved domain, the *mare Britannicum* of the cartographers of that time, the 'Channel', overseen and even guarded at that time by the town of Calais. The 'view', around 21 kilometres, generally accepted at that time as the approximate distance at which one could, in fair weather, sight and recognize a sail, served as an argument for the control of a strait from both its shores.

The notion of a territorial sea at the same time provided a basis for the claim to a salute at sea demanded, as we have seen, by an English author in the fifteenth century. That claim had a short life. In 1603 the French statesman Sully, going on a mission to London, was indignant that his boat was taken under fire by an English ship

demanding to be saluted. However, Sully was not a champion of
the maritime cause. Later, in 1662, there occurred the famous affair
of the flag in which Louis XIV, so as not to be outdone, had the
right recognized in London for his vessels 'also' to be saluted by
English ships on the ocean and in the Mediterranean.

The sea, a component of the power of the state

In Europe the sea had acquired the value of a component of the
power of a state, but not everywhere at the same time nor to the
same degree. In a general way, the role of the sea in the assertion of
power was inversely proportional to the extent of a given territory.
As far back as the thirteenth century, the Italian towns, Venice and
Genoa in particular, gave proof of their precociousness. Their
overseas possessions, stretching as far as the Black Sea, reactivated
the ancient concept of thalassocracy. And before England, Portugal, and later the United Provinces had founded – some on an
island, others on a narrow margin of the continent – their maritime
domination, the Mediterranean experienced, in the middle of the
fifteenth century, the expansion of the crown of Aragon. Starting
with a Catalan expansion as far as the Aegean Sea, the voluntarism
of Alfonso V the Magnanimous (1418–1456) had united in a sort of
federation Catalonia, the kingdom of Valencia, Sardinia, the
kingdom of Naples, and Sicily; in 1449 he proclaimed a programme which imposed on those states a few elements of maritime
imperialism: the prohibition of certain foreign imports, the growth
of naval construction, and a monopoly of the Aragonese flag. For
its part the kingdom of France, an integral part of the continent by
virtue of its borders as well as the attachment of its inhabitants to
the land, and torn between terrestrial imperatives and maritime
attractions, experienced hesitations and delay. It was perhaps one
of the merits of Charles VII's silversmith, Jacques Coeur, to have
demonstrated the importance of the maritime domain; Louis XI
confirmed its value. Charles VIII and Louis XII both took
advantage of its possibilities during the wars with Italy; but it fell
to the kings of the sixteenth century, from Francis I to Henry II, to
develop them. Independent of the organization of a military fleet,
of the establishment of Le Havre and of the impulse given to trade,
their awareness manifested itself even in the details of a kind of
political propaganda.

Francis I had read the chapter in the *Monarchie de France* in which Claude de Seyssel, around 1519, demonstrated 'how it would be expedient to have and to maintain an army at sea'. It was on the sea, he thought, and citing examples in support, that 'greater things than by those who have only an army on land', could be achieved; and from the sea would come 'the growth of the states of the prince', and for the inhabitants 'increased wealth'. Seyssel was not the only one to learn from the experience of the Italian wars. A famous example is that of a great lord from the Low Countries, Philippe of Cleves, lord of Ravenstein; related to all the dynasties and thus a true European, he served both the king of France and the emperor, as an admiral of the kingdom of Naples, as 'admiral of the sea' in the Low Countries, and as governor of Genoa. His *Instruction de toutes manières de guerroyer* accords to naval war the status corresponding to the importance with which he views it. Written at the beginning of the century, published in Paris in 1558, this book found convinced followers in King Henry II and the admiral de Coligny. The king then conceived a true naval programme.

However, the religious wars interrupted the efforts undertaken to ensure France maritime holds comparable to those which Elizabeth I, Philip II and the Estates-General of the United Provinces had respectively ensured for their countries. Political decisions seemed to be ahead of actions.

From the sea European individuality is born

The minds of a few men, in the fifteenth and especially the sixteenth century, saw further than the limited framework of state interests. Such thought simultaneously experienced both retrograde aspects and visionary premonitions. The word 'Europe' insinuated itself with the sense of a concept superior to particularisms. In truth, it was not all new, and the ideal of Christendom served as a reference and provided a mode of transition. Plans for crusades found a new stimulus with the taking of Constantinople by the Ottomans and continued to work for the union of the West as far as Lepanto and even beyond, until the fall of Crete in 1669. Pope Pius II had delivered a speech of a prophetic nature to the congress of Mantua in 1459 and, in writing to the sultan Muhammad II himself, defined Europe geographically as it could then be conceived in the face of the Turkish peril, and in terms which the twentieth century cannot refute. The Pope made his view explicit:

> It is in Europe itself, that is, in our homeland, that we are attacked. We cannot believe that you are so ignorant ... as not to see the power of the Christian people, how valiant is Spain, how warlike is France, how populated is Germany, how strong is [Great] Britain, how firm is Poland, how energetic Hungary, how rich, passionate and expert at arms is Italy.

This geographic tableau corresponded to the testimony of certain travellers who crossed Europe in the fifteenth century, such as Gilles le Bouvier, known as the Berry Herald, and later Jerome Munzer.

However, Europe's assimilation with old Christendom continued to prevail. It postulated the union of princes. Having learned from their failure at Varna in 1444, the princes of eastern Europe were particularly sensitive to the Turkish threat; for example, the king of Bohemia, George Podiebrad, invited the Christians of Europe to cooperate. The religious significance of the word *Christianitas* was to give way to *Europa*, less out of a misplaced concern than out of an obstinate humanist aversion to neologisms, as could be seen with Erasmus – without, however, his demonstrating a penchant for the sea, that man from Rotterdam who took God as his witness that he would never conceive the horrible idea of navigation.

The writings of Guillaume Postel, a great voyager by sea as well as on land, as well as a professor at the Collège de France, lacked a basis in reality, but were capable of a certain influence. He conceived in his *De orbis terrae concordia* a project of universal empire, where maritime and commercial law (the author was Norman) would contribute to the equilibrium of the state; to support that equilibrium, the visionary Postel proposed inventions in the military realm, notably the construction of unsinkable vessels. For him the 'good life' in this harmonious world would be achieved by the king of France – the issue, according to the time-honoured myth, of the Trojans, whose maritime migrations had reached from Scythia to the Pillars of Hercules. This ideal internationalism was thus confused with expansionist and imperialistic tendencies. The latter found a favoured place among the maritime populations, 'finer' and more aware than those of the 'interior', according to Jean Bodin (*La République*, 1576), a contemporary of Postel.

Furthermore, jurists developed the propositions formulated by Bartolomeo da Sassoferrato: the theory of the right of the people, that is, of nations, for Grotius reserved a privileged place to maritime relationships; commercial law was recognized as an article of the state. In addition, throughout the sixteenth century an effort was made to clarify, normalize and internationalize the rules and practices of commercial law; the success of the early maritime code, the *Guidon de la mer*, from Spain to the Low Countries and including Rouen, attests to this.

Nevertheless, towards the end of the sixteenth century, France, shaken by its religious disputes, had scarcely any other perspectives than to follow the advice of Sully and return to its two 'nurturing breasts, farming and breeding'. Marine horizons? That was for the future.

The teachings of the maritime experience were not, however, in vain for all Europeans. It was a man of the land, Cardinal de Granvelle, a native of Franche-Comté, who advised Philip II in 1586 to take advantage of the union of Portugal with his crown to transfer his capital to Lisbon, the crossroads, if ever there were one, of the great maritime routes. Significant counsel, but it went unheeded. The pack of Dutch 'sea beggars' put obstacles in the way of the Spanish on the sea and overseas. And as Sir Walter Raleigh said, 'Whosoever commands the sea commands trade; whosoever commands the trade of the world, commands the riches of the world, and consequently the world itself.'

The sea – the stakes of power: a coveted and guarded prey

A writer when he wanted to be, Cardinal Richelieu left an allegorical work entitled *L'Europa*. The 'Queen of Queens', Europe itself, courted by *Francion* and *Ibère*, whose names obviously designate France and Spain, repels the advances of *Ibère*, the false lover who seeks only to dominate it. It makes *Francion* its champion. Around the three principals, other participants serve as foils: *Germanique* (the Empire), *Austrasie* (Lorraine), *Mélanie* (Milan), *Parthénope* (Naples) and *Ausonie* (Italy). Curiously, England is absent. The argument does not lack symbolic significance. It corresponds to the political situation at the time of Louis XIII, and could well extend to later times, and even to our own by changing the characters. Europe pulled this way and that – the sea has contributed not a little to this. Offering its services to some, inviting others to request them, it was a place of competition or a battlefield, remaining until our own time the object of desire of heirs who were envious of each other. Those heirs, at the end of the twentieth century, still have difficulty conceiving of a balanced cooperation, which requires a transformation of mindsets as well as sacrifices.

For Europeans the sea has thus remained an object of possession, jealously guarded or avidly coveted. The former involved maritime nations formed into states earlier than others. Aside from Genoa and Venice in the Middle Ages, France, England, Spain and Portugal have since the beginning of the modern era been characteristic examples of powers based on the sea or seeking enjoyment, expansion and domination from it. The second category includes states motivated by political ambition, like the others, to obtain access to the sea, to ensure themselves unhindered maritime traffic, to participate in the advantages of expansion. So everything has taken place as if, for a state, advancement to superior rank had to pass through the stage of acquisition of a certain maritime power. It happened like this for Holland, Sweden, Prussia and Russia in the modern age, followed in the contemporary world by Bismarck's Germany, Austria-Hungary, Italy, Greece and the USSR.

The conquest of 'sea power' in the modern age

For each of the two categories mentioned above, the process of acquiring maritime power presented analogies, and sometimes similarities. The origin of this lay in the conviction that the sea provided a complement to power and a token of efficiency. The conquest of sea power first assumed a clear perception of the objectives to be attained and the means to use, then a deliberate and consistent activity. The most common cases were conflicting circumstances: commercial competition degenerating into hostilities born on or extended to the sea. There are abundant examples of this in Europe's past. The power of Venice and Genoa lasted beyond the Middle Ages. The maritime empire of Spain did not collapse until the nineteenth century; and that of Portugal, the oldest member of the group, held firm until decolonization in the second half of the twentieth century. The sea seems to have guarded the secret of perpetuity in the face of which the Invincible Armada on the one hand, or Dutch competition on the other, were only episodes or avatars.

For every state aspiring to possess the sea the first item of importance was to have many efficient ships, from both a commercial and a military point of view. 'Sea power' required that price. And 'price' is indeed the term to use, for a navy cost dearly and had to be profitable on economic, military and political levels. 'The sea', said Mahan, 'is above all a vehicle.' It permitted distant exchanges, migrations and activity. According to an American formula, the navy 'projects into the distance the influence or activity of the country it comes from, supports them, and prolongs them.' The strategies of the economy and of armed force were not mistaken. Navalism is again defined by Mahan as 'the indicator and the motor of imperialism'. Examples abound, and only a few can be cited here. In renewing and consolidating the Navigation Act in 1651, Cromwell had understood this. Richelieu, 'the great Master and Superintendent of Navigation', remembered his ancestor Guyon Le Roy du Chillou, to whom Francis I had entrusted the establishment of Le Havre. The founding fathers of the modern French fleets were Richelieu and Colbert, who achieved Richelieu's intentions like a clerk carrying out the plans of a statesman, as Henri Hauser said, somewhat unkindly. One might cite their successors up until Louis XVI, thanks to whom France possessed a navy such as she would never have again, except under Napoleon III and in the twentieth century thanks to Georges Leygues, the Minister for the Navy in 1925–1927. All of this has been said by contemporary historians such as E.H. Jenkins in England, Etienne Taillemite, Maurice Dupont, Jean Meyer and Philippe Masson in France, and José Merino in Spain. Continuity is always a condition for success. Naval power is a long-term proposition. And the term was not short in England, where the sea, being close to everyone, was of interest to the entire nation; the weaknesses of the

eighteenth century were only ephemeral. The French, following
their temperament and spoiled by the variety of their possibilities,
were less constant. At times they allowed themselves to be
overcome by theoretical discussions; thus under the influence of
the 'Jeune Ecole', around 1900, the temptations of fashion prevailed: there was a mania for technical performance of a few
experimental models in the realm of naval construction; above all,
in the eyes of a few generations obsessed by the fear of an invasion
by land, the sea appeared as a luxury rather than an opportunity.
On the Iberian side, the use of far from negligible assets lacked
economic and demographic roots, and with routine being substituted for consistency, equipment became outdated.

From the era of shipping companies
to maritime imperialisms

Trading companies to the rescue

Besides the continuity of naval effort, maritime power demanded a
balanced use of materials. On the civil level, modern societies have
conceived of the system of trading companies as being more
efficient than a military effort in interesting a nation in the sea and
in encouraging its expansion. The English Merchant Adventurers
in the sixteenth century, with the blessing of Elizabeth I, sought
paths in all directions, even in the one – the north-east passage – whose future was to open up only in the twentieth century.
The struggle against Spain established the maritime power of the
Netherlands and brought about the fortune in the East Indies of
the 'Gentlemen' of the famous Vereenigde Oostindische Compa-
nie, whose portraits were painted by artists including Rembrandt,
among others. The seventeenth and eighteenth centuries were the
era of trading companies; Richelieu's attempts in that domain
served as lessons for Colbert, who borrowed his models from the
United Provinces. His wish for prosperity broke the Netherlander
stronghold which had stifled the efforts of French merchants on
their own ground, in Nantes, 'Little Holland'. The Dutch war was
an economic conflict weighted, in an ephemeral way, in favour of
Louis XIV. In fact, the Anglo-Dutch union achieved by William of

Orange in 1688 was a great step towards British maritime predominance.

Military and civil fleets, a rational use of civil fleets within the framework of favoured companies, then of private ownership, were, on the European level, the foundations of a power expressed by numerical givens whose recent statistical analysis provides much to consider. They appeared in the numbers of vessels, frigates and store ships, with their accompanying sails and cannon, just as today the maritime power of a country is expressed in terms of tonnage and speed. Comparisons, revealing as to the level of power, highlight the competition between England and France, which reached a height that would have turned to France's advantage but for the Revolution and its costly wars. Henceforth, in the nineteenth century, British pre-eminence in the Victorian era was the fruit of the conjunction of a double military and commercial effort, in the service of expansion, the third panel of a triptych.

The ocean as a reflector of Europe

Expansion on the sea and overseas was the standard by which the role of oceans in the power of European states, starting with the Age of the Great Discoveries, was measured. Those discoveries projected the European image overseas; the geographic nomenclature explorers inscribed on the map of the world translates that intent, for example Hispaniola, Cartagena, New Spain, New Castile, Belem, New Amsterdam, Boston, New England, New France, Montreal, Louisiana, New Orleans and countless others as far as the antipodes. Emigration followed the impulses of discovery, transposing principally into North America European types of societies with their customs, languages and religious rifts. From Canada to Florida, along the present-day eastern coast of the United States, which Jean de Varassène (alias Giovanni Verrazano) was the first European to recognize on behalf of Francis I in 1524, Spanish, English, French, Portuguese (in Newfoundland), Netherlander and Danish (in the Antilles) Europe left its mark. It is not suprising that, despite the differences accentuated by time and a marginal position vis-à-vis the Old Continent, the sea maintained the ties it had made. The New World proved to the Old one its memory of its ancestry and parentage in the course of and following two world wars. At a time when Europe is defining its own identity and is seeking to organize itself, does America's connection to the western world truly pose a problem?

A new generation of maritime states

The second generation of European states acquiring maritime power includes those whose geographical location or degree of political evolution had until a certain point excluded them from the concert of states located close to the ocean. The role of straits played an important part in the first case, that of Sweden, Prussia and Russia. History has weighed heavily on the destiny of those living on the Baltic. Denmark demonstrated what it costs to have been a maritime power and how much courage it takes to safeguard what remains of it. From its former maritime empire and from its ability once again in the seventeenth century to spread to the Antilles and the Indies, there still remain Greenland and the Faeroe Islands, and the key position of Copenhagen. Denmark had to defend Copenhagen against Hitlerian Germany as it had done in 1801 and 1807 during the Napoleonic wars, and in the eighteenth century, on the eve of peace with the North, against Sweden. Denmark had to wage a constant struggle against destiny and to thwart the appetites of newcomers.

The navy of Gustavus Adolphus of Sweden (1594–1632) did not play a role beyond the Baltic, but without it, that is without transport ships, the Swedish armies would not have achieved their conquests. Gustavus Adolphus paid the very keen attention to his navy which his ambition required. He turned Karlskrona into a powerful naval base, the seat of the Admiralty and the Arsenal. Under his reign the fleet, which included only 50 ships in 1613, increased to 90 more powerful ships. Among them was the *Wasa*, a very beautiful vessel with sixty-four cannon, but too heavy in the shallows; it capsized on its first sortie in 1629. Taken out of the mud of the bay of Stockholm some thirty years ago, the wreckage, well preserved, remains a testimony to naval power as it was conceived in the first half of the seventeenth century.

The Thirty Years' War had maritime aspects which have often been misunderstood. Thus Emperor Ferdinand II, to fight at sea against Gustavus Adolphus, in 1628 added to his commander

Wallenstein's land functions that of 'Captain General of all imperial fleets and General of the Ocean Sea and the Baltic'. Wallenstein founded an arsenal at Wismar, but in less than four years the Swedish navy captured the imperial ships and put and end to the first attempts at an imperial navy. This lesson was well taken by the Great Elector of Brandenburg, Frederick William (1620–1688), who did not omit the sea in his role as founder of Prussian greatness. His great-grandson, Frederick II, at the time of the Great Elector's exhumation to lay his body with those of his ancestors in the new cathedral in Berlin, had, it is reported, this to say to his entourage: 'Sirs, this man achieved much.' Frederick William in his youth had contributed to taking the banks of Brandenburg and the island of Rügen from the Swedish, and, staying in Holland, where he was connected with the House of Orange, had assessed the maritime vitality of that country. That double experience led him to create out of an admittedly small navy, and to organize, with the help of a Dutch shipowner, Benjamin Raule, a trading company dealing with Africa and the Antilles, prefiguring, with its thirty-two ships, at a distance of two centuries, the ambitions of his distant successor, Emperor William II of Germany.

The Great Elector had learned his lessons in Holland. Peter the Great of Russia did his apprenticeship there, tools in hand, in the shipyards of Zaandam. He knew precisely what was needed to build a ship, how to do it, and how much to pay. A trip to Western Europe completed his education. It was thus with first-hand knowledge that he provided an impulse to a maritime policy based on direct and personal experience, inspired by examples sanctioned by Holland, but also by Venice. The tsar sent fifty young men (twenty-two to the United Provinces, and twenty-eight to Venice) to learn navigation; in Venice seventeen of the Russian apprentices received instruction from a Dalmatian, Marko Martinovič of Perast, whom Venice had hired as a professor; one of Martinovič's countrymen, Matija Zurajevič, was to become admiral of the Russian fleet. Peter the Great's first objective was to contain Sweden, whose fleet could prevent his opening 'a window onto the Baltic'. The founding of St Petersburg, with the naval fortress of Kronstadt, was a symbolic act, the price of which he made the Swedish pay; using the support of the Åland Islands, the Russian galleys were able to outclass the Swedish and even threaten

Stockholm. In addition, the tsar's will to power inspired him to construct ships of the line, able to cross the Sound: thirty-five of them in 1725.

Another objective was to have access to the Black Sea and the Mediterranean. For that he had to be patient because Russian politics were coming up against the thickness of the Ottoman Door, admittedly worm-eaten, as well as against British commercial interests and against the secular agreement between the French and the Turks. Catherine II, concerned, she said, with 'the honour of her flag' spared nothing. In 1770, a Russian fleet left Kronstadt to destroy a Turkish fleet at Cesme, opposite Chios, by going right round Europe; from afar, such events served as a prelude to the long detours which Russia's continental massiveness imposes upon it, such as the crossing of Admiral Rodjestvensky's squadron in 1905 around South Africa as far as Japan. By asserting itself as a maritime power Russia was delivering a double blow: to the Europeans it was showing its strength and asserting its presence in the Mediterranean by going through the Sound and around Gibraltar; in the Turks it inspired the fear of an attack on Constantinople, pincered between the Black Sea and the Aegean. Their progress into the Black Sea continued unabated. Azov, already attacked in 1736, was abandoned to the treaty of Kainardji (1774) by the sultan, who thus had to resign himself to freedom of navigation in the Black Sea and the Bosporus. At the same time the Crimea passed from being a disguised Russian protectorate to an open occupation (1784). The imperial fleet had some 50 ships and some 30 frigates; that was clearly many fewer than each of the three great Western navies (English, French, and Spanish), but the future trends would call upon it to assert itself in all directions: the Mediterranean (with the help of the liberation of Greece), the Indian Ocean (through the states of the Middle East), finally the Pacific at Vladivostok, all being crowned by the search for a summer route through the Great North from the White Sea to the Bering Straits; but this is another matter, beyond the limits of Europe.

The new maritime imperialisms

Around 1900 imperial Germany for its part showed that the domination of the sea was a necessity for a strong state. Its appearance on the oceans bears the mark of two men. The complaint of megalomania made against William II was not without foundation, but the conjunction of his ambitions first with the objectives of Admiral von Tirpitz, a man of experience as well as a theoretician in the use of the navy, then with the interests of the great ex-Hanseatic ports such as Hamburg, gave an awesome consistency to the practical developments of those intentions. Indeed, Mahan, whose work William II had had translated and disseminated, also learned much there. The emperor's parades, his speeches, his affectation, more genuine than has been thought, of presenting himself as a sailor (William thought he was pleasing his aunt, Queen Victoria, by wearing the uniform of an admiral of the British fleet, the rank of which she had conferred upon him), all of this was the manifestation of a true inclination on the part of the young emperor towards the domination of the sea.

Statistics show his presence on all the seas, the increase of his agents as far as the Pacific and his ability to establish colonies in Africa wherever land remained. Tirpitz's activity was representative of that policy. At the time when in Germany a technical controversy analogous to that of the'Jeune Ecole' in France was developing, Tirpitz managed to impose his concepts, for they gave substance to the dreams of the emperor. The latter, seduced by the clarity of the admiral's concepts and the strength of his convictions, made him chief of staff of the Navy High Command. Tirpitz, an advocate of the 'squadron war', advocated the 'risk' of a strategic offensive, but he needed much skill and imperial support to obtain the Reichstag's vote for the credits necessary for the realization of a naval programme which spread over fourteen years, beginning in 1898. The goal was first to outclass the Russian fleet in the Baltic and to face the French squadrons on the English Channel and the Atlantic, then to reach such a level that 'a first-rate naval power' would think twice before attempting to overwhelm the coasts of the empire. England could not mistake the meaning of that allusion. Thus the objective by 1912 was to raise the number of large ships to 61, where there had been only around 30 before Tirpitz took over. On 18 June, 1897 in Cologne, the emperor proclaimed that Germany had raised the 'Trident of Neptune' once again.

William II's ambitions were the product of a quest for military and political prestige more than a need for commercial outlets, which had already been acquired elsewhere. On the contrary, the

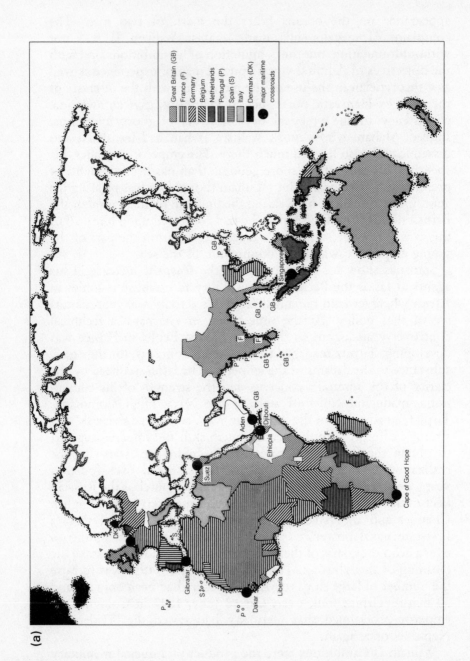

(a)

	Great Britain (GB)
	France (F)
	Germany
	Belgium
	Netherlands
	Portugal (P)
	Spain (S)
	Italy
	Denmark (DK)
	major maritime crossroads

Singapore

GB
P

F
F
F
GB
F
GB
P
P
GB
GB

Aden
Djibouti
GB
Ethiopia

Suez

F

F

DK
S
Gibraltar
S
P

P
Dakar
Liberia

Cape of Good Hope

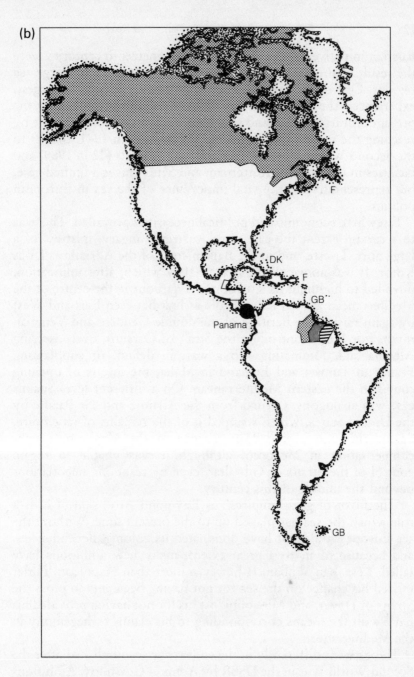

Figure 6.2 (a and b) Europe present on all the seas: the maritime heritage in 1914

Russian initiatives of the eighteenth and nineteenth centuries were the result of the geographical necessity for access to the large sea regions. One of the smallest European states, just like the largest, experienced the same necessity. Indeed, at the beginning of the present century Switzerland sought to break its continental vice by reaching the sea via the Rhine and the Rhône. In 1941, thanks to the Second World War, Switzerland had 36 boats (22 in 1989) and facilities in the ports of Rotterdam and Sète. This is a limited case, but representative of the vital importance of the sea in European politics.

Elsewhere economic and political necessities prevailed. This was to a certain extent the case with Austria-Hungary, mistress of a large port, Trieste, and of the Balkan coast of the Adriatic as far as Kotor. It was above all the case of Italy which, after unification, intended to highlight its situation as a harbour in the centre of the Mediterranean and its natural role as link between East and West by again raising the heritage of the double Genoese and Venetian myth. For Italy, controlling the Strait of Otranto, overpowering Albania and dominating Libya was, in default of supplanting France in Tunisia and England in Malta, the means of opening routes in the eastern Mediterranean. On a different level Spain's case was analogous. Ousted from the Atlantic and the Pacific by the United States, which stripped it of the remains of its empire, Spain, although preceded by France in the Maghreb, sought compensation in Morocco, although it was unable to regain control of the Straits of Gibraltar, even by resuming negotiations beyond the middle of this century.

'The pivot of great empires', as Raymond Aron said of it, is a role which the sea has played up to the present time. Without the sea Europe would not have dominated its colonial dependencies, and because of it, to a great extent, many new ambitions have failed. Less than William II but even more than Napoleon, Hitler missed his chance on the sea for not having been able to cross the Straits of Dover, and Mussolini lost his for not having provided his navy with the means corresponding to his claims to hegemony in the Mediterranean.

Things went differently in the endeavour accomplished after the Second World War in the USSR by Admiral Gorshkov. Ambitions to dominate were inscribed in its tradition and, ideology aside, and taking into account obvious technical insufficiencies, we must recognize in his work a clear perception of maritime problems in general; he was fortunate to have sufficient time and money. All the same, it is too early to know whether such an effort will have a future. In any event, the example is representative of the importance of the sea for a European state. 'History', Gorshkov has written, 'shows that states which do not have naval forces have not been able for very long to maintain their status as a great power ... the continents are only huge islands ...'. Quite aside from the Indian Ocean and the Pacific, the Soviet navy, under Gorshkov's guidance, asserted its presence in the Baltic and extended it as far as the Bay of Biscay, and organized a permanent base west of the straits in both the western and eastern Mediterranean, not to mention reserving for its own use the arctic route which starts in Northern Europe.

History is decided at sea

We need not cite other examples of the role of European navies on their own seas and on the oceans. Should we not subscribe to what Winston Churchill wrote in his memoirs and say that at every stage of European history the solution to great problems has come as much, if not more, from the sea as from the continent? At least, let us say that continental solutions have depended upon decisions taken beforehand on the sea. The list of examples would be long for Europe alone. Let us cite just a few: in the Middle Ages, Sluys (1340); in the sixteenth century, Wight (1545), Lepanto (1571) and the failure of the Armada (1588); in the seventeenth century, Agosta in Sicily (1676), Bévéziers (1690) and La Hougue (1692); in the eighteenth century, Chesapeake (1781), les Saintes (1782); in the nineteenth century Trafalgar (1805), Navarino/Pylos (1827); in the twentieth century, Jutland (1916) and the landing operations on the Italian coasts (July–August 1943) and on the coasts of Normandy (June 1944) and Provence (August 1944).

Let us conclude. The maritime ambition of Europeans has often been expressed in formulas or expressive acronyms, the very mention of which is in itself significant. We know the acronym conveying Charles V's claim to universal domination under the permanent watch of the Sun, AEIOU (*Austriae est imperium orbis universalis*); the programme contained in the words 'Britannia rules the waves!', in the proclamation of William II, 'Our future is on the water'; and Mussolini's claim to the Roman heritage of 'Mare nostrum'. Waves follow one another; the tide covers the shores, wiping out the sandcastles of children.

Part II

Europe and the Sea in Human Society

Introduction

We have followed Europe's relationship with the seas that surround it like the movement of an ancient classical ballet unfolding a continuous action in a defined framework – Europe – in a delimited time – close to three millennia.

In the first act, upstage, a group of actors, particularly ingenious and dynamic in the Mediterranean light, took advantage of the slightest opportunities for maritime activity. On another part of the stage, separate from the first group and at first as if in the background, another group, smaller, less favoured by the clarity and atmosphere of their climate, organized its life in a circuit limited to northern latitudes.

The second act saw the Mediterraneans, inclined to a social life and moved by financial interests, take the initiative in relationships with westerners and Nordics. Cutting isthmuses, crossing straits, venturing on a wide western route, they invited their partners to exchange of all kinds.

The response of those partners achieved a symbiosis and made possible the third act, a sort of synthetic apotheosis. From a tactic agreement and in a synchronic movement, from the Black Sea to the Baltic, Europeans from the North and the South spread out over the maritime expanses of the world, thus revealing an essential coherence, although different in its manifestations, of their hold over the seas.

But beyond considering the various seas of which the Europeans took control, there was 'the' sea in itself. To note its role in European history is one thing, to analyse it is another. Only in so doing will it be possible to understand

131

and explain the intimacy of the relationship between the European continent and the maritime element. Historically, how have Europeans lived with the sea? This question leads us to look at the ways in which they have seen it, understood it, felt it, and finally loved it. This is what we will investigate in the second part of this study.

7

Earning a Living from the Sea

The salt makers at their saltworks

For centuries a dialogue took place between the occupants of the coastal lands and the neighbouring sea. It was such a close dialogue that, even today, in France for example, the development of the shores depends both on agricultural administrative matters and on those of maritime affairs. Very early in history, that is from the eleventh and twelfth centuries in England (Dover) and in France (Dieppe, Carentan, the region of Nantes, Bayonne), tidal mills on certain rivers were used both in agriculture and to regulate the levels of harbour waters. The harvesting of seaweed, under the generic name of kelp, provided fertilizer and sea-sand, as it would later, in our own time, provide a component part of various food products; the seaweed farmer who cut it was in no way a mariner – he was a peasant. Similarly tied to the land were the collector of the pebbles which were used as building materials, or, on the beaches, the collector of sand intended for the manufacturing of window glass, whose quality and resistance has been appreciated by art historians. Above all the agricultural worker made the saltings, a stage in the development of the polders, the pasture *par excellence* for his sheep: all of Europe is familiar with this. But in the end salt was the wealth of almost all the seas, so much so that it was called 'white gold', as opposed and compared to the 'black gold' of our oil-based century. And yet in our age, Europe actively exploits the latter in the North Sea, not to be outdone by the sundrenched seas, rich in the former.

Following the course of time and the wake of ships enables us to perceive the mark of the salt makers' activity. The biological necessity of sodium chloride places the origins of mining tech-

133

niques far back into the night of centuries, and archaeological remains confirm documentary assertions. On the coasts of north-western Europe, from the Iron Age onwards, man has success-ively, then simultaneously, practised various processes for making salt on both sides of the North Sea and the English Channel, using clay basins, some of which were intended for concentration and evaporation of sea water and others for cooking the brine on a low fire in metal pans. The sites where this took place are remarkable: former dunes transformed into mounds 3–6 metres high, 100–600 metres wide, dominating an area that could be submerged during high tides, for example, the salt-hills of Lincolnshire. These sites were particularly important on the English coasts, since in the eleventh century Domesday Book points out close on 2000 of them.

Other techniques have left their traces, noted from the twelfth to the seventeenth century, for example on the southern beaches of the Channel; for instance, the collection of salty sand, followed by its washing in a ditch to obtain a brine which was then boiled several times in pots on a continuous flame; at night their flames on the beaches made navigators suspect the ruses of shipwreckers.

J.-C. Hocquet, who has specialized in continuing the inquiry into salt in history which was begun more than thirty years ago by Jacques Le Goff and P. Jeannin, provides much additional proof of the role of marine salt in Europe's past. Thus the Frisian and Zealand *terpen* provided a counterpart to the British salt-hills, used as they were for the manufacture of ignigenous salt from salty ash resulting from the burning of dried peat bricks. This technique too was practised from the eighth to the sixteenth century. Later, in the eighteenth century, the Germans perfected a method of gradua-tion; two pumping operations raised the water to the top of a building in order to use in a vertical plane the energy exploited in sunnier climates on the horizontal plane of the marshes.

Human ingenuity was especially tenacious when, in response to a vital need, it attempted experiments whose outcomes were doubtful under the Nordic sky. It is believed that salt marshes existed in the Gallo-Roman era not far from Bruges and Ostend, analogous to those on the Atlantic shores of Europe; but it was necessary to use ovens to obtain the salt.

Out of the preceding observations there results the possibility of relationships between the land and European salt production in early times. In 1970 in the Scheldt archaeologists found 130 altars dedicated to the goddess Nehalennia with inscriptions attesting to the activity of *negociatores salarii* in the Rhine valley and on the coasts of the North Sea. Salt already appeared as a linking feature and the southern example favoured by the sun as a model. It has remained so. A comparison shows similarities and relationships between Atlantic and Mediterranean saltworks. The priority and profitability belong to the latter, but the essential techniques differ from each other in terminological rather than technical differences.

Nothing could be closer than the layouts of Atlantic and Mediterranean salt marshes. They obey the same principles, as stated by J.-C. Hocquet: to get the most out of the sun and the winds, drain off the rain water and distribute the flow of salt water into basins to improve the harvested salt in quality and quantity. These principles guided the establishment of salt marshes first in Venice, notably in Chioggia in the eleventh century, then in its dependent territories, for example in Piran in Istria, Pago in Dalmatia, in Cyprus or on the African coasts, as well as in Tuscany (around Livorno), Provence (Hyères) and Languedoc (Saintes-Maries-de-la-Mer) in Sardinia (Cagliari), Spain (especially Ibiza and La Mata), Portugal (Setúbal), Aunis and Saintonge (Oléron), Poitou (the 'Bay of Bourgneuf') and Brittany (Guérande, Morbihan). The water's path followed a similar route. A conduit (*callio* in Venice, *cui* in Guérande) was placed into the breakwaters separating the compartments of the marsh. Gravity caused the water to flow toward a reservoir (*moraro*, a tidal reservoir) where concentration began, then through little canals toward the salt beds; at the lowest level (*capitini*, evaporating pans), the salt crystallized. Technical progress, depending on climatic conditions, consisted of obtaining a series of stronger and stronger concentrations through increasingly accentuated compartimentalization, of improving to the maximum the removal of fresh water brought by rain or seepage, and finally, of diversifying the presentation of production according to the size, quality and colour of the salt crystals.

The work was much the same everywhere; the maintenance of the conduits, dams, basins and salt beds did not differ very much from one nation to another, and the harvest, carried out using long wooden rakes (the wooden shovel of the Guérande, the fire rake of Poitou), was assembled into heaps on a flat space set up on one of the dams, while waiting to be stored in dry buildings (the salt

salt marshes

sea traffic routes

Chiarenza ports for salt traffic

Figure 7.1   The international importance of salt

silos). These tasks were naturally subject to bad weather; however, the same problems having analogous solutions, it is possible to make a comparison in equivalent terms of the relationship between the conditions of those who undertook similar efforts.

Indeed, those who were here called salt workers and there salt marsh workers, carried out the same tasks under slightly different living conditions throughout the year. With a few exceptions, in Poitou for example, the labour force on the salt marshes was free; at worst one heard rare mention of freed serfs in Venice. Saltworks were new lands, and when one said new lands, they meant free men. In the Middle Ages any struggle against nature, as well as against men, required or conferred freedom: how could it have been otherwise for those concerned with the conquest of the marshes, salt or otherwise, on the sea? It is nevertheless true that the small family-run saltworks seem throughout Europe to have shared the common fate which tended to incorporate them into a concentrated system.

Three successive phases can be distinguished in the history of salt in Europe, with certain local variations. Although it is not necessary to go back to the remarks by Cassiodorus on the exploitation of marine salt, our study shows a first phase, approximately from the ninth to the thirteenth century, which was incontestably domanial, since the Venetian patriciate fed its inheritance by holding on to the saltworks of their former indebted owners as a chattel mortgage. 'Domanial' – that first phase could, according to Jacques Le Goff, be better called 'monastic'. The saltworks were above all elements of the very large abbeys, beneficiaries of lay donations, even those located far from the coasts. The incomplete, though long, listing of them forms a fan-shape across Europe, beginning in the seventh century with St Demetrios of Thessalonica, continuing in the Adriatic with the possessions of the patriarch of Aquileia, of the bishop of Torcello, of the monasteries of Santa Maria in Murano, of San Giorgio Maggiore in Venice itself; in Commachio, the abbeys of Bobbio and Novalaise; in Cervia, the churches of Ravenna, notably San Appolinare Nuovo. The circuit continued in the western Mediterranean with the saltworks of Hyères, Toulon, Marseille, Berre and, in Sardinia, of Cagliari, owned by the monks of St-Honorat of Lérins and St-Victor of Marseille, finally, the Languedoc saltworks of the abbeys of Psalmodi, Aniane and La Grasse, then, going through the Pyrenees, the important abbey of Gerri de la Sal. The same can be seen in the Atlantic salt marshes; the most important ones were owned by monasteries near the coast, such as St-Jean d'Angely and St-Michel en l'Herm in Saintonge and Poitou, or St-Sauveur de Redon, St-Gildas de Rhuys, Prières and Ste-Croix of Quimperlé in Brittany; but the inland convents owned saltworks on those coasts as well (Ronceray in Angers, Trinity in Vendôme). All of that, based on the importance of salt in daily life, attests to the strong ties between the continent and its maritime shores, where the organization of salt mining was moulded into the framework of rural estates. The consumption of salt was carried out in a closed circuit, for the needs of the inhabitants and the livestock of the estate, the distribution of the product being carried out with the help of what were called the 'fleets of the abbey'.

A second phase began in the twelfth century, then developed in the thirteenth century in the Mediterranean region, perhaps based on the models of the Byzantine and Arab institutions, and first of all in the Italian towns, especially Venice. The state, at the onset of progress, had a tendency to recuperate for its own benefit the revenues which sometimes profited individuals. A key product, salt, particularly marine salt, became the pawn of powers which, through the institution of the salt tax, begun in Italy and disseminated into other countries in the fourteenth century, turned salt into one of the components of public taxation.

It became tempting to speculate on such a commodity; and the third phase was economic. The southern saltworks increased their production of good quality salt at lower cost than the Nordic salt obtained at high prices through a cooking process. For their part, merchants with circulating capital speculated on trade and tax farming. This phase took on an international character, with the help of maritime routes between the North and the South. We have only to recall the voyages of the Hanseatic ships between the Baltic and Portugal in numbers exceeding one hundred in the middle of the fifteenth century, or the activity of Breton coasters distributing salt in the ports of western Europe.

At the foundation of a Europe of merchants, salt makers of all genres, without forming a homogeneous group, represented a type of man and types of societies which took on similar characteristics. Of these, poverty was the most striking among the marsh workers, even more so than among the workers involved in the heat processes of the North. Their poverty was primarily the result of the precariousness of an undertaking subject to meteorological caprices; sometimes there was not enough sun, sometimes there were rainy summers, sometimes there were devastating storms. Poverty came from the mediocrity of the pay for a task demanding constant vigilance, that is, a constant maintenance of the dams, the canals and salt beds throughout the entire year; even women were compelled to work, and not all salt marsh workers had the advantage of also being farmers. Moreover, the profits from the marshes were unequally divided between the workers and their sovereign; thus, in Noirmoutier in the fourteenth century the salt workers kept only a third of the profit from sales, as compared to the two-thirds given to the abbey of La Blanche; though it is true that the abbey, when misfortune struck, for example in 1365, relinquished its share to the salt marsh workers to make possible the restoration of the marshes. In the eighteenth century the salt workers of Séné, in Morbihan, gave three-quarters of the revenue from the sale of their salt to the canons of Vannes, and kept only one-quarter for themselves. As for Venice, in the twelfth century it had the quit-rent system, indefinitely and tacitly renewable. On the other hand, the owners of the saltworks earned considerable profits when they were able to stockpile the salt and wait for the higher price resulting from bad harvests; but such speculation was hardly within the grasp of the humble salt workers, and it primarily benefited merchants, tax collectors and the urban bourgeoisie who acquired saltworks, until the nineteenth century.

The poverty of the salt workers was seen in their daily life. At the Venetian saltworks in the twelfth century, the properties were already too small to support a family. On the Atlantic marshes in southern Brittany, for example, subdivision was accentuated in the fifteenth century. Families were big there; the land was covered with hamlets. Situated on the edge of the marsh, the houses turned their backs to the sea, occupying a narrow parcel of land on rocky soil, apart from the outbuildings (tool sheds, salt silos); they were made of quarry stones and whitewashed, with a thatch or tile roof. Their rustic appearance has been preserved to the present day.

The salt workers' condition was very poor on the Mediterranean and the Atlantic, for example in Poitou and Saintonge in the middle of the fifteenth and sixteenth centuries, for in the first case the complaints were loud, and in the second there was open revolt.

The grievances formulated in Poitou in 1451, despite the inevitable exaggeration in such a case, leave us in no doubt. In them one reads that the salt workers were 'the poorest people of all the surrounding region, living day to day by expedients, burdened with large families, with debts owed to their sovereigns (here two-thirds of all profits) and to salt merchants with whom they had mortgaged in advance their share of the harvest to come'. It is not surprising that a little later, under Louis XI, a lampoon attributed this complaint to those who were called 'the labourers of the salt works': 'We are obliged to season our vegetables with the salt of our tears.' In the following century, in 1548, anger grew, this time armed, in Saintonge, against the agents of the salt tax, who, 'made up of lean and hungry men landed like locusts over the provinces, devouring the substance of the people and leaving only after they had made their fortune'. King Henry II, faced with this distress, reduced the fiscal burden of those people, and rendered homage to the harshness of their work as well as to their role in the safety of the coasts of the kingdom: 'peoples hardened by adversity, familiar with the tides, the ruses, the perils and dangers of the sea, capable of becoming just as warlike, adventurous and capable in war, both on sea and land, as no other coastal-dwellers'. This late recognition of social usefulness was not the first nor the only one. The Church, admittedly rather modestly, authorized their working on Sunday, 'in order', wrote Henri de Gorkum around 1420–30, 'not to stop up the sources whence comes the water which provides the materials for salt'. Water, salt: two sacred elements; two components of the baptismal rite.

Certainly peasants, at least in part, the salt workers everywhere exploited the sea, but they also assured a watch over the coasts and could on occasion or when asked even change into navigators. Good at everything, modest, often miserable, Europe owed much to them.

The worlds of fishing

Until the recent invention of conservation techniques using refrigeration, salt found its most ancient clients among fishermen. This historical detail brings a factor of unity to fishermen beyond any differences in the climate of their fishing grounds, in the nature of their catches and in the organization of tasks. Landsmen themselves, in their hasty view of the marine environment, are not mistaken, but they over-simplify the diversity of fishing societies. To understand the difficulties currently encountered in the organization of what is called 'Blue Europe', an historical reminder within a geographical perspective will be useful.

The coastal topography on the one hand, marine hydrological conditions, climates, technical factors (boats and engines) were the circumstances under which the evolution of different types of fishing occurred in each region. Progressive stages went from fishing on foot on the shores to offshore fishing a short distance from the coast, to long-term open-sea fishing, and finally to distant fishing demanding suitable equipment and the competency of deep-sea navigators.

Each type of fishing had its own techniques, fashioned original human types, and demanded particular forms of social organization. The time factor also played a role; it accelerated communications and improved technical exchanges, opened the doors to the harvests of fishing, encouraged opportunities for the intervention of capital, enabled the building of certain fortunes and left in modest conditions the less lucky or the less talented.

Mediterranean coastal fishing

Each of the two great European maritime regions has conserved its particular fishing traditions. Acknowledging the differences corresponding to the nature of the Mediterranean and ocean waters, a comparison of fishing practices brings to light resemblances and oppositions, often veiled by language differences. Time-honoured fishing practices were followed for a long time on the Mediterranean coasts. Archaeologists have discovered the wreckage of small fishing boats, commented on their carvings, and in piles of shells have found confirmation that oysters were eaten, as mentioned by Ausonius. Ancient literature mentions coastal and offshore fishing; hagiographic tales took up the story. Mosaics from Ostia and Tunisia represent fishermen at work, and merchants offering fish at their stalls; in turn, miniatures from the High Middle Ages, in Greek or Latin manuscripts, lend themselves to precise commentaries; the collection gathered by Christiane Villain-Gandossi is rich in both secular and religious scenes (for example, the miraculous draught of fishes of the Gospels) in which the shape of boats, equipment and fishing practices can be recognized: fishing lines and especially nets, upright or flat, close-woven drag-nets to capture sardines and anchovies, a *lamparo* or torch on the boat used to attract the fish, fishing with 'steers', where two boats tow a drag-net with a large pocket, the fishing net which, like a trawl, devastated such a large area that it was prohibited in Marseille in the fifteenth century.

Fixed traps were installed in places where fish travelled along the Mediterranean coast, notably in the fairways, or *roubines*: large traps (as big as 100 metres) forming the receptacle, whose compartments formed a labyrinth, the *bourdigues*; or simple or complex devices made of cylindrical or conical nets attached to a post, the hoop nets.

Sponge and coral

Near the shores in certain favourable locations two types of fishing traditionally originated in the Mediterranean: sponge and coral. Europe exploits a few zones for sponge fishing, off the coast of Turkey and in Greek waters, especially around Rhodes; but the Europeans obtained their supplies above all off the Kerkenna Islands, off Djerba, in the Gulf of Syrtes, and off the Syrian coasts. Coral fishing was undertaken on the Sardinian coasts around Alghero, and between Naples and Sicily. Tied to thermic conditions, these two types of fishing were carried out from spring to autumn, and their technical demands were similar. Naked sponge divers descended to a depth of 25 fathoms (45 metres), as often as ten times a day, for around three minutes each time; today, the use of a diving suit enables a diver to reach a depth of 70 metres and to prolong his dives. The tools used are similar in both cases: a sort of drag-net made from a pocket net, with large links, mounted on a frame, rectangular for sponge fishing (the *gangava*), and in the form of a St Andrew's cross for coral; dragged along the ocean bottom, it was pulled up on board by a winch. Barcelona, Leghorn, Marseille and Genoa for a long time controlled these once profitable fishing industries, profitable at least for the shipowners; but in consolidating them the industries lost their artisanal character and their spread over a great number of small ports, for example in Liguria, and at Sestri Ponente among others.

Offshore fishing in ocean waters

According to Henri Touchard, it was only in the fourteenth century that offshore fishing in Brittany was added to fishing on foot. Until then the fear of the sea and of pirates had dissuaded men from adventuring beyond the point where the land disappeared from the horizon. Furthermore, what profit could be expected from fishing too far away for it to be possible to bring back and sell fish while it was fresh, since in those early days there was no efficient salting technique? One had to remain a 'fisherman on the edge of the sea', according to a formula of Tréguier of around 1300. Moreover, one had to come back with the incoming tide so as not to risk having the cod, the conger eels, the mackerel and the morays captured by net or by line, go bad during the good season, from May to September.

In addition, the offshore fisherman was constrained by the restrictions placed by the lord of the manor on his fishing, as on the piece of land he cultivated for the rest of the year. He had to take time off, which, however, did not permit him to go off to sea for longer than the time it took to consume the single day's provisions which he was allowed to take with him. The seigneurial decree fixed the opening and the duration of the fishing season, as it did rural work. The lord took his share. He also possessed fishing grounds, such as the *esperqueries* of the bay of Mont-St-Michel and the Anglo-Norman islands, and he reserved for himself, by virtue of his ownership, the flesh of the cetaceans washed up on his shores.

Without venturing out to sea, those living on the coasts of the Atlantic and the English Channel, like their Mediterranean counterparts, set up traps made of wood or stone on the shallow coasts, 'locks' to contain the fish as the tide went out; in the eighteenth century, one could still count close to 400 of them between Bayeux and Oleron Island.

These examples from France had parallels in England and in the Low Countries. For centuries, offshore fishing everywhere remained an artisanal, local undertaking; however, in the traditional seigneurial framework its extension gave it a European importance. This importance appeared when offshore fishing began to supply the hinterlands, notably the towns, in the thirteenth century. A beginning of commercialization led Italian and Basque business-men, for example, to rent out fish-drying establishments in Léon and Cornouaille. In the fourteenth century certain centres assured the redistribution of the fish. Thus each day Paris was supplied with fresh fish through the services of beasts of burden coming from the ports of the Channel, the 'fish carts'. This organization was the result of fundamental transformations: the development of long-distance fishing and far-reaching technical innovations.

The reign of herring and tuna

Red tuna fishing in the Mediterranean was an occasion for large gatherings of fishing boats in a festive atmosphere where instincts of violence could be liberated. Each boat carried at least four men armed with pitchforks and the operation lasted several consecutive nights. Fishermen from Marseille often went home each evening. The season depended on the migration of schools of fish from Catalan and Provençal waters towards those of Sicily; fishing took place from mid-April to St John's Day, 24 June. The tool used was a special net, hence its name, *tonnaire* or *tonayra*, around two metres long, which was 'dragged' along the bottom six fathoms deep in another net large enough to form an enclosure, the *ceinche*. From on board ship the fishermen harpooned the tuna that were caught in the net. The *madraque*, used in the thirteenth century in Sicily, developed from a transformation of the *ceinche* into a bow-net compartmentalized into chambers which the fish went through until it hit a pocket of fine links (the *corpou*); when it was full, the men on the four boats raised it and indulged in a real massacre: Joseph Vernet, in his picture of the Gulf of Bandol, did not exaggerate the savagery of the scene in which the *madraque* became what Mistral would later describe as a 'bloody arena'. This 'work' demanded strength and a know-how handed down from generation to generation by the *rais*, whose name sufficed to convey the primacy of that technique.

Herring fishing was a northern counterpart of tuna fishing, but it had greater economic importance, for at the end of the fourteenth century herring fishing was extended from the Baltic and the Danish straits to the entire North Sea and the English Channel. In addition, it developed economic, social and political consequences over the whole of Europe. For the northern regions herring was a sort of 'unifying symbol of a maritime civilization'.

Fishing for herring was particularly European, beginning in the Middle Ages. The semantics of the word 'herring' convey its uniquely European cultural origins. A Greek root, *hals*, designating salt and the sea, was latinized in the forms *hales, alex, alecium*, out of which developed the French, English and German words *hareng*, herring, *haring*. The regular migrations of the varieties of those *clupidae* were of concern to all those living on the shores of the Baltic, the North Sea and the Channel, a considerable part of European maritime populations. Fishing began at the end of June in the Shetlands and the Orkneys, in mid-July in Scotland, around the end of August in Dogger Bank; it ended in October in Yarmouth, in November on the Flemish coast and around Christmas or even Candlemas (2 February) between Upper Normandy and the Sussex coast. The presence of schools of herring gave rise to an international gathering; one of the first descriptions of this was given in the fourteenth century by Philippe de Mézières, adviser to Charles V, on his return from his voyage to Prussia. His book, *Le Songe d'un vieil pèlerin* (Dream of an Old Pilgrim), presents in the following terms the influx of fishermen and the abundance of fish in the Danish straits:

> Between the kingdom of Norway and the kingdom of Denmark there is a long arm of the sea, which separates the island and kingdom of Norway from the mainland. This strait stretches for fifteen leagues, but is only a league or two wide ... in September and October, the herring makes its passage through the strait from one sea to the other in marvellously great number. The number is so great, indeed, that in many parts of this fifteen leagues one could cut through them with a sword ... every year ships from the whole of Germany and Prussia assemble in those two months to catch herring ... and it is common knowledge that there are 40,000 vessels ... It seemed to me desirable that I should

record these wonders for two reasons. First, so that we should be aware of the bounty of God towards Christian men in furnishing an abundance of herrings by which all Germany, France, and England are fed in Lent ... (Philippe de Mézières, *Le Songe d'un vieil pèlerin*, vol. I, ed. G. W. Coopland, Cambridge University Press, 1969, pp. 129–30.)

Chance had it that around 1400 technical innovations permitted improvements in preservation and the long-distance and abundant distribution of a food product at a price affordable, as Mézières continued, 'for poor Christians ... who cannot afford a big fish'. Indeed, around that time the development of salt production and trade from the Atlantic, and the perfecting of salting procedures, formed a conjunction beneficial to all of western Europe. Without going into details, the essential thing was, first of all, the practice of a first salting of the catch on board the boats; this presupposed an increase in the boats' tonnage, to allow for the loading of the indispensable quantity of salt, and allowed them to stay longer in the fishing grounds, thus a more abundant catch of fish. A portion of them, salted on board, could be sent on immediately to the large cities relatively close to the port of unloading. The rest, intended for rather longer preservation, was treated following a procedure attributed to a Zealander, Van Beukhelsz: fish were piled into barrels, or kegs, in alternating layers of salt and fish (kegged herring), or after soaking in brine, were desalted in fresh water, then smoked (smoked herring). Such procedures made it possible to send them long distances, for example in the fourteenth century from the banks of the English Channel or from Flanders as far as Avignon for the pontifical court.

This level of organization and commercialization was subsequently perfected; however, the directions taken were maintained. Long-distance fishing, such as that around Newfoundland, initiated at the time of the Great Discoveries, was inspired by earlier organizational models, which it went on to develop in volume.

Long-distance fishing

The initiatives of Cabot and of merchants from Bristol in Newfoundland were the result less of exploration than of a branching out of European fishing. This was the classic schema: those excluded from an intermediate market went to other sources to find what they sought – the cod, the traffic in which was controlled by Bergen. What was new was that Europe grafted a very distant region onto its own traffic and supply systems. The shipments of Newfoundland cod became regular and copious around 1540 and that activity was integrated completely into European routes. There developed the Atlantic custom of a triangular route. Needing salt in large quantities to bring the fruits of their fishing back to Europe, the Newfoundland fishermen loaded it up before their Atlantic crossing. Instead of encumbering themselves at the outset, though, they loaded it at their final stop, at French or Portuguese saltworks. On the return trip some ships traced the same geometric figure and unloaded, for example, all or part of their fish in Marseille.

Thus the new fishing grounds contributed to the maritime symbiosis of Northern and Southern Europe as it did to the incorporation of transatlantic traffic into European maritime life. If the French held an honourable place, sometimes the first place in the sixteenth and seventeenth centuries, they were not the only ones to include Newfoundland in the system of European fishing. In the sixteenth century some fifty ports took part in it and around 1580 the French cod fleet grew to over 500 units, as compared to 200–300 Iberian ships, mainly Basque and Portuguese, and only some 50 English vessels, because they went much more often to Iceland. This distribution changed in the seventeenth century; at the end of the eighteenth century Europe had left to the 'Americans' a part of Newfoundland fishing, which was no longer totally an extension of European fishing grounds, except on the French Shore preserved by France until the beginning of the twentieth century.

The cod-fishing boats were not alone. Starting in 1540 there were many whalers, accustomed as they were to the practices of a hunt in which for three centuries they had proved masters in the Bay of Biscay, which was rich in cetaceans. The Basques followed the animals' Atlantic migrations and transferred their whaling techniques to Newfoundland, the Gulf of St Lawrence and the coasts of Labrador; recent excavations of the Red Bay have produced one of their installations and one of their boats. The decline of catches at the end of the sixteenth century led them to transfer their activity more to the North, to Greenland, Norway and Spitzbergen; cooperation between St-Jean-de-Luz, Bayonne and Le Havre, fruitful in the seventeenth and eighteenth centuries, still existed in the middle of the nineteenth century at the time of the sinking of the *Winslow*, which bore the name of its Franco-American owner. Whale hunting had become international, beyond its centuries-old European preeminence.

Solidarity: shared values and constraints

Two traits characterize the different types of fishing and fishermen in all ages and throughout Europe: the interdependence of activities and the solidarity necessary among mariners was perceptible on all levels. The small coastal fishing ports were inserted into the framework of the rural seigniory whose fiscal demands and legal competence went beyond the coastline and the limits of the foreshore. Fishermen were very often also farmers and did not escape the masters of the land. The fisherman belonged to a land parish and was attached to it: he was born there, baptized there, and hoped to be buried there, if the 'great eater' did not swallow him up first; his parish was generally that of his father and mother, the one where his wife awaited his return from sea, the one where his children were born. To that community of familial ties were added those of the working community. The fisherman learned his profession young, on the boat of his father or an uncle, in the company of cousins and childhood friends. Jacques Bernard has given us a remarkable description of the community on board ship, and his account, based on Bordelaise information, can be applied to all the shore-dwellers from Cape Finisterre to Ouessant, and appears valid far beyond. Examples of this are not lacking either in the British Isles or in Flemish, Dutch, German, Scandinavian and Slavic lands; moreover, all differences aside, the Mediterranean shores offered just as self-contained coastal units. Islands, due to their geographical location, have particularly preserved that type of social life where the stranger is admitted only after a long period of probation. What was true from Portugal to Norway and from the Baltic to Ireland concerned the harshest islands off the French coast – Ouessant, for example, the 'sentinel island' at the meeting of the English Channel and the Atlantic Ocean, and Sein, where in 1940 the men unanimously decided to rally England to continue the struggle. Also unanimously collective still today are the decisions of the fishermen of the Island of Houat, off the coast of Morbihan, concerning the starting date of the fishing 'season' and the 'equipment', in other words, the technique chosen for such and such a type of fishing depending upon the 'appearance' of the sea. This communal will must not be confused with a retrograde tendency. Here are three examples ranging from Portugal to Iceland. At the beginning of this century fishermen from Povõa de Varzim, not far from Oporto, fought to maintain their local mutualist traditions, the origin of which went back to the four-teenth century and certain aspects of which were related to Nordic, Scandinavian and Celtic practices. For their part, Irish fishermen preserve strong solidarities, a conviviality which is expressed in the feasts of St John, an occasion to elect from among them, in Galway, for example, a leader and sheriffs to govern their com-munity. However, not everything has an out-dated air. On the point of Brittany the little port of Conquet, with a prestigious past, was completely renovated in the 1970s by some one hundred young men, whose average age was thirty-one, and who wanted to prove that artisanry remains practicable on the coasts if it is adapted to new conditions: thus they gave up lobster to look for crabs. There is a difference here between the Mediterranean environment, where individualism borders on noisy conviviality, and the worlds of the fishermen of the West and the North, upon whom the dangers of the ocean impose more silent solidarities.

The 'great profession', as long-distance fishing in Newfound-land, Iceland and Spitzbergen was called, not to mention the excursions into the Antarctic, multiplied the demands for solidar-ity. The causes for this were the length of the trip, the distance, the risks of the sea and of the work, the rigours, perhaps inevitable, of an iron discipline; those conditions existed from Spain and Por-tugal to Norway, including France and the British Isles. An abundant literature enables us to have an idea of the close quarters in a restricted space endured by the Newfoundland fishermen: the reciprocity of favours and of help balanced that of animosities, if not of hatreds, repressed to the point that a minor incident might cause them to explode into violence. Being exposed to the same dangers meant that not the slightest negligence harmful to the entire crew or to the ship itself would be tolerated, whether carelessness on a dory, a clumsy gesture while raising a net or the involuntary wounding of a companion where hygiene conditions

prevented healing. Any infringement of elementary discipline led
to punishment, more or less harsh depending upon national
temperaments. Rules must have been pitiless, even on ships where
discipline was relaxed, for someone sentenced by common law, a
former Newfoundlander, to shout in the face of a brutal prison
guard: 'We're not out big-time fishing, you know!'

The necessity which made solidarity compulsory was made clear
very early on, with the help of pecuniary conditions, in the
economic organization of the ship and the sale of fish. Nowhere
could the small, isolated fisherman, owner of his own fishing
smack, go for very long without the cooperation of others; unless
he exercised another activity at the same time, either agricultural or
artisanal, he had to 'make his profit from the sea alone', like the
inhabitants of the Island of Bréhat in 1429. For centuries that was
also the frequent fate of the 'très povres et indigens' inhabitants of
the neighbourhoods or suburbs inhabited by simple fishermen in
the principal ports: in Dieppe le Pollet, in Sables-d'Olonne, La
Chaume, in Boulogne the Basse Ville, in Lisbon the Alfama, in
London that quarter downstream from the Tower described by
Dickens. More and more frequently the fisherman possessed his
boat, when he had one, in co-ownership, and it was his sole capital.
But many rented out their services, living only on their share of the
catch. Boats' tonnage increased towards the end of the Middle
Ages throughout Europe, as did the duration of trips out to sea,
with a consequent increase in risks. These were some of the many
stimulants towards cooperation that could be perceived at the end
of the twelfth century and which became increasingly evident with
the development of long-distance and deep-sea fishing.

A cooperative spirit added new ways of distributing the profits
of fishing to the co-ownership of boats. The commonly admitted
base was remuneration by shares, that is, a predetermined lot of
fish allocated to each worker who brought his nets. Functions and
responsibilities also came into play, for example, those of the
boatswain and the 'sturman', who was responsible for steering the
ship. Such were the principles which, in the world of the North Sea
and the English Channel, underlay the solidarity among fishermen.
The Latin term *socius*, designating the participants, and Old French
associages, defining the ties which joined them, are the very
expressions of rules of solidarity in practice among fishermen up
until recent times.

As selling the catch could not be undertaken by the fishermen
themselves, since they had to return to sea, they worked with

middlemen possessing funds, personnel, time and contacts, who were able to greet them upon their return from sea, take over their fish, keep accounts of the sales, distribute the product and, if need be, pay them in instalments and agree to loans. This system is documented for Dieppe, but its functioning, found as far as Holland at least, was particularly known in Wenduine, a small Flemish port, in 1467. Developing the importance of his services, the middleman contributed to the fitting-out of a boat; by associating himself closely with the enterprise he increased his share of the profit. He played the role of wholesaler. Middlemen and fishermen needing each other's services, the longevity of the system, in spite of inequality, is not surprising. Keeping tally, which was substituted for the middleman system after the French Revolution, functioned according to very similar rules, before making way for modern practices. And out of the accentuated separation of work and capital, an entirely new form of solidarity, the union, was born in the world of fishermen, at the beginning of the twentieth century.

The instinct for solidarity also took on forms of social concern whose aspects resembled each other greatly from country to country. Whether it was in France, Flanders, Germany, England, Scandinavia, the Basque country or Portugal, fishermen, with the endorsement of public powers, endowed themselves with professional organizations supported by religious fraternities. As in other professions, religious life also gave lay solidarities the consecration of a sort of spiritual mutualism. To the gestures of mutual material aid were added works of charity to help old, poor and sick fishermen, and more frequently widows and orphans of those 'lost at sea'.

Finally, considering the fishing environments on a European level, one question must be raised. From one country to another, fishermen could not ignore the existence of groups similar to their own. Of course, one must not accord to the instinct of solidarity an absolutism which it never had. Indeed, history retains the memory of reciprocal violence among Norman and Basque fishermen at the end of the thirteenth century and at the beginning of the Hundred Years' War, as well as repeated fist fights between Breton, English and Flemish fishermen during that war. The reciprocal tricks, assaults on boats, broken nets and deaths of men cannot be counted. Moreover, privateering in the Mediterranean as well as in the North-West was in large part the act of fishermen who found in it a way to supplement their income. However, if we are able to use the expression 'international herring community', certain details contribute to justify the extension of that phrase to various fishing environments. The North Sea was a space whose inhabitants shared too many similar interests to be constantly at daggers drawn.

Alongside dramatic incidents at the worst moments of the Hundred Years' War and of the conflicts in the seventeenth and eighteenth centuries, there was a true concern for safeguarding closely overlapping interests. Total war was a posthumous and bitter fruit of the speculations of the Age of Reason and of the myth of the progress of humanity. The Hundred Years' War was dotted with truces called 'fishing truces', which enabled fishermen to carry out their activities with the help of rather generously granted safe-conducts. The duke of Brittany, in instituting a system of briefs, and the duke of Burgundy, by organizing the fishing convoy (1471), responded to the expectations and the needs of fishermen. This awareness of problems is documented in a few texts. Thus in the eighteenth century (1747), the Estates-General of the United Provinces made a decision authorizing 'the French fishermen to continue fishing off the coasts of England', in exchange for which the king of France 'forbids under any pretext the disturbance of the [Netherlander] ships used for fishing'.

To conclude, let us cite the great chronicler Froissart, who in the fourteenth century stated:

> These sea fishermen, whatever war there is between France and England, never hurt each other; but they are friends and help each other in need, and on the sea sell and buy their fish to and from each other when some have more than others, for if they were at war there would be no fish to eat.

We might recommend these words to the consideration of all those who in Europe in our time are closely connected with the issues of fishing. Froissart! A reference for the study, if not the solution, of the issue of fishing 'quotas'? One can always hope.

8

The European Community of Seamen

Who were they?

From the salt workers to the fishermen – first coastal then deep-sea – a hierarchy was established which corresponded to the extent and the constancy of their relationship with the sea. The salt worker was still, in many respects, a peasant who worked the shores. The fisherman, however, lived on the sea and from the sea, but in direct proportion to his distance from the fishing locations which were as familiar to him as were fields to a farmer. The further away the adventure, the more the sea became dominating, if not dominant. Not content to be just a workplace, it took complete possession of the men, women and children who lived from it; it fashioned their lives, their mentality, their gestures; it was a cultural mould. It turned them into 'people of the sea', that is, people – or better, communities – living from the sea, through it and for it.

The Romans called these people *maritimi*, a plural term, because it was applied to social groups. Europe followed their example, and its languages invented words or phrases expressing the same notion: *gens de mer* in French, *genti di mare* in Italian, *gente de mar* in Spanish, 'seamen' in English and *Seeleute* in German.

An analysis of the tripartite relationship of man-sea-ship has revealed the individualization of specialized professional functions. Thus the use of the singular, first in Latin (*marinarius, navigans, navigator, nauta*), then in the various languages, for example in French with *marinier* (waterman) and its derivations (*marinel, maronier, mareant*), *navigateur* (navigator) and *nautonier* (pilot). Covering the whole area, the expressions *ars maris*, the art of navigation, of seamanship, have designated a knowledge of the arts of the sea.

153

By extension, the terminology diversified the designation of technical specialities and hierarchical levels. Languages distinguish the functions of master, owner, captain, crewman, page and cabin boy, pilot, steersman, steward, boatswain, purser, scribe etc.; terms correspond to precise activities involving steering (from *gubernator*, 'sturman', and *locman*, boatman and pilot) or speed (the ancient heritage having bequeathed *remigatores*, *vogatores*, rowers). On land the gamut included the personnel of the ship-yards: chief shipwrights, caulkers, carpenters, rope-makers, black-smiths etc.

Subservience to the sea spread to their entourage, beginning with the family. Young boys set sail very early as cabin boys, for the sea was their first and only horizon. Dare one say that they inhaled the sea air in their infancy and that the salt was on their lips with their mother's milk? For women, too, belonged to the community of 'seamen'. They endured the same risks, particularly solitude and waiting: conjugal solitude during their husband's absences, with all the accompanying anxieties, anguish and jealousies that sometimes brought; solitude in the responsibility for the education of their sometimes numerous children, depending upon the rhythm of the father's return – physical solitude and solitude of the heart; all literatures have described them. But women also worked for the sea: they fished on foot, maintained nets, sails and ropes; the treatment of fish, as well as selling it, did not wait for the industrialization of modern fishing, for from the end of the Middle Ages women, often widows, took on the management of compa-nies. In all languages nouns and adjectives, not always laudatory, designate those female 'seamen'.

A certain masochism might have contested such an enlargment of the notion of seamen and have refused to include those who did not actually set sail – those who on land baptized, taught, married, took care of or buried the sailors, that is, teachers, doctors and priests; they nevertheless shared the same life and feelings. There was, however, a distinction made between the totality of popula-tions living in dependence on the sea and the restricted group of sailors. In the first case the sense is social, psychological and ethical; in the second, professional and technical, economic or military.

The definition of the environment of seamen includes two other dimensions, one historical, the other geographical, both of which are intimately enmeshed. When Charlemagne, at the beginning of the ninth century, solicited the services of the *maritimi* against the Vikings, he envisaged the inhabitants of the coastal regions, the *marages* or *marines*, as reaching as far inland as around 25 kilometres. But later this coastal zone was redefined to limit the service of watchkeeping. In England the *Act for the Mayntenance of the Navy* of 1540, after expressing concern to 'produce many masters, mariners and seamen instructed in the art and science of navigation', added this important observation:

> They, their wives and their children, derive their sustenance from the sea and are at the same time the support of cities, towns, villages and ports and harbours on the coast; bakers, tavern keepers, butchers, blacksmiths, rope-makers, ship builders, tailors, shoesmiths and other suppliers and artisans living in the neighbourhood of the said shores derive from the same source a large part of their sustenance.

The range was large. And other states did not conceive of it otherwise, for example in the Iberian peninsula, in the Low Countries, in Italy, notably in Venice, as well as in Sweden under Gustavus Adolphus and in the kingdom of France. In Richelieu's time, later under Louis XVI and, even later, under the Restoration, the entire coastal population was, just as in England, considered a breeding ground for sailors. The Code Michaud, promulgated under Louis XIII (1629) was applied to all men who made theirs the 'profession of the sea'. The monumental *Hydrographie* by the Jesuit Georges Fournier, published in 1643, republished in 1667, and reprinted in 1973, based the value of navigators on 'experience, preferably from birth', and Richelieu himself gave the *Commandeur de la Porte*, who served in the Mediterranean, these instructions: 'I prefer large, brave sailors, fed on sea water and battle, rather than clean-shaven horsemen, for the former serve the king better'. Colbert gave its rightful place to this circle of the best sailors; the institution of the system of 'classes' aimed to include 'all people capable of serving in the Navy' and to keep them in it. There was even a sort of precocious social service which extended to the wives of those 'enlisted' in the navy the benefits of its allowances. The Ordonnance de la Marine of 1681 and the later commentary upon it by Valin conceived of the notion of seamen in a broad sense. That group was 'precious', as Sartine, the Naval

Minister under Louis XVI, in turn wrote. The French Revolution took care, despite all its destruction, to renounce such teachings, and in a memorandum composed in 1794–5 one finds expressed with exceptional clarity and strength the importance of the *environment* in which seamen were born and raised: 'We need men born in maritime towns; they must early on breathe the air of the sea, play a little with the marine element while they are still in the cradle . . . A man born on the shores of the sea is worth two others at least' . . .

More similarities than differences

Time relaxed geographical differences without altering professional diversities. Granted, despite growing communications between maritime sectors, the Mediterranean and the Ocean in particular, contrasts persisted between the Ponant and the Levant. However, at all levels of maritime existence, the demands of life at sea engendered parallel, though not identical, reactions.

On land the habitats of fishermen in Catalonia, in the Basque country, in Brittany, in Holland, on the Flemish and Danish shores and in the Norwegian fjords, offer analogous layouts. What essential differences, besides exuberance or a certain reserve, were there between the sailors' inns of Genoa, Marseille, Barcelona and Lisbon on the one hand, and those of Bordeaux, Nantes, London, Antwerp, Rotterdam and Hamburg on the other?

On board ship daily life was conditioned by the ratio between the available space and the number of men called to spend days, months and years in it. Although a few men connected by family or national ties, or by friendship, sufficed to man a coastal fishing boat, the same was no longer true for fishing on the high seas, or for international trade, especially in its more exotic forms such as Negro slave trading, where the embarking of slaves almost doubled the number of bodies on board; nor did it hold good for privateering, demanding one or two prize crews, or for warships in which purely military personnel was added to that of the mariners.

These living conditions cannot be expressed only by numbers. Theoretically, as in housing, the possibility of occupation was determined by the number of square metres available, and one might, from the number of inhabitable tons (in weight or volume) corresponding to one man on board, estimate the space available to each person. The attempt was made in Venice in the Middle Ages; the amount seemed to go from one-third of a ton to one ton between the middle of the thirteenth century and that of the fourteenth. According to F.C. Lane, technical progress at the end of the Middle Ages (square-rigging, stern rudders) should have enabled an economy of personnel on board, if piracy had not cancelled out that advantage through the necessity of embarking soldiers.

This tendency accompanied the technical evolution, economic conditions and general circumstances, in the North as well as the South, until the end of the era of sailing ships. An estimation of the amount of material and the number of men on board is only possible with sufficient numerical documentation. The correlation between the metric tonne and the Nordic *last* and the Mediterranean 'deux bottes' enables an approach; but more precise data appeared at the end of the seventeenth century: for France, the Ordonnance de la Marine of 1681 evaluated the tonne at 979 kg and at 1.44 m. Thus the tonnage/man ratio for three destinations (Newfoundland, the Antilles, Africa) rose respectively from 3.9 to 7.3, from 4.8 to 10.5, and from 4.1 to 7.9. The economy in use is obvious, but assumes a rational utilization of it and postulates an increase in tonnage, favoured by technical progress.

Next, one may ask whether the rise in the tonnage/man ratio on the large ships did not favour the maximum use of the holding capacity at the expense of the space left for crew members. Living in close quarters was one of the trials of life on board ship, especially when it went on for some time. Seamen from the North and those from the South coped with it differently, due to the difference in their social habits and cultures. Mediterranean exuberance was in contrast to the natural reserve of the Nordics; but anger could be quick and violent among both groups. Going below decks for a moment, whereas to forward the senior officers and the petty officers enjoyed some comfort in the seventeenth and eighteenth centuries on the king's ships or on those of the large companies, the crew members had to make do in the stern with badly ventilated, smelly, noisy rooms; taking turns sleeping, on the rhythm of the watches, on the same 'beds', was a practice which can only be explained by fatigue, the sea air and youth. The oarsmen did not move from their benches; they slept on them, ate, and satisfied their other needs on them.

The quality of food was characterized by its adaptation to local resources and a sufficient number of calories. On the medieval Mediterranean naves and the vessels of modern centuries alike, a variety of menus was unknown by crew members and sometimes by the officers too. European navies rather early on developed a hierarchy of several 'tables' (as many as four on Venetian ships), corresponding to functions and ranks. Meat was more easily available on the Mediterranean than on northern boats, which had herring and cod in abundance. Salt provisions always constituted the essential food, along with biscuits, so hard that they had to be dunked in water, wine, beer or broth. It is better not to dwell on the food of the oarsmen, although a concern for their efficiency maintained a minimum nutritive level. There was, if one may put it like that, a 'Europe of Calories': in the fourteenth century, sailors consumed 3920 calories per day on the Venetian ships, and hardly more (4000) on Swedish ships; but much more (6500, because of the beer) on the large Dutch vessels in the eighteenth century. On the other hand, the minimum was found in the Russian navy, whose sober diet contained around 3000 calories per day. Between these extremes were the other diets, French, English, Iberian. Thus the emaciated and famished European navy is only a legend, even if it did seem constantly parched: the salt air dries one out.

The quality of the air could not, however, compensate for the lack of hygiene, frequent until the twentieth century due to the cleaning agents available, the lack of different clothes, which were slow to dry, body lice and other vermin which were encouraged by the warm dampness of the ship's interior, where the humidity of the 'nautical marsh' persisted; simple sores degenerated into purulent wounds, inflammation of the eye and pulmonary tuberculosis were rife. Along with lice and fleas, rats were the sailors' companions until the moment when a leak forced them to leave the ship and find refuge, like the men, on the smallest plank. Such an environment maintained a constant death toll, especially during long-distance voyages. Then scurvy, resulting from a vitamin deficiency, wreaked havoc to the point of suspending all activity and defeating even the biggest vessels; this happened until in the eighteenth century the antiscurval virtues of citrus fruits were discovered. European navies did not really have efficient medical services worthy of that name until the eighteenth century. To resist so many health threats, ships needed very healthy sailors, hardened by experience beginning in their adolescence.

A rigorous discipline contributed to strengthening characters and personalities. Its harshness on galleys has remained legendary, to the point that, increasing its richness, legend has added more. In the Mediterranean as on the Baltic Sea, on the anachronistic galleys of Sweden and Russia in the eighteenth century, the absence of consideration for the workers was injurious to service. Meanwhile, some charitable souls had reacted in favour of more humanity: the German Dominican Felix Faber in the fifteenth century was shocked at the passiveness of the oarsmen who were beaten on board the Venetian galley taking him to the Holy Land; and everyone knows the charitable initiatives taken by St Vincent de Paul in Toulon in the seventeenth century. Without reaching constant violence, the harshness of the relationships between men equalled that of the elements. One figure has, in this connection, become legendary: the *boss* or *bosco*, the boatswain, the interpreter of the orders of the master, or the *pasha*; but without rigour, with regard to the crew members who were themselves peasants, what would have become of discipline, indispensable on a sea which is itself without the least consideration?

The same dangers, the same need for security

The sudden tempests of the Mediterranean were no less dangerous than the torments of the ocean. The fog of the Bosporus, of Gibraltar and the Berlenga Islands off the coast of Portugal, or those of the Breton reefs, the banks of Flanders and the Danish straits, presented risks of running aground on the sandbanks, of drifting into rocks and of collisions. Alongside those catastrophes, masts falling onto decks or into the water appeared as the small change of dangers, of which landsmen could have no idea. Rich in contrasts, the sea is celebrated, not without reason, as a source of life and nourishment: it has been called the 'plasma of Europe'. But it is also called, with just as much justification, a 'place of mortality'.

Security, a problem common to all seas, in Europe took on particular importance due to the intensity of navigation. Paying especial attention has obtained remarkable results, at the price, it is true, of tragic experiences and serious material and human losses. The peoples of Europe have cooperated with an unequal intensity, but an equal tension has permitted, in the course of centuries, the sharing of similar results. It is useful to note the convergence of technical, legal, social and moral progress. On the technical level research in the realm of naval construction resulted in the development of the three-master characteristic of European navigation. As it was not enough just to have a good ship, mariners from the North and the South cooperated, some bringing the experimental knowledge and empirical intuition of consummate sailors, the others their astronomical calculations and the use of the nautical chart.

The search for security brought about the initiatives of convoys and armed escorts, and developed the practice of piloting at sea and of inshore piloting in estuaries. Inspired once again by the Roman example, Europeans dotted their shores with illuminated points of reference, the multiplication of which at the end of the seventeenth century was the result of solutions to architectural problems, the resilience of materials, sources of energy and optics posed by the construction of lighthouses. We will see that the placement of lighthouses, sometimes close together, offered a landscape similar to a balcony on feast days in certain areas of the European coasts, which helped to diminish the number of accidents at sea.

Research into the prevention of catastrophes at sea engendered the development of maritime insurance. The most fertile initiative came from the Mediterraneans. There had been ancient precedents, but the acceleration of maritime trade stimulated the ingeniousness of traders, in Florence in particular. In the fourteenth century Féderigo Mélis discovered their precociousness in the practice of premium insurance, whose variance reflects the intensity, different according to the areas and the moments, of natural risks or those brought on by men (wars and piracy). Its use reached the ocean ports, then those of the North. Castilian businessmen, in particular those from Burgos and Bilbao, continued the practice and in the sixteenth century diffused a code of international usage as far as Antwerp. In turn the Hanseatics substituted these practices for less refined ones such as loans for great adventures, to which their caution and habits remained attached.

A few episodes will illustrate the swift spread of preoccupations with security, notably from a technical point of view. The two which follow contrast both geographically and psychologically. One, already mentioned, is the affair of the *Pierre* from La Rochelle, whose hull the municipal authorities of Gdańsk used and restored to serve as a model, in the second half of the fifteenth century. The other, a Venetian text from the beginning of the eighteenth century which, paradoxically discouraging, eulogizes northern ships: 'With the westerners', it says, 'one cannot compete either in ability, or in profits, and even less in the security of vessels'.

Insecurity also resulted from human malice, and it took time before charitable initiatives shook up consciences and organized help for the shipwrecked. It would be unjust to make a general pejorative judgement on the attitude of the 'wreckers'. Populations whose island location enabled them to escape legal repression attracted ships in distress with fake fires or signals on the rocks of the furthest points of Europe. Another malicious ruse pretended to mount a disinterested rescue operation, but had it paid for, expensively, by the 'beneficiaries', who were stripped of their property and held until they paid a ransom: the misadventure of Jacques Coeur near Calvi in 1432 is an example. On the other hand, one must not equate the wreckers with those who, in our time, in Ouessant, recovered a cargo of espadrilles from the Far East, lost in a tempest by its transporter, which was broken up on the rocky cliffs.

The duty of helping people in danger did not move from a moral to an institutional level until recent times. At the end of the eighteenth century the spirit of mutual help incited the development of organisations for rescue at sea. This development resulted from traditional Christian inspiration and from the spirit of 'Reason'; it was stimulated by the double influence of wars and shipwrecks, whose numbers increased with the growth of maritime traffic. Even in our own time, the summer flow of tourists each year brings to the coasts millions of inexperienced landsmen, whose unawareness causes many accidents.

The movement began on the shores where the frequency and seriousness of catastrophes revealed a necessity for them. For example, the shipwrecks in the Irish Sea at the end of the eighteenth century, others on the coasts of Denmark and Holland (1811, 1824), those, more famous, of the *Méduse* on the Moroccan coasts in 1816 and above all that of the *Sémillante* in 1855 in the mouths of Bonifacio, which caused the death of several hundred soldiers *en route* to the Crimea. All of Europe was moved by that disaster, and that emotion resulted in the creation of the International Red Cross. The construction of British *Wreck Charts* and French charts of shipwrecks made it possible to determine where rescue stations should be placed.

Institutions appeared simultaneously in the British Isles and in France before 1800 through the initiatives of Sir William Hillary and M. de Bernières (1775 in Le Havre). A few dates attest to the extension of these foundations: Ireland (around 1800), Holland (1824), Belgium (1838), Denmark (1844) etc. The most powerful institutions made their débuts in France and England. The Société Humaine des Naufragés (Le Havre, 1825) gave way to the Société Centrale des Naufragés and to the Société des Hospitaliers-Sauveteurs Bretons, fused in 1967 into the current Société Nationale de Sauvetage en Mer. The Royal National Lifeboat Institution dates from 1849, the Deutsche Gesellschaft zur Rettung Schiffbrüchiger from 1865; there followed the Instituto de Soccoros a Naufragos (Lisbon, 1892) and the Sociedad Española de Salvamento de Naufragos.

There is no question of the unanimity of efforts, nor of the nature of them. They consist of a stock of lifeboats, unsinkable and fast, spread out between the most sensitive points, manned by volunteer rescuers wherever private initiative prevailed. This is the case notably with German, English, French, Norwegian and Swedish institutions; however, in other countries (for example, Belgium, Denmark, Spain, Finland, Greece, Italy, the Low Countries, Poland and Portugal), help at sea, financed in large part by the state, managed by ministers of the navy, are a public service. This diversity does not damage the solidarity of rescuing institutions; they are in almost daily contact in Western Europe and every four years hold a conference to coordinate their technology and their initiatives. European rescue at sea is in action, day and night, in all seasons, regardless of bad weather, without expecting anything more than well-deserved gratitude. Even before a wished-for coordination in 1992, the Europe of rescuers at sea is more than an idea: it exists.

The victims of the sea have not only been those drowned. There are also invalids through old age or accidents, as well as widows and orphans. The system (a precursor of social security) instituted in France by Colbert had emulators in other countries; itself, it came out of initiatives sometimes going back to the Middle Ages, where the inspiration had been charity. Ancient Athens during the

Peloponnesian War in the fifth century BC, and Rome in the squadron of Cape Miseno of the first century AD, had a kind of ship-hospitals: the first with the *Therapia*, the second with the *Aesculapius*. Medical assistance served the Byzantine fleet in the seventh century. In its turn, medieval Europe had rest homes for disabled or senile sailors, and facilities for the orphans of those who disappeared. Venice reserved the St-Martin home (1272) and the St-Anthony hospice (1317) for them; the Great Council agreed to the apportioning of a percentage of customs receipts for mariners out of their right to security in old age: 'It is an act of charity and pity to help the poor men of the sea, sixty years old, who spent their youth in the service of the state, and then became useless.' The candidates were so numerous that in 1385 they extended the Misericordia, and in 1500 the hospital San Nicolò di Castello, until then intended for pilgrims, was used for mariners no longer able to work. Without being comprehensive, we should not fail to mention among the pawnshops founded in the sixteenth century the Monti delle Arte del Mare in the kingdom of Naples, as well as the Iberian foundations benefiting fishermen in Valencia (1396), and oarsmen in Puerto de Santa Maria (1512) and Oporto (1443); near that city, in Matosinhos, a navy hospital today is still faithful to its goal. In La Rochelle tradition has it that a rich merchant, Alexandre Auffredi, in the thirteenth century founded the hospital which still bears his name. In the fourteenth century foundations spread to Nordic shores. In ports, as in other cities, orphans were a preoccupation; special officers, the *garde-orphènes* in France, watched over them; in London the Court of Orphans dealt with them. The same thing occurred throughout Europe in the seventeenth and eighteenth centuries with the founding of navy hospitals in Pisa (1627), Civitavecchia (1645, 1660), Rochefort (1666), Brest and Toulon (1689), Greenwich (1695) and Rotterdam (1740). In Sweden the Maritime Code renewed a disposition of the Laws of Visby, apportioning to works of charity a third of the fines inflicted on sailors for negligence in their service. Old and disabled sailors, widows and orphans, thus made up a group of people affected by insecurity. It is impossible to count them, even though they were the most numerous victims of the sea. Furthermore, dying at sea was not always by drowning. Fatal illnesses killed many on board, and throwing cadavers into the sea in sacks weighed down by a stone made up a defined ceremonial; on the black slavers of the eighteenth century more whites than blacks died. Alain Cabantous has calculated that in Dunkirk between 1662 and 1791 accidents on board were responsible for 37.4 per cent of all deaths, and battles for only 2.25 per cent. We can imagine the anguish of the one who knew he was dying, sick or declining, far from his family and native land. C.E. Dufourcq noted, in the course of his research into Catalan archives, a prayer composed and written with emotion by an anonymous mariner on a single sheet of paper in a register; he has translated it thus: 'Lord! please let me escape from perils!'

Ultimately, in a Europe which remained unanimous in its fundamental beliefs in spite of the Reformation, the ultimate recourse of sailors remained a view towards Heaven, in the hope of final security. Hope existed in all times and did not belong to any single civilization. Everything happened, at sea, in the desert and in the mountains, as if the confrontation with the constraining power of nature led one to invoke an extra- or supernatural force exercising itself at sea, with an oppressive infiniteness. Before making contact with the sea the consecration of the ship was an act whose rituals foresaw, at the foot of the main mast, the evangelical reading of the miracle of the calmed tempest and a benediction from the prow to the poop. The ship received a name, the choice of which in the fifteenth century reflected the faith of its owner. The religion of seamen, similar to that of landsmen, was, however, different in the at least apparent intensity of its relationship with Heaven. From the middle of the fourteenth century until the sixteenth, appeals were principally addressed, except in England, to the Virgin Mary, invoked as *Stella Maris*; the other intercessors were generally St Peter and St Nicholas, whose legend was known everywhere in the twelfth century, and, in particular areas, certain regional saints unique to the Mediterranean, the ocean and the Nordic seas. God, with reference to the Saviour, to the Cross, or to the Holy Spirit, was Himself sometimes made responsible for the protection of the ship. Modes varied: St Francis conquered Mediterranean space; Saint Ursula and Saint Barbara preserved the North. Purely secular words, small in number in the Middle Ages, on the contrary, confirmed the search for extra-natural security alongside beneficent feminine allegories (*Gloria, Benedicta*) or animal ones evoking strength (the *Eagle*, the *Lion*, for example). Nordic Protestantism changed those practices. The immediate protection of God took over from the intercession of the saints. The saints, however, until the middle of the sixteenth century, were willing patrons of the boats sent from the northern countries to the Mediterranean ports; for the Lutheran mariners there were supplementary guarantees against the suspicions of the Inquisition, severe in certain places such as Malta. The appeal to the Lord alone, directly or indirectly through the intermediary of his Mother or his saints, was animated by equal sincerity. In the seventeenth century the collection of prayers by the pastor Théophile Barbauld, from l'Ile de Ré, for all forms of danger was inspired by a spirituality comparable to that of Father Fournier regarding the 'good use of shipwrecks', because the sea, a sacred space because it was perilous, was itself redeeming. Worried tension and assured confidence were joined. The spirituality of the 'Ecole française' of the seventeenth century finally found its place there, even at the heart of the superstitious backwardness of the sailors.

The call for help became more ardent at the moment of supreme peril, when the mast was broken, the sails torn, the rudder shattered; even the anchor of charity was powerless. The crew was at a loss. Only Heaven could save them. It was the moment for promises: one promised, if he escaped death, to go on a pilgrimage to such and such a marine sanctuary scattered along the European coasts, and bring to the chosen miracle worker an object which, commemorating the tragedy, was meant to represent the donor. The marine votive offering or *ex-voto* might have been a piece of the hull on which the escapee floated, one of the articles of clothing he was wearing at the time of the shipwreck and which he put on once again to make his offering, a model of the ship, or an image (a painting or a simple drawing) portraying the drama. This type of practice is of an anthropological as much as spiritual nature. In use in Antiquity and also among primitive peoples, the *ex-voto* has left testimonies on all European shores, in the Greek and Dalmatian islands, for example in Cattaro; they are numerous in the Annunziata near Naples, in the Monte Nero, near Leghorn, in Antibes, at Notre-Dame-de-la-Garde in Marseille; in Seville, the large painting of *Nuestra Señora de Navegadores* evokes the Discoveries; they are found at Notre-Dame-de-Montuzet on the Gironde, in Sainte-Anne-d'Auray and in the smallest Breton chapel, in Honfleur and Fécamp, in Notre-Dame de Boulogne and in Notre-

Dame-des-Dunes near Dunkirk, as well as in Bruges. Protestantism did not make them all disappear in the English, Germanic and
Scandinavian sanctuaries; Dutch and Danish churches possess
models whose commemorative character could be substituted for a
votive intent, without the latter being completely obliterated. Even
in Poland, despite the wars, the coastal churches have preserved a
few *ex-votos*.

The painted *ex-voto* holds the attention with its psychological
and spiritual content. Bernard Cousin has minutely analysed
Mediterranean paintings by comparing them with those of other
regions in Europe. Three registers share the pictorial space: one
deals with nature, the sea in fury and threatening clouds; the
second relates to man and his boat(s); the highest register is
occupied by the image of invoked celestial figures. 'Gestures'
expresses the religious content of the object. Waves symbolize the
trial endured by man. Between him and celestial beings, gestures
and looks evoke a dialogue: the begging arms and imploring looks
of those shipwrecked aimed towards Heaven, the outstretched
hand of the saint to pull the unfortunate from death with a look of
pity. Meaning is at its highest when the Virgin holds the Baby Jesus
on her arm; Mary stretches her hand towards the supplicant, but
exercising her role as intercessor, she watches her Son from whom
every decision depends. The work then achieves a theological
dimension rare to the degree that it comes from among simple
sailors, but expressive of the function of security, of which Jean
Delumeau has made the title of one of his best books: *Rassurer et
Protéger*.

Sociability and independence

Decidedly not very comprehensible to land-dwellers, seamen – Mediterraneans, northerners and Nordics – found the
means to compensate for their differences by sharing two opposite
character traits: sociability and independence, just as capable of
firm solidarities as of explosive antagonisms.

The 'ship's board' has already been discussed, with the both
monotone and fantastic appearance of an artificial, but constraining, masculine community (except on the little fishing boats). The
cement, truly vital, came from the demands of security. The

frequent co-ownership of little fishing boats explains that solidarity. Added to that was the co-responsibility for the fate of the ship, especially on long voyages. The various codes of the sea, which we will mention again, refer to it. Aware of the interdependence of their tasks, the seamen had the habit of holding councils, especially when their common fate was at stake. That council was more or less large depending on the nature of the decisions to be made, on an economic level (stops to make or to prolong) or a technical level (repairs and caulking, changing a route due to weather or the presence of pirates, jettisoning cargo due to an imminent threat). The expression 'company on board' has its meaning, represented, for its part, by the Venetian institution of the Council of Twelve.

Solidarity on board rooted itself in a multiplicity of sociabilities on land. The council just mentioned resembled a family council on the little boats manned by close relatives, friends, or at least 'countrymen'. Even if they were not from the same parish, their origins were in the same region and, unless there were personal animosities, they had the same mindsets. On land they gathered for religious or secular holidays and belonged to fraternities or guilds, specialized according to professional categories in the large ports, from small fishermen to caulkers, carpenters and ship's masters, under the patronage of the saints of the professions we have already mentioned. The organization of the fraternities of seamen resembled that of similar organizations of landsmen and, like them, had first of all a charitable end, to the benefit of widows, orphans and old or infirm sailors. One of their concerns was looking for the bodies of drowned men in order to give them a burial in holy ground; if they could not be found, a simulated religious burial took place; this was, for example in Ouessant, the *proëlla* (etymologically *pro illa anima*), in use until the middle of the twentieth century. The London guilds demonstrated a great activity on behalf of the poor, and for their part the Neapolitan fraternities contributed until the end of the eighteenth century to the financing of the pawn shops reserved only for seamen, with the help of receipts from a tax on fishing. Some fraternities saw to the education of cabin boys and young sailors by encouraging swimming and rowing competitions through prizes, or by organizing – in Le Havre in the seventeenth century, for example – courses in hydrography which were accompanied by moral and religious training.

On the professional level, guilds used fines to punish drunkenness on board, the cause of accidents; they confiscated fish caught off-season, the dates of which they regulated; and suspended pilots who went against regulations. In Germany and in the Baltic Sea they fixed the salaries of sailors. Joyful sociableness too sometimes exercised its rights, to celebrate, for example in the herring ports, the end of the fishing season; in Dieppe this was the occasion for the banquet of the *oue* (*oie*, or goose). Another fraternity organized literary competitions (from the Norman *puys*), in which the poets of the sea expressed themselves, not the least at the time of the Renaissance.

The sense of solidarity pushed to the point of sacrifice had as its counterpart – one is tempted to say, as its complement – a very lively spirit of independence from all points of view: moral, religious and sometimes disciplinary. There is nothing surprising in this. Young men, setting sail on the threshold of adolescence to follow the example of their father or brother, or to ease the poverty of a large family, risked becoming perverse early on through an uncontrolled initiation into life's problems. If they were a little more watched over on the little boats, in a familial or, at least, known environment, on board the large ships, on the contrary, mutual intentions conspired to lead them astray.

Certainly practices tended to keep religion in mind: the benediction of the ship at the time of its launching and upon its fitting-out for a distant destination (Jacques Cartier, on 15 August 1534, received the Eucharist with all his men before leaving for Canada). In passing them, men saluted the bell towers of preferred sanctuaries. Every day prayers were recited *en masse* under the direction of the ship's master. Before the sixteenth century there were rarely chaplains on board, even on ships of pilgrims *en route* to the Holy Land from Venice, Genoa, Marseille or Barcelona. For lack of a priest, prayers of the mass were read without consecration: this was called a 'dry mass'. The Church recognized the need to dispense with common practices at the end of the twelfth century, when it permitted Flemish fishermen to go to sea on Sunday. It was only after the long oceanic voyages that there were chaplains or pastors on board large ships, after the Protestant Reformation. At that time there developed a pastoral effort among crew members.

Indeed, the diversity, sometimes the confrontation of Christian confessions, as well as the discovery of other religions overseas, inclined many sailors to scepticism and to religious or at least practical indifference. And yet those sailors, not bad boys, many of whom were attached to ancestral traditions, appealed to divine help at the ultimate moment when they could no longer pretend or brazen it out.

Being brazen was an easy attitude for those who were young and free of social constraints. Once the jetties had been passed, the air of the open sea swept away prohibitions and loosened all shackles. 'Facts at sea', said a French royal ordinance of 1400, 'are not the same as those on land.' Gestures and rituals carried out on board ship remained strict and misunderstood, but taking God, the Virgin and the saints (a way of recognizing their existence!) as witnesses, men blasphemed constantly, and curses rained from the top of the masts down on the deck and criss-crossed from the forecastle to the poop, like stimulants and proofs of liberation

Anger was expressed with the violence of the great winds. It would burst forth like a storm, set off by the smallest incidents of collective life and by repressed resentments. Theft was small change next to the rifts that occurred on board or, more often, on land, in a tavern, with the help of drink. Jealousies over women happened too, for conjugal morality was sometimes put to the test during stopovers; but stopovers were rarely long, and conjugal fidelity resumed its rights upon a sailor's return and continued once again. There were also quarrels about money, for many sailors were almost penniless when they set sail, and the moment they landed they spent the sum of their earnings on carousing. Some violence had more noble motives: there was the defence, for example, of a servant girl in Dunkirk whom other sailors were planning to rape, or the sudden solidarity which would reconcile sailors of rival origins, such as Bretons and Gascons, Normans and Flemish, English and French, Germans and Scandinavians.

Rebellions

Sometimes the spirit of independence went further, beyond the limits of discipline, and threatened the necessary solidarity. Individual insubordination was subject to rigorous punishment and ended up in desertions which the French system of 'Classes' and the English custom of the 'Press' attempted to prevent with unequal success.

Collective insubordination took the path of mutiny, which had much more serious consequences. In *La Vergue et les fers*, Alain Cabantous has analysed very well the phenomenon of rebellion in the various aspects of what is called (from Flemish) the *groume*. The protesting murmur implied by this term, mute at first, took on the volume of a rumble, and the grumbling swelled to the point of assembling a more or less large group, one capable of exerting pressure on the ship's command by taking over the ship's poop deck. The origins of discontent were sometimes a minor episode which became amplified in inverse proportion to the masculine microcosm of the ship: a simple remark made to a subordinate, bad treatment, the demands of the *bosco*, dissatisfaction with the food, protests against the choice of route, grudges about the distribution of fish caught, and, on ships armed for privateering, recriminations over the division of the booty. The objective varied depending on the complaints and the extent of the movement. Every age experienced this with more or less solid or legitimate goals. Legal files of all kinds in Venice or Genoa, in Iberian and Hanseatic ports, in England and in France, the archives of admiralties, as well as letters of remission, reveal such circumstances in a vivid fashion. These are the terms in which a ringleader on a Catalan ship incited his men to hold the captain so they would be able to engage in piracy: 'Fellows! Do you want to fill your pockets? Well then, let's grab anything that belongs to anyone!' Without going to such lengths, the crew of a British ship went on strike in 1757 in London and threatened to desert if the owners did not agree to leave the sailors a large proportion of the hold to store their private merchandise. This share of the sailors' cargo, which had to be carried on the deck and was therefore exposed to bad weather, was a way of supplementing their wages, recognized communally (in Venice, it was known as the *portata*) and defined in England (1786) as destined for the sailor's family.

The ringleaders were rarely simple sailors, but rather second-rank or petty officers moved by old grudges or jealousies and having a certain level of education. The most famous example of this is that of the *Bounty*, too well known to need discussion here.

Some dozen years later, the seriousness and duration of the mutinies of the Royal Navy in 1797 almost led England to disaster. They enjoyed considerable success until the mutinies of the Black Sea in 1917.

Desertions, less important but more frequent, continued until the eighteenth century to be a scourge for all the navies, beginning with those of the Italian towns in the Middle Ages. The case of Genoa in the fourteenth and fifteenth centuries was so significant that a *Manuel des fugitifs des galées de la commune* made known that in 1356, from thirteen galleys, 190 men had deserted, disgusted by life on board ship, to seek less strenuous and better-paid work. However, less than twenty years earlier (1339) a regulation had taken steps to limit the number of desertions. They disturbed sea traffic so much that ships had to recruit workers to fill gaps in their workforce even during the course of a voyage.

Corsairs and pirates

For centuries an outlet for the seamen's spirit of independence was found in adventures in privateering and piracy. However, since the nineteenth century, in Europe at least, they have continued to exist only in the work of novelists and in the minds of the general public. For several decades historians have been attempting to define and distinguish the characteristics of those adventures, to assess their extent and to evaluate their significance, which is not an easy task.

At the end of the Middle Ages the authority of the state sought to limit the damage, that is, to channel the use of violence on the seas. There was much to be done to dominate such an anarchic situation, for individuals and certain public powers were organizing enterprises without control. In the fourteenth century in the North Sea, the Vitalienbrüder in the English Channel and on the Atlantic Ocean English, French, Breton and Castilian pirates or corsairs took advantage of the Hundred Years' War, even during truces, to obtain lucrative booty; in the Mediterranean neither the Tyrrhenian nor the Adriatic nor the Aegean Seas escaped the raids of both Christians and Saracens.

The state's efforts consisted of introducing into international law distinctions between privateering and piracy. In this it was helped by the reflections of jurists such as Bartolus and Grotius, and progress was made thanks to bilateral treaties at the end of the fifteenth century between France, the Hanseatic League, Castile and England. From that time a corsair was someone who was armed at sea with the authorization of the prince against the enemies of the crown, and who left the issue of legitimizing or invalidating his loot to the authority of the Admiralty. On the other hand, a pirate was someone who, without control, attacked and plundered anyone. The corsair became respectable; the pirate became a bandit.

The results, inevitably imperfect on the oceanic and Nordic side, left a share to the privateers; we can evaluate their role in the Franco-English wars from Louis XIV to Napoleon, in the Anglo-Dutch wars of the mid-seventeenth century, and in the Baltic region during the Thirty Years' War and the period of Russo-Swedish rivalry The situation was more complex in the Mediterranean. In the sixteenth century the Uskoks came out of their Dalmatian islands to disturb traffic. But the entire Mediterranean was the privileged region of an armed competition between Christians and Barbary pirates, for the distinction between privateering and piracy remained confused there: everyone insulted everyone else with accusations of piracy, combined with insults of religious infidelity.

To bring this to an end in the nineteenth century, it took the cessation of the Barbary pirates' activity and the international prohibition of privateering – although one must recognize that in the two world wars there were vestiges of privateering and, in a few cases, of piracy. For several centuries the state took advantage of the results of the seamen's spirit of adventure; it seized the profits without always being aware that privateering itself, and not just piracy, was a parasite on the economy, for without producing anything it deflected both goods and energies away from their final goals.

Composite crews

Though marked by conflicts, rivalries and competition, though restrained by ethnic, political, social and religious differences, a compenetration was evident in the increasingly mixed nature of crews. At the time of the voyages of Mediterranean galleys the necessity of compensating for desertions by hiring, depending on availability in the workers' markets, had been recognized. Since medieval times that tendency has remained constant.

The Genoese finally stabilized a fluid situation by providently initiating, at the time they hired sailors, the agreement before a notary of guarantors standing surety to ensure a replacement, whom the conscripts could, moreover, choose themselves. Those recruited naturally included a large Genoese, or at least Ligurian, contingent, but complements were sought elsewhere too, and not only on Tyrrhenian shores. Thus, Michel Balard has calculated that of the 7508 sailors on eight armed galleys between 1369 and 1409, four-fifths came from Liguria (1400 from Genoa and 207 from the northern shore); the last fifth were natives of the neighbouring coasts and the Genoese agencies in the Orient: they were thus Greek or Slavic. For their part, the Venetian fleets recruited a great number of Greeks from Crete, Negroponte and the Cyclades. Travellers, Felix Faber among others, observed on the ships of *la Serenissima* [Venice] an odd assortment of 'Macedonians, Greek Slavonians, Turks and Saracens'; but the Infidels did not hesitate to force their Christian captives to wield the oars on their galleys. The disparate recruitment of mariners in the service of Venice ended up by forming an ethnic mosaic. Less than in the Italian ports, this composite character nevertheless affected Marseille, Barcelona and Valencia. Discoveries in the Atlantic attracted a labour force in search of profit and adventure; alongside confirmed seamen, those living in the interior, lured by the news of discovered lands, flooded to Lisbon, Seville and Cádiz to join the fleets of Vasco de Gama, Cabral and above all Magellan.

Types of twin-city arrangements linked ports in different countries. The *Contratación* associating Nantes and Bilbao in the sixteenth century had certain aspects of an international fraternity, with common prayers for the dead. In other, more numerous, cases an association was a simple effect of frequency of contact, for example between the ports of northern Brittany and those of Devon and Cornwall (notably Roscoff and Lannion, Exeter and Dartmouth), or between the coasts of Caux and Essex (Dieppe, Fécamp, Rye and Hastings), or between Calais and Dover, between Flanders, Zealand and East Anglia. There were other examples of this as far as the Baltic, where Germanic and Slavic shores were in such strict symbiosis with the Scandinavian coasts that their ties served as bases for the maritime ambitions of the Wasas' Sweden and the Romanovs' Russia.

The labour markets

In this context a few places and regions played the role of international market-places for marine labour, in the North and on the Mediterranean. The sailor became a salaried worker. Hiring depended on demographic location, for example in Brittany and Norway, as well as on economic conditions and technical necessities. The professional competence acquired on the banks of Newfoundland in the seventeenth and eighteenth centuries thus made deep-sea fishing the breeding-ground for the British navy and the royal navies of France and Spain. Crews, on trading vessels above all, were very mixed. At the beginning of the seventeenth century, Flemish Jesuits saw them as 'assemblies of the dregs of nations'. Diversity was not just ethnic. Vauban wrote to Louis XIV that one-seventh of the 'classified' ships were Protestant. The pluriconfessional composition of the crews undoubtedly contributed to the development of a tolerance characteristic of the relationships between men of the ocean. In the Mediterranean the mixing went even further on the merchant or military galleys, since it included, even on the European side, Saracens alongside Christians (or nominal Christians). It is true that although seamen were forced to accept a hard existence, they also counted on potential profit from privateering or unadmitted piracy.

Supply and demand played a role. Whereas Northern Europe had an excess of sailors at its disposal and Holland, Denmark and the Hanseatic towns satisfied their needs, France and England took measures to hold on to their mariners. The British Navigation Act of 1660 established that three-quarters of all crews would be British; Colbert's intention was to keep French sailors in the service of the king of France and to dissuade them from finding work on Dutch ships. Out of an estimated total of between 300,000 and 400,000 European mariners, fishermen and sailors included, France would have had a maximum of between 43,000 at the end of the seventeenth century and 55,000 in 1789; but England far exceeded France. To make up for a deficit meant not only keeping one's own sailors, but also, for trade, seeking labour from other countries. This is what Bordeaux and Nantes wanted; in 1730 Nantes solicited from the royal administration 'every ability to hire foreign sailors and to encourage them to settle' in the kingdom.

The example of Dunkirk

The case of Dunkirk, which Alain Cabantous has studied, is an interesting example of a European maritime labour market in the seventeenth and eighteenth centuries. By virtue of its location between the North Sea and the English Channel, its proficiency in small- and large-scale fishing, in international coastal trade and colonial traffic, and its experience with privateering, this port was prepared to profit from, as well as to suffer from, the long-standing ambiguous political position of belonging to the Austrian Low Countries, of being connected with the Dutch, and of having necessary relations with England. That ended in the time of Jean Bart, under Louis XIV, with a definitive attachment to monarchic France. There is no better place to apply the formula: 'the maritime world escapes borders and, to a large degree, time, as well' (M. Bogucka). Dunkirk had the appearance of a 'melting pot'. There was no preeminent national group there, such as the Spanish in Bordeaux or the Dutch colony in Nantes, but there was a fluctuating environment of needy sailors in search of work. Between the middle of the seventeenth century and that of the eighteenth, the majority came from England, the Germanic and Scandinavian countries; then around 1740 came the Italians, the Spanish and the Flemish. Despite the instability of families, the distribution by origin of married foreign sailors in Dunkirk between 1710 and 1790 puts the Venetians and the Genoese in the lead (close to 25 per cent), followed by the Spanish (12.5 per cent), the British and the Germans in equal proportion (11 per cent), with the Dutch coming in at scarcely 8 per cent, and the Scandinavians at 3 per cent. The approximation of the numbers is less important than the nature of the facts. The case of Dunkirk appears modest alongside the ports of the United Provinces, where the proportion of foreigners among the seamen rose to more than 40 per cent, and beyond what London, Seville, Marseille and Genoa were able to count. The result of all this was that in the large ports of the old continent, by the end of the eighteenth century the maritime population had become a mosaic of nationalities.

9

Familiar Images

Landscapes

Maps and route charts

Europe was not so big that a little distance could not allow one to perceive its nuances. The mariner, a man of distances and distancing, could do so better than anyone. He went around it on the west, which he easily recognized from landscapes that had been predicted, and were even expected, thanks to the plotting of the maps and the descriptions of the route charts, which the Mediterranean was the first to give him, beginning in the thirteenth century. Having measured with his compass the angle of his route to the direction of the winds marked on his portolan chart, he soon recognized the coastlines and the seamarks pointed out by the author of the route chart in simple language:

> If you want to go to Loyre [i.e. Nantes] be aware that the island of Pilier and the point of Chémoulin lie north-north-east and south-south-west. The point of Chémoulin is below Saint-Lesayres [Nazaire] and above it is a chapel and a black point, and to follow the channel well . . . one must see a mill made of earth . . . at the centre of the Sand cove below Chémoulin.

The mariner could thus discern the outline of the shores whose silhouette was more or less reproduced by awkward drawings.

Thus it was until the end of the journey; but 'in the Baltic', noted the cartographer Fra Mauro in 1459, 'one navigates neither with the map nor with the compass, but with the sounding line.'

That was already necessary for a landing on the Flemish and Zealand coasts to reach Sluys, Middelburg and Antwerp. But, the *Seebuch*, picking up from the *Routier de la mer*, went on:

> If you wish to sail from Zwin towards the reefs of Jutland, distancing yourself from the land by 27 fathoms, you must go north-north-east . . . and maintain that direction until you no longer have a depth of 40 fathoms; then go north-east until you see Jutland . . . Once you pass the reefs of Skagen, sink the sounding line until you have no more than 10 fathoms . . . Finally you will arrive before the town of Rostock.

An improvement in the 'language of geographers' (Fr. de Dainville) enabled geographers to inform navigators with more precision, by inventing signs indicating rocks, sand banks, anchorages and, using soundings, sandy bottoms and even schools of fish. In Italy in the fifteenth century an innovation close to pictorial art consisted of framing the map or of furnishing it with vignettes portraying the monumental appearance of the ports. The prototype of this genre was the work of Cristoforo Buondelmonte, the descendant of a large Florentine family who in 1420 dedicated to Cardinal Giordano Orsini a sort of guide to the Cyclades and the Ionian Isles, the *Liber insularum archipelagi*, a work containing around eighty images which the author comments on in these terms, addressed to the cardinal: ' . . . there you will see green mountains white with snow, springs, plains, ports with capes and neighbouring shelves, fortified towns, expanses of sea.' The town of Chios, 'a very safe port', appears with the two lighthouses looking out over the approach to the harbour and the enclosure of Kastro, which still exists. Buondelmonte was the founder of a school, and his work was recopied several times, translated into Greek and imitated, notably by Bartolomeo delli Sonetti (1485) and Benedetto Bordone (1528); the cartographic genre of the *isolario* prospered in the seventeenth century and left representations of Mediterranean islands through precise drawings. The harmony of colours in them equalled the quality of miniatures in manuscripts from the end of the fifteenth century, representing Rhodes, Constantinople, Venice, Naples, Genoa and Marseille.

The *isolario* shared the privilege of representing harbour sites with maps in the strict sense. In the time of Buondelmonte, a map of the Mediterranean by the Majorcan Gabriele de Vallsecha (1447) is decorated with rather conventional bird's eye views, among which one can recognize Genoa by its jutting-out breakwater. The cartographic schools did not lag behind. In 1559 Diego Homem provided an image of Lisbon. Examples are numerous in the seventeenth century. The nautical atlas by the pilot from Enkhuizen, Lucas Waghenauer, published in 1584-5 and translated into English under the title *The Mariner's Mirror*, with its 23 marine maps, was a fundamental work for European navigators until the publication of *Neptune français* in 1693. Whether Waghenauer had emulators, notably in the Mediterranean and Dieppe schools, or whether he provided models for them, is unknown, but portraits of harbour towns multiplied on maps. In 1603 Barcelona, Marseille, Genoa, Venice and Ragusa appeared on the maps of Francesco Oliva, of Majorcan descent. In 1620 there were bird's eye views of ports in the *Atlas* of Charlat Ambrosin from Marseille. And Jean Guérard from Dieppe decorated the margins of his *Description hydrographique de la France* (1627) and of his map of the *Océan septentrional* (1628) with insets and commentaries providing images of Atlantic ports, that of Dieppe in particular, of the English Channel and the Nordic seas, with an almost photographic precision.

Thus if one also takes into account the manuals which constituted the scientific tools of mariners from the fifteenth century (piloting manuals, tide tables, declination tables), which enabled them to establish the position of ports, and if one considers their wide diffusion, one may conclude that the image of the European coastline held no secrets for the navigators sailing between the Bosporus and the Danish straits.

Coastal sites

Certain coastal sites lent themselves to comparisons which did not escape the attention of travellers. One of the most obvious shows the similarity of salt marshes. The same landscape of salt beds and estuaries placed in a chequerboard pattern on an orthogonal plan is found on the shores of both the Mediterranean and the Atlantic. Thus the Hanseatics were in no way out of their element when going from the marshes of Guérande to those of the 'Bay' of Bourgneuf and Saintonge, then to Portugal; it was the same for the

Genoese who, returning in ballast from their ocean voyage, took on salt similar to that of Languedoc or Hyères in Ibiza. For their part, the Venetians thought only of the cost of loading salt in Crete or on Dalmatian shores. Nothing was more like itself than the landscape of the saltworks.

On the contrary, the different types of coasts lent themselves to a differentiated typology, the perception of which in past centuries was conveyed by the notations of voyagers and the behaviour of mariners: a low coast, raised cliffs, shelves at water level, all were dangerous in various ways, and in bad weather it was better to stay off-shore, and set one's 'nose', that is the ship's bow, into the wind and wait for clear weather. Islands were perceived differently. Tales of navigation in the Mediterranean are eloquent: alongside islands used as refuges from the wind, others had been feared since Antiquity. The differences from the ocean islands, fewer in number and less sporadic, are notable. But there were many pirate nests; the danger was greatest on the great trade routes, and when the layout of the archipelagos was favourable to traps and surprises, for example on the coasts of Asia Minor, in the Ionian islands, in the Dalmatian 'canals', at the Mouths of Bonifacio between Corsica and Sardinia, near the Berlenga Islands off the coast of Portugal, in the narrows of Saintonge and Aunis, in the Breton reefs, in the Irish Sea, and at the approaches to the Danish straits. However, there was security as well as insecurity in the island sectors; they were refuges as well as pirates' nests.

Watchtowers, lighthouses, beacons

Boldness, anxiety and caution have been served or tempered all along the European coasts by the progressive placement through the centuries of a security arrangement. In certain regions the western shores have taken on the look of well-signed and well-watched boulevards.

Two complementary functions have thus been established. One, that of watch-keeping, had as its first objective the security of the shores. The other, that of signalling, aimed to guide navigators. The Mediterranean, in both cases, was at the forefront and made its initiatives available to the Atlantic and Nordic shores. The first typical landscape included the placement of watchtowers which dotted the shores of the 'Great Blue Sea', perhaps since prehistoric times. In Corsica and Sardinia they are happy to call them Genoese; they could also be called Catalan. This is of little importance, for documentation confirms the facts. Thus fourteenth-century Provençal archives enable one to map the network of those towers, around 20 to 25 kilometres apart – that is, the optimum space for optical signalling by fires or signals announcing enemy sails on the horizon – from the Rhône as far as la Turbie. Suspicious sails were often those of enemies of the city or the state; and always those of pirates. This is why, as the same causes produced the same effects, the western shores showed a comparable layout. The Viking menace reflecting that of the Saracens, the Carolingians initiated the watch in the ninth century, forcing the inhabitants of the coast to keep surveillance posts on the shores. The French coastal castles and the British cliff-castles also played the same role as the Mediterranean towers. Later the monarchic states took up that policy; for example, under Louis XIV Vauban organized the defence of the French ocean coastline.

Since Antiquity and the Middle Ages lighthouses have been a symbol of Europe's awakening to maritime life, and the increase in their number and power throughout the centuries conveys a growing attention to issues of the sea. In Antiquity they had dotted the shores known at that time: at the approaches to the Danube, on the shores of the Bosporus, the Strait of Otranto (at Dyrrhachium [Durres]), at Ravenna, whose towers are portrayed on mosaics, in Messina and in Reggio di Calabria to accompany the natural signals of the volcanoes, then five beacons very close together between Naples and Ostia. The chain continued along the Ligurian coast to Albenga, then in Fréjus and Marseille (the Pharo), and in Port-Vendres. The lighthouse of Gades [Cádiz] signalled arrivals into the ocean and announced the ocean route; that of Corunna, which has been quite well conserved, was put back into service in the eighteenth century; after which there remain ruins at the end of the route, in Dover, and in Boulogne those of the famous Tour d'Ordre, demolished in 1644.

The Middle Ages completed that heritage in the twelfth century, for example in Genoa, where the lighthouse, at the end of the breakwater, was entrusted to a Columbus, the uncle of Christopher, in the mid-fifteenth century; Meloria, to the east, also had one (1157), which was replaced by that of Leghorn around 1300.

The ocean coasts and those of the North, until then darkly sinister, finally lit a few beacons (*fouyers*) on dangerous sites, at the entrance to a few ports and on church steeples. These were bonfires of brushwood, dim lights difficult to see from afar: lanterns rather than lighthouses, taking the place at night of seamarks visible in daylight. This was so at the entrance to the Gironde, where Edward, the Black Prince, who administered English Aquitaine in the second half of the fourteenth century, in 1362 kept a fire burning on a tower sixteen metres high, built on the rock of Cordouan, to indicate to mariners the access to Bordeaux and its vineyards. The same service was provided by the towers of La Rochelle (1498) and by the bell-tower of the collegiate church of Guérande to the Hanseatic navigators who came to get salt from 'the Bay'. Upon their return north, they benefited, beyond Calais, from about ten lighthouses, notably those of Ostend, Blankenberghe and Walcheren; their route then passed in front of that of Falsterbo, which marked the Sound. And whoever wanted to reach Lübeck found a beacon signalling the entrance to the Trave, while from afar the town of Rostock was announced by a steeple 122 metres high. Around 1600 the German, Slavic and Scandinavian coasts were dotted as far as Riga with more than fifteen lighthouses.

European coastal equipment, which improved in the seventeenth century, benefited in the technical realm from the constant progress of 'pharology' up to the present time. A remarkable fact, despite the frequency of wars, was Franco-English emulation, sometimes cooperation, in signalling in the trouble spots of the Straits of Dover and the entrance to the English Channel.

If lighthouses could tell their stories Cordouan and Eddystone would be among the most talkative. Both of them have undergone at least four restorations, so necessary have they been. Cordouan was mentioned in portolan charts. The man responsible for its third restoration, at the end of the sixteenth century, Louis de Foix, one of the architects of the Spanish Escorial, turned it into a work of art, and it was classed as an historical monument at the same time as Notre-Dame in Paris in the nineteenth century; it now has to be protected less from the sea than from the vandalism of tourists. Eddystone, near Plymouth, caused a sensation around 1700 at the time it was first built (the current one, the fourth, dates from 1882). An interesting episode of international cooperation marked this event. A drawing was sent at that time from Plymouth by the commander of the Royal Navy to the Intendant of the French Navy in Brest, in order to avoid any confusion with the lighthouse recently constructed in Ouessant; as a precaution the latter had been painted white, and the *Gazette de France* announced in 1700 the construction of the Ouessant lighthouse 'to all nations whose vessels enter the Channel and leave it, so that those who come from afar do not mistake this tower for that of the Scilly Islands'. Ouessant was the continuation of a beacon-light which 'according to ancient treaties with England the kings of France would have been obliged to maintain in times of war as in times of peace'. Fortunate times! if one may say so, remembering that Cordouan was dark from September 1939 to July 1945.

Emulation reigned on both sides. In 1686 an inquiry was made on the orders of Louis XIV, who wanted 'to be informed of the way in which beacons were established in England', in order to do just as well. Vauban took care of it. Everywhere the impulse was provided by the demands of traffic and by technical possibilities. Thus England, in particular at the time of the Napoleonic wars, multiplied signalling on its eastern coast to take advantage of the proximity of the energy resources of its coalfields. For its part France, which had 24 lighthouses in 1800, had 360 in 1885, and 1088 lighthouses and beacons in 1987.

The development of energy sources and optics accompanied a general progress. In less than a century the move was made from coal to vegetable and mineral oils, to petroleum gas (1907), to fuel oil (1948), and to electricity. Optical equipment changed entirely with the adoption of the mirrors of Teuler and Borda, then with the lens of Fresnel (1882), and with a system progressing from fixed lights to intermittent flashes (1854), to occultations grouped with beams of different coloured light (white, green, red). The range of light projection is remarkable: the lighthouse of Creac'h in Ouessant has a reach of fifty-five kilometres, the duplication of which aims to ensure more security for the some 50,000 ships which each year take the 'RAIL', the major artery of European maritime traffic.

An international agreement, primarily European, was called for, so that the security of the very busy seas would not be lost. International codes regulate the colour of lights, their flashing and their frequency; any change is the object of reciprocal and concerted notifications. Moreover, going beyond the European framework, the International Association of Lighthouse Authorities holds regular meetings and publishes information, playing the role of one of the common institutions in which Europe is finding the foundations of its unification.

Outports

Mariners from the north and the south gradually became familiar with types of ports that they did not previously know. The topography of sites, the movement or absence of tides, produced conditions to which they were undoubtedly the most sensitive. The Mediterraneans were used to certain sites, whose differences from the usual harbour landscape of the Ponant were gradually affirmed.

Western Europe opened itself up more widely and more deeply, and also in a more protected way, through estuaries where maritime life was carried on to the point where the tide ceased, where the dialogue between the land and the water took over. The harbour landscape thus extended itself. The increase in the tonnage of ships and in their draught, combined with the intensity of silting in the estuaries, posed problems in their fitting-out. There was a risk of vulnerability for harbour installations on the coast, which was compensated for by a gain in time, diminishing or completely avoiding the delays of going up river. The development of outports became characteristic of the end of the Middle Ages and the modern age.

Certain ports dispensed with them, for various reasons. Lisbon had no need of one. On the contrary, Bordeaux, ensconced back on the Gironde, which could have built one in the Middle Ages, chose to do without one, concentrating on its own quays almost the whole of its essential, and seasonal, traffic, wine. Moreover, before industrial implantations, there was no obvious site to play that role. The same was true for a long time in Nantes, which was even closer to the sea. Bristol had no need of one, either, nor did London, which was both close to the sea and far enough away to be sheltered; moreover, the secondary ports of East Anglia, Sussex and Kent are so close that nature seems to have destined them to serve as outports for London; even Southampton played that role at the end of the Middle Ages.

On the other hand, the issue of outports was a matter of concern for Rouen, the ports of the Low Countries (in the broad sense) and those of the plain of Northern Europe. For Rouen the question was posed on two levels, by reason of the river navigation and of the length of the journey both up and downstream. Access to the estuary was difficult due to currents and alluvial shallows. The channel, sinuous and unstable, was subject to tidal waves. Even at the beginning of the modern era it took three tides to reach Rouen. If it had not been for the economic value of the hinterlands, the Paris region, it would have been of little interest (as in Nantes and Bordeaux) to create an outport. Those living in Rouen felt so strongly about it that they wanted the new port, Le Havre, to remain in their dependency. Le Havre resulted from the will of the king, Francis I, whose name it initially bore, 'Ville Françoise de Grace', but the economic, fluvial and political conditions of its establishment illustrated rather well the problem of outports.

The former Low Countries offered two opposite cases (see figure 5.2). That of Bruges was a battle against nature: two successive outports, between the twelfth and the fifteenth centuries, Damme and Sluys, were victims of an inexorable silting-up. In the eyes of the famous Nuremburg traveller, Jerome Munzer (Monetarius), who visited Bruges during his European travels in 1495, it had a charm that was already old-fashioned; but, according to the traveller, Damme remained a 'very beautiful city' and Sluys 'a magnificent port'. At that time Antwerp was beginning its rise in importance. The Scheldt river was and remains a very beautiful waterway, but not all the navigators of the fifteenth and sixteenth centuries went up the eighty kilometres which would have taken them to Antwerp, but made do with the intermediary relay stations of its outports; through the islands of Zealand, the passages are numerous, and nature made its choice there. Man, too. Until the fifteenth century access was from the east, useful for whoever was coming from that direction, but a detour in relationship to Sluys; storms and a positive movement of the sea opened up the western branch of the Scheldt, the Honte, to navigation. Without ruining the old outport of the eastern Scheldt, Bergen-ap-zoom, whose fairs preserve its fame, moorings and new warehouses were developed in the middle of the fifteenth century on the Honte, on the island of Walcheren, in Arnemuiden, Veere, Flushing (Vlissingen), and especially in Middelburg, which was particularly well-placed to greet ships arriving from the west and to serve the same function for Antwerp as Le Havre did for Rouen; large ships did not risk going up river. Transactions were carried out in Antwerp which, as a business centre, was equipped with new specialized quays depending on the merchandise, and soon with three hoists, the old one in wood and the new ones made of stone, near the fortress of Steen, in the centre of the town and sheltered by a wall on the river's edge connecting towers posted upstream and downstream to watch over the river traffic.

Lübeck illustrates the problem of outports with particular originality. The town had been established in 1158–9 at the confluence of the Wakenitz and the Trave, 20 kilometres upstream from the mouth of the latter on the Baltic Sea. Until the end of the Middle Ages the depth of the Trave was sufficient for seafaring vessels. But Lübeck's location placed the little neighbouring ports on the isthmus of Holstein within its field of influence. In addition, the short distance between Lübeck and Hamburg, some 50 kilometres, made it a sort of outport on the North Sea, at least until the sixteenth century. Then Hamburg began to develop, tripled its population, doubled its tonnage, and, endowed with a stock exchange, replaced Lübeck at the head of the Hanseatic League – not without in turn being faced, due to its distance from the sea, with the problem of an outport.

The physiognomy of harbour towns

The layout of urban spaces was obviously different in the Mediterranean, Atlantic and Nordic ports. However, alongside notable contrasts in human arrangements and behaviours, analogies ensured that, even in passing through, seamen did not feel like strangers. Certain constants enable us to define a specific type of maritime town.

The port was either within or outside the city limits. It was often outside in the case of river ports whose ramparts bordered the edge of the water, for example in Rouen and Bordeaux, Antwerp and London, likewise in Palermo and Constantinople, whose wall goes along the Golden Horn. In other cases the enclosure encompassed the stretch of water where the ships were anchored; this was the case with La Rochelle, Marseille, Genoa and Ragusa. Anchored in open water or alongside a dock, the ship then had contact with an element which, present everywhere, solidified its presence in the port: the quay.

The poetry of the quay was real, however commonplace it may have been. The quay was synonymous with stopovers, thus with rest, or with the completion of a voyage, in a 'haven of refuge'. Gone were the anxieties of the open sea, the absence of news and the monotony of masculine company on board. Everywhere, in Bergen and Palermo, Gdańsk and Hamburg, Genoa, Antwerp, Lisbon or Seville, in Rouen, Nantes or Bordeaux, as in Marseille, the quay was a place of warehouses and stores, administrative buildings where formalities of ships' stays ('lay days') were carried out, as were fiscal declarations and legal inquiries. Near the ports were the jurisdictional seats of admiralties and specialized authorities, such as the military police, water bailiffs, consular jurisdictions, whose names, while they varied depending on the countries, corresponded to similar institutions.

There were many different sounds on the quay, such as the screeching of the pulleys of the hoists, and in certain ports, the cranes. But the quay also rang with other sounds: the loud voices of the stevedores, the curses of cart pushers, the clomping of horses' shoes. And odours were added to the sounds: the very strong smell of herring or the intoxicating odour of wine, the perfume of resin and of spices; but in addition to those were the stenches exhaled by the ships' holds and the cesspools of the barges. Even in the eighteenth century all the recesses of the quays were not elegant salons.

Travellers added their accounts to the engravings and the paintings representing ports. Certainly the Mediterranean brothels did not have the same ambiance as those of the North; but the personnel and the clientèle had similar appearances, if not identities. For example, there is an analogy between the small streets going up the Genoese *ripa* towards the top of the city, those of Marseille which once formed a maze from the port to the Major, the brothels of the Quai des Chartrons in Bordeaux and of the Fosse in Nantes, those of London's East End described by Dickens, and the bawdy houses of Antwerp, Amsterdam and Hamburg. And we must not forget that there was a Europe of sailors' bistros earlier than that of the shady bars of the twentieth century.

The quay was all of these things, but this did not exhaust the complete significance of harbour life. Little streets fanned out from

the quay; some, in Palermo and in Bruges, bore the names of the
'nations' whose members had their homes there; others, sometimes
the same ones, bore the names of the professions whose artisans
had opened a store there and worked within view of passers by,
even on the sidewalks, A living organism, the harbour town,
whether Mediterranean, oceanic or Nordic, evolved with the
rhythm of the evolution of maritime traffic; it developed, moved
its centre, retreated, following the movement of business. As for
the people, they showed a concern for social segregation in the
quality of their homes more than in their topographical localiza-
tion. The houses and mansions of the foreigners whose presence
we have noted in Bruges, Antwerp, Venice, Lisbon and London,
stood next door to those of local descent, allied to rich immigrant
families; the merchant aristocracy willingly grouped themselves in
certain parishes or certain smart neighbourhoods: the banks of the
Grand Canal in Venice, the Via San Luca in Genoa, St-Michel in
Bordeaux, St-Nicolas in Nantes, St-Etienne des Tonneliers and
St-Jean in Rouen, the Strand in London . . . In the neighbourhoods
around these well-to-do homes the European port placed public
buildings where business was transacted: the Merchants' Lodges
on the edge of the Mediterranean (Genoa, Montpellier, Barcelona,
Valencia), the Bourse or Stock Exchange in Bruges, Antwerp,
Amsterdam, London and Hamburg.

On the other hand, the humble population of sailors were
grouped in the sometimes squalid neighbourhoods around the
port, for example in Genoa, Lisbon and London. In the most
ancient towns, the original castle looked out over everything or
stood in the centre of the town: in Lisbon, the Castelo overlooked
Alfama; in London, the Tower controlled the course of the
Thames as the Vieux Château near the Seine did in Rouen, the
Steen on the Scheldt did in Antwerp, and the medieval castles did
in Brest and Boulogne.

Thus, at the end of the Middle Ages the harbour town was an
organism, a model, on which the modern port was modelled
without disturbing the layout of the whole.

Arsenals

There is one component of the harbour town which the centuries,
especially modern ones, have seen as part of its historical core,

both in the North and in the South: the arsenal, or naval dockyard. Comparative studies carried out in the course of the last few years enable us to determine the common characteristics of this phenomenon in the European arena.

We must first make the distinction between shipyard and arsenal. The first was a specialized workshop, arising mostly out of private initiative, and whose activity was limited to a sector of naval construction. The smallest port, the most isolated coast, could have a shipyard. The arsenal, on the other hand, was an institution established by an authority so that it could have a fleet; this function involved specific equipment, specialized personnel, and the carrying out of complementary tasks: stocking of materials, construction, fitting out, maintenance. For these reasons, the origin of arsenals is linked to the moment when, for technical, economic and political motives, improvisation no longer paid off, because what was simultaneously needed was a large volume of capital and a continuity of competence, at the best prices. The development of arsenals coincided with the growth of states.

The Arabic etymology of the word 'arsenal' (*darsenaa*) carries with it the Mediterranean heritage of the institution, not received from the caliphate, but from Rome and Athens through Byzantium. The mention of that city and the evocation of Themistocles are sufficient to remind us that Europe, in its beginnings, triumphed over Persian imperialism to secure its freedom, thanks to ships built in Greek shipyards. Are we forcing comparisons too much in drawing a parallel between Hellenic maritime genius (in the strict sense) during the Medean wars and that of the western Mediterranean, led by Venice, in the era of Lepanto?

Until the end of the seventeenth century, the model of the arsenal, according to José Merino, remained Mediterranean, before ceding primacy to the Atlantic ports. It then changed its appearance, all the while remaining a homogeneous unity in the harbour ensemble. The specificity of its tasks determined the specialization of its administrative personnel, that of administration and execution, from engineers to chief shipwrights; in human terms, the arsenal was a world apart, both technically and administratively – topographically and architecturally, too. In relation to the harbour town, the arsenal could be outside or integrated into it. The space it needed could justify placing it in close proximity to Venice, Messina, Barcelona, Seville and Lisbon. On those models, at the end of the thirteenth century, the first French royal arsenal

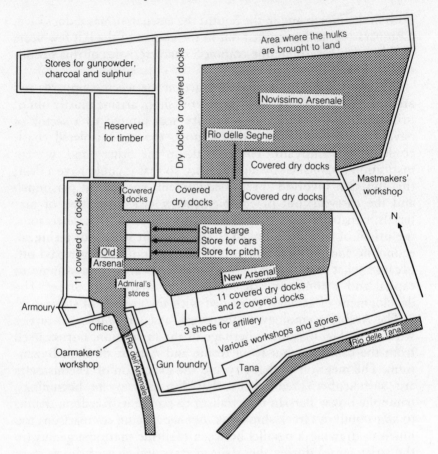

Figure 9.1   The Arsenal at Venice

was established on the empty grounds of the left bank of the Seine opposite Rouen, thus outside its walls, and was called the Royal Arsenal; it remained there until the sixteenth century, the moment when Francis I founded Le Havre with an arsenal for the construction of his own ships.

Modern arsenals were often created out of nothing, sometimes on new land, sometimes in immediate proximity to an already ancient town. This was, for example, the case at Pisa, which, in the fifteenth century, saw the Medici's *tersana* and its nine oared galleys fitted out on land bought from the extra-urban monastery of San Vito. In the north, all the Hanseatic arsenals were set up outside the town walls, either on a river island, as at Cologne, or on a peninsula, as at Hamburg and Bremen. Iconography confirms documentation of this. In Genoa a famous painting by Cristoforo Grasso, as well as later maps, show the shipyards right next to the town wall, but outside it.

The great era of European arsenals, starting at the end of the seventeenth century, also placed them on the immediate periphery of the large harbour cities. That of Marseille, described in 1670, was constructed to the east of the Vieux Port on the grounds of the Formigier square, opposite the medieval city and at a distance from the residential neighbourhoods in the east. In Lorient it was the city which the Compagnie des Indes built next to its shipyards. Rochefort developed around its arsenal; Brest grouped its workshops at the foot of the castle and next to the city, on a ria site where, as in Ferrol, a narrow bottleneck could, depending on the situation, be either a protection or a trap.

The geographical distribution and the arrangement of arsenals corresponded to the growing intervention of the state. Their role lost its local character in favour of a purpose in the service of wide-reaching politics. This is verified in Brest, Toulon, and again in Marseille, in Cartagena as in Ferrol, and in Cádiz, which took the place of Seville. It was true in England; to Southampton, installed at the end of the Middle Ages, were added Chatham in the middle of the sixteenth century and Devonport in 1689. In the northern countries the shipyards of Antwerp, Amsterdam, Copenhagen, Karlskrona, Stockholm and Kronstadt completed the map of the great arsenals of eighteenth-century Europe.

State intervention accentuated the specific nature of the harbour town: it took on the very noticeable technical characteristics of an industrial complex in the seventeenth and eighteenth centuries. The arsenal, a factory for constructing ships, stocked its own primary materials, made what it needed and assigned special buildings to each stage of production: basins for the treatment of wood, forges, hoists, mast-making machines, careening basins in Rochefort and Portsmouth at the end of the seventeenth century. Finally, special mention should be made of the majestic rope-making buildings: that of Chatham, surviving those of Woolwich, Portsmouth and Devonport, functioned until 1984. That of Rochefort, restored after the Second World War, remains the pride of that city; its monumental appearance gives proof of the importance of an arsenal in a maritime city.

Images in the mind: the challenges of the sea

The images familiar and common to mariners were not only material and visual. Others were of a mental order, some based on experienced facts and convictions, others on imaginary data and myths. Their relationship with the maritime world confers upon them the value of messages, bearers of the challenges of the sea. Braving time and space, the sea opposes its perenniality and its immensity to the ephemeral generations of humans fixed on a defined land. The sea defies continental constancy by the irregularity of its whims. It defies the agitation of men by the demands of its silences, insisting that one abandon oneself to it, for it is the mistress of the absolute.

Europe shares the threat of those challenges with other marine regions of the world; but it has its own way of facing them. We have seen it at work as much in the North as in the South, but it is not without interest to make a choice from among the observed reactions. A sort of gradation thus leads from attitudes of fear in face of the marine element to dreams of happiness, to a search for the infinite, and finally to the conviction of a vocation suggested by the immensity of the sea.

Fears, phantasms and beliefs

The ambiguity of the sea, both a source of life and a realm of death, has made it equally a maleficent and a benevolent power. It had to be tamed, and when it showed itself to be mean, mariners were forced, according to their own expression, to 'work along with it'. This explains, from the 36th parallel to the Arctic Circle, a collection of fantasies, legends and practices which Christianity attempted to exorcise. Anthropology, ethnography, sociology and the history of religions have stood shoulder to shoulder in an attempt to explain them. The Greco-Latin cultural foundation has not limited its predominance to the Mediterranean world, for we have noted its confrontation with Celtic, Scandinavian, Slavic and

Germanic mythology. The Greek and Roman divinities of the sea have encountered the competition of those of the pagan peoples of the North; the identity of their functions has often given rise to the commutability of their names, so much so that scholarly literature has, depending on the country, used them all. Legends have followed the same evolution, by attributing to the forces of marine nature a personality whose maleficence has everywhere been affirmed. Meteorological phenomena, storms and tidal waves, fog and flat calms, with their after-effects of bad fishing, the destruction of saltworks, shipwrecks, attacks by monstrous animals, made up a fearsome universe; fighting against these misfortunes, Mediterranean and Nordic magic had multiplied the charms which Christianity gathered in the pagan heritage. The hermits and the missionaries spread out over the coasts of Ireland, Britain, Gaul and Germania in the high Middle Ages did not succeed, despite alternatively patient and violent efforts, in eradicating or at least baptizing ancestral practices. Some have left traces up to the present time, in the form of traditional taboos (on the presence of a pregnant woman on board, the loading and consumption of rabbit meat), of divinatory gestures (the interpretation of the movements of the sea and of the direction of winds on certain days of the year, premonitions in dreams), propitiatory gestures (hiding coins in the step of the main mast), precautions made before setting off to sea (resorting to an astrologer, the embarkation of a magician armed with a knife to cut the hurricane accompanied by magical formulae). What is important in these actions is their intimate motive, perceived or not, conscious or unconscious. Their universality, noted throughout the centuries, in the Adriatic, in the Baltic, in the English Channel and on the banks of Newfoundland, was the result of the general conviction that the sea, however fertile it may be, was the favourite dwelling-place of the powers of Evil – that is, for Christian Europe, of Satan.

Ancient maritime societies were very attentive to benevolent or maleficent signs. Just about everywhere the former have engendered popular devotions which have been accepted or tolerated by the ecclesiastical authorities. Those authorities, however, were not able to prevent legends from misting over the original facts, nor superstitious practices from overcoming and deforming authentic devotions. Not without ill-will, the Church recalled the true significance of malpractices. Pilgrimages were organized to the

places where tradition fixed the beaching of empty boats transporting perhaps the body, or perhaps the statue, of a saint: Saint James
at Compostella, Our Lady in Boulogne, to cite only two famous
cases. On the contrary, the demon and his henchmen expressed
themselves in the presence of the sacred, for example, in the
violence of the wind. One night, during the monastic services, the
door of the abbey church of the Dunes was blown open by the
tempest: 'the Devil', concluded the narrator, 'was there, in person.'
A common belief was that the cry of the seagulls in their
never-ending flight expressed the wailing of the souls of the dead
who inhabited them, especially those lost at sea, who had been
deprived of a tomb.

Death at sea was an obsession. To die on board from an accident,
or from an illness, scurvy or typhus, was to die without ever seeing
again one's family, one's house or one's village: the body was
thrown into the water in a sewn sack weighed down with a stone
or a metal bar; it became the prey of marine fauna; of course, the
cadaver had a right to the farewells of its companions and to their
collective prayers. Dying in combat did not include even such
ceremony as this. The families of mariners experienced the an-
guished waiting for news until the moment when, with the passing
of time, the inevitable certainty became clear.

Certainly life reclaimed its dues. For example, one April day in
1516 the bells of the church of Penmarc'h in Brittany rang in
collective celebration of the remarriage of the young widows of
those shipwrecked on the *Pierre*, lost at sea the preceding January.
However, the depths of emotions remained alive, for it was
thought that the souls of the dead without graves were doomed to
wander, expressing their woes in the whistling of the wind and the
cries of the birds. The greatest fear was that at the end of time the
bodies of the shipwrecked would not be found for the general
resurrection.

Not being able to gather together at the grave of their departed,
the families of seamen and their fraternities multiplied prayers for
the repose of their souls, in spontaneous forms such as the *proëlla*
of Ouessant, or more authentically canonical such as the celebration of masses. Maritime milieux were predisposed to accept
devotion honouring the souls in purgatory, the development of
which, beginning in the twelfth century, has been established by
Jacques Le Goff. The localizaion of this final resting place of

spiritual justification, accepted from Ireland as far as Calabria, found its way onto the maritime routes from traditions going back to St Patrick. Was it not a source of consolation for families anxious about the salvation of their drowned men?

Did the official rejection of the belief in purgatory in the countries which became Protestant, beginning in the sixteenth century, completely rid popular consciousness of a belief in the spiritual presence of disappeared souls? Is not the placement of plaques in their memory, analogous to the 'walls of those lost at sea' in Breton parishes, in the Nordic countries but a commemorative tradition, deprived of an invitation to prayer, at least personal, for the dead? The use of such reminders characterizes those countries where Germanic and Anglo-Saxon mythology seems rooted, where 'legends of marine ghosts, phantom vessels and other flying Dutchmen awaken so many tales of the forecastle'. Alain Cabantous, in those words, poses a problem which has not yet been resolved. But it seems possible to accept that on such an important point the mental picture of seamen in Western Europe preserves, to the present time, an essential coherence.

Dreams of happiness: the island myth

The psychological contrasts of marine environments place morbid tendencies side by side with the search for compensations through paths of hope – a natural aspect of societies, such as that of seamen, where waiting is commonplace. But to hope is always a little to dream, and the form this usually takes is anticipation of a better life and a better way of living. Among maritime societies mirages, or better, myths of the islands of happiness were constant and significant.

This dream was found, in the earliest days of Europe's history, in the classical legacy and in Celtic legends. The nature of the myth has varied not only because the dreamed-of islands were not to be found, but above all because, since encountered realities did not correspond to hopes, it was necessary endlessly to search for happiness elsewhere. The legendary story of the whale that revealed itself at the moment when St Brendan was celebrating mass on its back is symbolic. Hoped-for happiness, an illusion of discovery, lost happiness, a new search: the cycle is representative of the human adventure.

The quest for happiness comes from the yearning for that primordial terrestrial paradise which was placed by medieval cartographers somewhere in the northern hemisphere, on an island or in an isolated location, circumscribed by a barrier or by mountains on the continent. The island ideal takes on all imaginable forms, depending on tastes, temperaments and the age. The distance at sea and the absence of troublesome neighbours were conditions as valid for hermits of the High Middle Ages as for lovers of Celtic romances, in the Iles de Lérins or in the Breton, Anglo-Norman, Irish or Scottish islands.

Idealized, those islands could be either the purgatory of asceticism (one thinks of those in the North), or the paradise of all enjoyments (Antilia, the Islands of the Blest), a realm of boundless love, of wealth because the Sun was believed to create gold, of an ease of existence without pain or work, for nature would provide everything necessary to live. If the islands were inhabited, their rare occupants were happy, naturally good, disposed to share. Let us add that those islands were steps towards the vast regions of wealth and happiness: for Christopher Columbus, the Antilles were stops on the route to enchanted Cathay. Marvels (*mirabilia*) as exceptional as they were admirable fed the Atlantic dreams as well as those of the Indian Ocean.

The persistence of the island myth had many manifestations. Their favourable nature was the most frequent. It incited Scandinavian migrations, the search for the banks of Newfoundland, launched the Prince of Castile on the conquest of the Islands of the Blest in the fourteenth century, led Jean de Béthencourt and Gadifer de La Salle to the Canaries at the beginning of the fifteenth century, took the Genoese, the Portuguese and the Castilians to Madeira and the Azores. On an even more oneiric level, the image of the 'noble savage' ran right through from the *Roman de la Rose* to *Paul et Virginie* and to Bougainville; it inspired More's *Utopia*, guided tourists by Tendre's map; it took shape in *Robinson Crusoe*; and the adolescents of the nineteenth and twentieth centuries found in Jules Verne a pilot to guide them to the *Mysterious Island*.

The island myth seemed to favour distant archipelagos. The French missionaries of the twelfth and thirteenth centuries saw the

Atlantic islands close to the continent with the eyes of faith. Like the Franciscan preachers of the fifteenth century who renewed eremitism there, Michel Le Nobletz, Julien Maunoir and Louis Grignion de Montfort saw the islands 'as a reflection of terrestrial paradise without the apple tree or the tempting snake'; this idyllic portrait was perhaps their work, if one takes into account the influence of laypeople such as François Le Su, the fisherman of Sein, and in Ouessant Françoise Troadec, whose cartographic knowledge, inherited from her ancestor Brouscon, from Conquet, enabled her to imagine maps (the *toalonnou*) describing, with supporting technical details, navigation towards Heaven on difficult seas: an apostolic reflection of the *Carte du Tendre*.

The dream did not always have the rosy hues of happiness, even in the Age of Reason. Some doubted; others were disappointed, especially by the islands close to Europe; islands too large for isolation, too well-known to incline one to dream. An original example of this is the opinion of Frederick the Great. Reflecting on Machiavelli, he dismissed both the English and the Corsicans with a pitiless lucidity; in 1740, less than thirty years before the birth of Napoleon, he wrote:

> The Romans, who had conquered Great Britain but could not keep it at peace because of the turbulent and war-loving character of its peoples, attempted to weaken them, which succeeded ... As for the Corsicans, these are a handful of men as brave and resolute as the English; they will only be subdued, I believe, by caution and kindness.

The need for an absolute

The permanence of a religious element in maritime civilization, beyond European experiences of the Christian religion, from the sixteenth century in particular, begs an explanation, or at least an inquiry. The Atlantic islands were not the only beneficiaries of an effort on the part of the Catholic missionaries. The coastline of the Latin countries has given proof of an attachment to its beliefs; its resort to the intercession of St Anne, starting in Auray in the seventeenth century, spread over all of Western Europe and beyond the Atlantic Ocean, onto the banks of the St Lawrence

River. The post-Tridentine Church extended to seamen their efforts at deepening their understanding, which went beyond the simple maintenance of an acquired situation. The generation of St Vincent de Paul, 'the apostle of the galleys', in France and in Spain had the *Missio navalis*, the distant ancestor of the contemporary 'Mission of the Sea'; and the work already cited by the Jesuit Georges Fournier, *L'Hydrographie*, develops what, *mutatis mutandis*, would correspond to a pastoral of the sea. With the help of a routine, but also with that of chaplains embarked on the largest ships, daily prayer on board remained 'an indispensable element of common life'. The ideas of 'Reason' having penetrated the crews less than it did bureaucrats, the French Revolution itself neither profoundly nor lastingly upset beliefs and practices.

Protestant Europe had the same experience. In England and Scotland, for example, the rigour with which traditional devotions were hunted out might have disturbed some minds. But some mariners continued to make vows and to set out on pilgrimages, or, for example in Danzig, they asked their companions who had remained Catholic to do so in their name. The persistence of such practices has been noted throughout the seventeenth and eighteenth centuries. However, a few reformed pastors in the sixteenth century, perceiving the danger, composed prayer books in English for the use of mariners and stimulated the struggle against immorality and blasphemy. These efforts had varied success, and yet at the end of the eighteenth century a religious 'revival' resulting from a widespread distribution of the Bible was manifest in the British Navy, even during the mutiny of 1797.

There is a possible reason for the perenniality of a religious sense among seamen. It is a commonplace (but must the commonplace necessarily be wrong?) to attribute it to contact with the immensity of the sea. Like mountains and deserts, the sea invites reflection; because it is immense it can draw the spirit towards the infinite. Facing danger incites personal humility in the presence of superior forces. In conjunction with cohabitation with companions, that confrontation demanded, in the name of a necessary solidarity, going beyond oneself and the accomplishment of one's part in the common task. What imposed itself, with an awareness of one's own relativity, was the need for an absolute.

Appeals

The incitements of the sea were so many invitations. It offered at the same time near and distant routes: those which made up the network of coastal relationships in Europe, then those which wove a sort of spider's web on the oceans similar to the schema of the portolan charts and their compass cards. To set out one needed a lot of imagination, initiative, courage, and a brave spirit which, knowing one's own possibilities, would exploit them to the full and even go beyond them. The dialogue between mariners and the sea was made up of questions and answers.

At the beginning there was curiosity, a desire to know and a taste for risk. The history of risk deserves a study of its motives, its stakes and results. The imagination that animates the undertaking foresees the various aspects and the unfolding of it, creates its object and projects it in an image, first mental, then made concrete. Is that not one of the lessons of the Great Discoveries, a lesson which could be put to good use at the moment of their five hundredth anniversary celebrations, when a united Europe is seeking a way forward?

One might consider it impertinent to call Europe's response to the seductions of the sea a vocation. To repel them would have been an evasion, and similar offers have also been made by the sea to other peoples. Europe's fortune in its dialogue with the ocean is that it had long been prepared for it. Athenian thalassocracy was an inheritance; the Celtic and Viking adventures, an experience; the Venetian and Genoese successes, an instruction; the Portuguese initiatives, a bold act.

The nature of the solicitations to which seamen have been sensitive reveals the type of calling to which they have responded. In whatever direction one turned in Europe there were the same movements, generally at the same time. It is obvious but necessary to point out the economic motives of maritime expansion at the end of the Middle Ages; they were joined by political and colonial ambitions from the sixteenth century. Europe believed itself called upon to assume the maritime activity of the world, and almost all states believed their role was to participate in that calling: after Portugal and Spain, France and England, Denmark and the United Provinces, while waiting for a unified Germany and Italy. Russia took a different path to arrive at a similar result on the Eurasian continent. Thus the notion of colonialism remained tied to that of overseas travel until, just recently, the dismantling of the Soviet Union clearly showed the colonial character of its empire.

In addition, Europe began to believe that it was also to guide souls by way of the sea. The Christian Churches judged it their duty to propose, and sometimes to impose, the evangelical truths it upheld. Missionaries sailed in the wake of the sailors and the beginnings of propaganda even used that word in the seventeenth century to designate the Roman congregation responsible for converting peoples.

The diversity of these economic, political, intellectual, moral and religious vocations did not exhaust only the geographical dimension of Europe in its ensemble. It had and still preserves a social dimension in the most varied aspects. This is why the resonances of maritime life can be perceived in different sectors of European civilization, through with differences of tone.

10

A Cultural Dimension: Seeing, Feeling and Understanding the Sea

At the conclusion of this rapid stroll along the edge of the European sea, it seems appropriate to consult some witnesses who, in one capacity or another and from different points of view, have looked at the sea, sought or fled its company, listened to its voice, or spread its messages. Indeed, history has perceived, through time and space, how Europeans have seen, felt and understood the sea.

Literary voices

Literature has reflected the wealth of the maritime theme. This wealth, without having either the same volume or value from one age to another, contributed to a European identity. Ways of looking at the sea might be contrasting depending on whether they come from a Mediterranean or from a Nordic, but their nature is not essentially different, and the processes of description offer singular resemblances. Taking into account the diversity of languages, temperaments and circumstances, reference to the sea presents analogies and similarities in texts of different natures and from different eras. Some, of a conventional nature, are peopled by *topoi*; others, coming later, it seems, seek to express a realist vision of marine phenomena. In both cases, that vision either may have a pessimistic and unfavourable hue, or an optimistic and favourable one. Those aspects are frequently blended. In Europe there was dual inspiration, and the two aspects have been transmitted from generation to generation while overlapping each other. Its Mediterranean face, luminous, alternating fantasy and melancholy, contrasts with its oceanic aspect, shaded with softer hues, subject to the caprices of the tide and to terrifying fits of anger. In both, doubt and fear alternate with reassuring calms. These instabilities of the marine humour are perceptible in the Greco-Latin heritage and in the 'barbarian' tradition of the North. Homer, Thucydides and Virgil rub shoulders with the Celtic, Scandinavian and Slavic sagas, to the point, as we have seen, of being the object of mutual contamination and of suffering the partial superimposition of their gods and legends.

Christianity, taking the place of pagan cults, engaged in a merciless struggle against such mythology. Maritime references in medieval literature have preserved the mark of that conflict, in the most varied realms: hagiography and chivalrous romances and courtly poetry, liturgical texts and sermons, theological and moral treatises, 'mirrors' of the world and correspondence. Medieval society, like ancient society, had an ambiguous attitude towards the sea, considering it simultaneously as an empire of evil and misfortune, and also a source of good fortune and wealth. Christianized, the Middle Ages saw the sea disputed by Satan and God. Fear and hope coexisted. Texts express this sense that the sea was beyond common law. It is sometimes difficult to discern the clichés and the redundancies of style without relating them to facts. In order to reassure the faithful troubled by heresies and the Schism, around 1400, the evangelical tale of the tempest calmed by Christ served as a model for the *exempla* on the vicissitudes of the ship of the Church and its pilot, the sovereign pontiff. Caution is needed in the interpretation of the theme of the sea. The search for stylistic effect and for impressionistic images blends with reflections of an authentic reality. The narrators of voyages, such as pilgrimages to the Orient, were miserly with precise details of their navigations, which they judged commonplace, but they lingered on the fabulous episodes and the phantasmagorical evocations with which they mingled classical references attesting to the level of their biblical or secular learning: mermaids encountered Noah and Jonah. The nautical observations of chroniclers such as Joinville hold our attention.

Some authors had seafaring experience. We may recall the precision of the notations of Adam of Bremen on the Nordic seas and the naval competence of the Norman poet Wace. At the end of the twelfth century, in June 1178, Peter of Blois described a terrible crossing from England to France: the helmsman had to heave to, the only manoeuvre that would enable them to wait for the calm of the next morning: then, he concluded, 'it was as if I was being resuscitated from the dead.' In the fourteenth century, in Florence, the writings of Boccaccio placed fictional episodes in the arena, which he knew, of Mediterranean activity between the Balearics and Egypt, from Naples to Trapani in Sicily; he describes the customs operations in Palermo and the traffic in the markets of Barletta. Piracy provided him with fictional episodes: a poor captive Christian woman in the service of a Saracen woman learned Arabic with her while working with silk, palm fibres and leather; another woman, thrown onto the Island of Pongo by a tempest in which her husband had perished, lived there for several months as a 'true savage' until a Genoese ship rescued her by chance. Tempests are presented as divine punishments. For his part, Petrarch knew enough about the customs of sailors to compare the inhumation of plague victims in 1348 to the stowing of cargo: 'Just as in the bowels of a ship they pile up merchandise, they covered up the cadavers with a shovelful of dirt, until they reached the top of the grave.' In France, Eustache Deschamps had experience with the sea only from his crossings of the English Channel, but he did not burden himself with clichés in describing the disadvantages of it: 'To hear the sound of the great sea' prevented him from sleeping, he said (*Ballade 84*),

> In a full-blown tempest
> You must descend below,
> Stretch out with your mouth gaping wide,
> Because of the foul stench of vomit.

Another example comes from a Castilian, D. Pedro Niño; in his *Victorial*, he tells of his sailing from the Iberian coasts as far as Flanders, at the beginning of the fifteenth century. It took courage to venture into the strong current of Sein at night: 'The waves', he noted, 'were so high they hid the moon.' On the Aberwrac'h, in the cove of the Fairies, the will-o'-the-wisps of the neighbouring marshes seemed to be maleficent genies.

Literature showed even less proof of concern for realism in representing maritime episodes on the stage. If directors made an attempt at verisimilitude, the public trembled with pleasure at representations of shipwrecks.

One might believe that in the age of the great maritime discourses realism would have ultimately won out over literary conventionalism. But the two currents persisted and were blended. Erasmus was frankly pessimistic; his description of the *Shipwreck*, which, under the pseudonym of Adolf, he presented to Anthony, evoked in the latter this disparaging exclamation: 'What a horrible tale! Is that sailing? God save me from ever forming such a plan!' Speaking up in turn, with the tone of a man in the know, Rabelais introduced humour into his evocation of a tempest; Panurge and Brother Jean des Entommeures refer simultaneously to demons and saints to conjure out 'the rotten plague of all the millions of devils who are holding a meeting for the election of their new rector'. 'What madness', Erasmus again said, 'to give oneself to the sea!'

Were ocean explorers madmen? Even worse, the crews which some captains, Magellan among others, recruited included former convicts. In the middle of the fifteenth century the hagiographer of Henry the Navigator, Gomes Eanes de Zurara, scorned the *genta baixa* who embarked on the boats of discovery, whom Louis Vivès, in the following century also put down with the untranslatable condemnation, *faex maris*. In the literature of the Age of Discoveries, seamen often shared the detestable reputation of the sea itself, though they sometimes enjoyed praise comparable to that of the heroes of ancient navigations. After Zurara, the representatives of the king of Portugal at the Roman court at the end of the fifteenth century presented the exploits of their countrymen in epic terms. João de Barros and Camões followed in their footsteps. The literature inspired by the discoveries of Christopher Columbus, Magellan and Verrazano in Spain, Italy and France had echoes that are too well known for us to repeat them here. These echoes reached all the social strata, for example in Normandy, where maritime subjects were, in the age of Jean Ango, the theme of annual literary competitions, the laurels of which the greatest poets, such as Clément Marot, did not scorn. What is more, certain navigators were themselves humanists, such as Jean Parmentier from Dieppe, who was both a Latinist, a Hellenist and a confirmed mariner.

Thus, despite the detestable reputation of the sailor population and the fear inspired by the marine element, the sea was accepted in European literatures. In the time of humanism, everything, however, was blended: the evocation of the pelagic divinities of Antiquity with the invocation of the Virgin Mary, Stella Maris, the popular myths and the *Légende dorée*, nautical science with routine empiricism. Neptune would not have recognized his own fish.

Two genres developed. One, literary, made sacrifices to symbolic imagery; the other was progressively scientific. The two currents have continued in evolving forms and Europeans have recognized themselves in both. Although we need not describe these currents at length, let us note here a few of their stages and some accounts of them.

The description of lands was an ancient and lively genre. The Castilian author of the *Libro del conoscimiento* and the book by his fourteenth-century contemporary, Sir John Mandeville, continued to be read and translated into all the European languages. Their enumerative and descriptive 'geography' included, with a few cautious reservations, many traditional fables. André Thevet has also been accused of this; his work, from the sixteenth century, contains remarkable mixtures in which imagination is clearly present. These works existed side by side with serious accounts, including the travel journals of Munzer covering the entire West, of Claude de Bronseval on the Iberian peninsula, of Sigismund of Herberstein in Russia and of Montaigne in Italy, all contributing to European knowledge of their time, testimonies whose personalities contrasted strongly with the conventional characters of their predecessors.

Although the subjects of many travel writings in the sixteenth and seventeenth centuries were not European, their maritime character conveyed the attention their authors paid to things of the sea and they do not leave us indifferent. The distances writers travelled beyond the ocean horizons of Europe are full of significance. Of his travels to Brazil, Jean de Léry had observed that 'those who have not been at sea . . . have seen only half the world.' This remark remained valid for the following centuries, and the present author begs indulgence for saying that he only felt truly European and that he understood Europe thanks to a visit to Brazil in 1962.

A distinction between the concrete, sometimes scientific reference to the sea and its literary evocation is discernible from the seventeenth century, particularly in France, England, Spain and Italy. The literary evocation is impregnated with classicism; the Mediterranean holds a much larger place in it than does the Atlantic. In the narrative and dramatic genres, as in poetry, the number and importance of maritime adventures corresponded to a taste for fiction, for sensation and for spectacle. A thesis by Mme Bournaz-Baccar has analysed this closely. Authors, even Corneille, despite the maritime relationships of his city, Rouen, rarely had direct knowledge of the sea. A curiosity about the marine world and its distant horizons and the ambivalence of the sea took its place most of the time. Nevertheless, through its evocative strength, nautical vocabulary has often passed into the regular language of writers. Some show proof of sensitivity towards the sea: 'One dreams quite sweetly when one rides upon the sea', wrote the Grande Mademoiselle, cousin to Louis XIV, to Mme de Motteville.

However, the sea was rarely described in its own right, given the caution it inspired. In the novels and plays inspired by the sea the dramatic concept of it favoured tragic adventures in a procession of metaphors and hyperbole. The theme of a flight enabling one to change one's identity and to make a new life, like that of being kidnapped by pirates and ending up as a slave, was inspired by ancient legends and by true stories of the Barbary pirates; sea monsters vied with the fury of waves and the wind, and also with human cruelty.

It took the exceptional talent of Shakespeare in *The Tempest* to escape from this mythological conventionality, and in the dialogue between Prospero and Ariel, to express the reality of a shipwreck: 'All but the mariners', says Ariel, 'Plunged in the foaming brine'; and he sings: 'Full fathom five thy father lies; Of his bones are coral made.' The author gives to the king's son Ferdinand this cry, imitated perhaps from the *Quart Livre* of Rabelais: ' "Hell is empty, And all the devils are here!" '(*The Tempest* Act I, sc.ii).

Among other authors, such as Corneille, the presentation remained bookish, as in the staging of *Andromède* or with Rotrou in *Iphigénie en Aulide*. The marine reference would be more direct in Madeleine de Scudéry's novel *Artamène ou le Grand Cyrus* if one accepts the relationship between her picturesque description of the burning of some twenty galleys and the painting of the *Troyennes incendiant des navires* by Claude Lorrain, painted six years before the novel was written. Among some other authors, setting aside literary merit, sensitivity to the sea appears, for example in the descriptions of the Straits of Gibraltar and of Belle-Île by the Norman author St-Amant, despite criticism by Boileau. Finally, we are grateful to Tristan for having entitled one poem simply *La Mer*.

The beginning of the eighteenth century initiated throughout Europe a wave of tales of marine adventure. After 1699 *Télémaque*, written by Fénelon for the instruction of the duke of Burgundy, grandson of Louis XIV, sold well, but what at least three or four generations found in it was an ancient Mediterranean where Neptune, Amphitrite and the Nereids would let their imagination wander from Tyre to Carthage and from Corinth to Syracuse. England, growing out of those schoolboy dreams, proposed others based on reality. In 1719 Daniel Defoe wrote his novel on the misadventures of the Scotsman Alexander Selkirk, *alias* Robinson Crusoe, and seven years later a similar success greeted Jonathan Swift's *Gulliver's Travels*; both were translated or imitated abroad for decades, as for instance by Nicolas Chamfort's *Jeune Indienne* of 1764. The French had to wait until the eve of the Revolution (1788) to be moved by the shipwreck, highly realistic in presentation, of the *St-Geran* in Bernardin de Saint-Pierre's novel *Paul et Virginie*. To enable himself to write from first-hand knowledge Bernardin de Saint-Pierre had visited Port-Louis, the headquarters of the Compagnie des Indes. This brings to mind the enormous European success of the travel accounts of Cook and Bougainville. Even if European seas were not involved, Europeans' interest in the sea wherever it may have been appears as a sign of those times.

This concern was henceforth affirmed in several literary genres: the pedagogic work (in so far as it was one), the travel account, the novel, poetry and sometimes plays. These were various means of grasping the influences under which the sea and sailors entered the stage in the first half of the nineteenth century, and of understanding how the maritime world was perceived and what was the evolution of that perception.

Books written for young readers are naturally the reflection of the mental images of adults. *Télémaque*'s successors have become commonplace, but in the French case the presentation of the sea was done with an attempt at pedagogical realism of the 'lessons of things' of the past, for which television has now been substituted. During a century of successive reprintings (1877–1976), *Le Tour de France par deux enfants* led its young readers from Marseille to Dunkirk. Then two other twentieth-century children, born after the Second World War, continued the journey from Le Havre as far as Bayonne (1977). In the interval, *Le voyage d'Edgar*, begun in Marseille, took its passengers to the Baltic and from there to Greenland; it was written in 1938, but its European opening deserves mention, justified by the humour of a chapter entitled 'Of a Few Characters who Haunt Gibraltar'. The reader is introduced into a salon where a conversation is taking place between a little princess, 'Mediterranean', a young woman with a supple body and black skin, 'Madame Africa', a large, powerful man given to sudden and violent anger who is called 'Atlantic', and 'Madame Europe', an old, well-preserved lady, with a very high collar, very conservative: a ribbon hides her wrinkled neck; she is wearing a hat from the time of Queen Victoria and watches Madame Africa through a lorgnette.

The development of a maritime literature in Europe was a herald of Romanticism, as has been shown in a study by Monique Brosse. Its precursor was Bernardin de Saint-Pierre, to whom it owed the theme of the tempest, at once a spectacle, an epic confrontation with magical and baleful interventions, and a meteorological phenomenon. It lent itself to ceremony and to a sort of convention which did not exclude technical details. True mariners such as Byron and Fenimore Cooper were initiators of the maritime novel. Cooper is considered to be responsible for the popularization of the heroic figure of the 'old salt'. His *The Pilot* (1823) was probably inspired by Sir Walter Scott's *The Pirate*, written two years earlier (1821). In his generation, but also later on, it was still mariners who were sensitive to the drama and who admired heroes. Some of them willingly situated the tempest in the Nordic fogs evoked by the legend of Ossian, popular at the time, and in the Norwegian fjords, also quite popular, pandering to the sentimental softness of the 'dandies'. Emotion found pity elsewhere for the victims of pirates, much as it exalted the boldness of the corsairs, whom the twentieth century turned into idols or 'supermen'.

The success of maritime literature is attributable to its relationship to the romantic leaning towards the cult of heroes and to 'dolorism' – the doctrine of the usefulness, the (moral) worth of pain – but above all to the professional quality of the authors. If Chateaubriand had not hailed from St-Malo, he would not have been able to convey the soul of his city, nor express the emotion of his first encounter with Brest, nor recount his dramatic crossing of the Atlantic, nor describe the splendour of the victorious royal fleet returning from the American War. In his time, and after him, mariners have been able to evoke and describe their lives. Several were poets and painters, even though they did not all attain the level of Garneray, whom we will discuss below. Let us cite contemporaries on both sides of the English Channel: Frederick Marryat, an officer in the Royal Navy who received from Louis-Philippe the cross of the Légion d'Honneur 'for services rendered to science and navigation'; he remains well-known for his novel, *The Phantom Ship*. In that generation Edouard Corbière is considered the first maritime novelist worthy of that name, along with Augustin Jal, from Lyon, who, like Chateaubriand, was completely bowled over by his first sight of the port of Brest.

In France, at least, little can compare with the 'flamboyant expressionism' of Eugène Sue, a navy surgeon; present at the battle of Navarino, he evoked the *Salamandre* in combat, 'thundering, furious, dishevelled, biting an enemy frigate with its grappling irons'; he was also able to evoke the shipwreck of the *Méduse* and construct a fictional epic around the character of Jean Bart.

The generation that supported Greek independence applauded at the news of Navarino, and was enthusiastic about the English and French discoveries in the South Seas, the progress of which it followed in the London and Paris press (the 'Voyages' column of the *Globe*), was also moved by Charles Dickens's description of the fate of David Copperfield, by that of the widows of mariners from the Island of Norderney, by Heinrich Heine in the *Reisebilder*, and by the poverty of the Guérande salt marsh workers as described by Honoré de Balzac.

In the middle of the nineteenth century, around 1860, and since that time, maritime literature changed its tone to respond, through a didactic concern, to the demands of a public thirsting for knowledge. A more serious form of literature, it considered the sea in a frequently more objective way and described professions and technology. 'De-dramatized after romanticism, the sea became the object of a gloomy and monotonous practice', argues Monique Brosse. Are we sure she is absolutely right? How, then, can we explain the vigorous sensitivity of Hugo's *Travailleurs de la mer*, and the power of the evocation of Jules Michelet's *La Mer*? And how can we explain the extraordinary success of Jules Verne, whose works, translated into every language, combine a talent for suspense with psychological analysis and with the technical exactness of his time, indeed, even ahead of it – though this is too well-known to dwell upon here.

The turning point, if there was one, was not a change in course. Sensibility did not lose its rights in affirming itself more virile, at least among the greatest. The tempest still made its voice heard. After its evocation in the Great North by Edgar Poe, we see how in *Oceano Nox* Victor Hugo gives a solemn echo to the roaring of 'the stormy dwelling of God'. For his part Alphonse Daudet sublimated the passing of the *Sémillante* in *L'Agonie de la Sémillante*, opening one winter's night the 'tomb to which chance had brought' those drowned on the Lavezzi Islands. Talent could also sometimes take the place of experience at sea. Arthur Rimbaud had never seen the sea before composing *Le Bateau ivre*. Talent enables one to feel and express everything. Without it Stéphane Mallarmé would not have evoked in *Brise marine* the yearning to 'go where the birds are, to wander between the sea, between the waves'. Charles Baudelaire, in a single play on words in *Spleen*, evoked the flickering of the lighthouses, the harmonious oscillations of the swell and the movements of those who leave and those who return. But there were also those who did not return. Paul Valéry in *Le Cimetière marin* paid them tribute with a sensitivity which can only be suggested by the list of those lost at sea which is engraved on the wall in nearby Gruissan (Aude).

Although they are not all poets, seamen themselves even now bear witness about the sea which veracity renders even stronger. All of Europe from generation to generation works together in this. The North produced Hans Andersen with his *Tales*, Henrik Ibsen and Alexander Kielland, novelist of *Skipper Worse*. Tempests of the North Atlantic suggested *Captains Courageous* to Rudyard Kipling and *Pêcheurs d'Islande* to Pierre Loti. With Loti we have already sailed as far as the Bosporus. But there are other convergences, for example, in two humanist diplomats: Alexis Léger (St-John Perse) to some extent reflected his colleague and predecessor, Paul Claudel, in a cosmic vision of the world and of Europe. But the most complete, the most European, and in addition, a mariner, was perhaps Joseph Conrad, born in Poland, who took English nationality after having served for twenty years in the French and British merchant marines. Better than anyone, Conrad was able to evoke in *Typhoon* the authority of the west wind, 'that king of the West who reigns as master over the North Atlantic, from the Azores to Cape Farewell, and who reserves bad nights for ships that are *en route* to the English Channel'. But

Conrad also experienced the 'tender seduction' inspired by the Mediterranean, 'the cradle of maritime traffic and of the naval war', 'great chamber of an old dwelling where numerous generations have taken their first steps'; for, he adds, 'all sailors form only one family.' A single family! Conrad wrote that in 1906. Fifty years later, after two world wars, St-John Perse exclaimed, in *Seamarks* (*Amers*):

> '. . . O plenary Sea of alliance and of discord! . . . '
> 'She also who is questioned . . . by the great federators of pacific peoples . . . '
> 'Federal sea and sea of alliance!'
> (trans. Wallace Fowlie, in St-John Perse, *Collected Poems*, Princeton University Press, 1971, p. 553)

The ink on the Treaty of Rome, foundation of the European Community, was scarcely dry. Would the visionary-diplomat of the Quai d'Orsay be heard? Later!

Marine reflections in iconography and the minor arts

The arts were not far behind literature. Impressionism and a concern to record were expressed in Europe by graphic images and by musical evocations, as well as in poetry, tales, plays and pedagogical literature.

The motives behind iconographic representation of maritime scenes were varied. Some were aesthetic, others came out of curiosity and a search for the picturesque; many responded to a demand of the collective memory inspired by a concern for military or political glory. In this last genre, in the eleventh century Europe produced such imagery in tapestries, of which the Bayeux Tapestry is the perfect example. In the form of a comic strip, it recounts the conquest of England by William, duke of Normandy, in 1066; the work, as Lucien Musset has analysed it, represents with the support of legend the construction of boats, the embarkation, a combat at sea and the disembarkation; the sea is awkwardly portrayed by waves, but the ships and crews convey an attempt at exactitude.

Another area, that of manuscript illustration, covers the entire European Middle Ages. Its richness expresses readers' taste for the maritime tales which the miniatures accompanied. The precision of the drawings, despite evident lack of knowledge, quite frequently throws light on the technical evolution of the types and rigging of ships, the activity of seamen and the location of ports. The choice of images, the manner of portraying them, their peaceful or tragic character, reveal a certain way of viewing, or of conceiving, the marine world. Moreover, the fact that very often the miniaturists had not been familiar with the sea was compensated for on their part, and on that of their clientèle, by a certain interest in it. The work of Christiane Villain-Gandossi, based on a very rich corpus of miniatures gathered in the libraries of Europe and America, proves the importance of these works for a knowledge of the role played by the sea in medieval European culture.

Seals and blazons, other sources of equal interest, have the advantage of corresponding directly to an experienced and evolving reality in a defined social and institutional milieu. Numismatics and heraldry were not without ties to the sea, especially the former, for they symbolized the ambition and the destiny of harbour towns and of maritime states. Sometimes the blazons joined their original elements with symbols corresponding to their political allegiances and to their successive manifestations; in that way they were able to perpetuate the memory of past glories.

The seals of European harbour towns are interesting in that they reflect their history and contribute in clarifying the history of the ship. The outline of boats which, for example, form part of the seals of La Rochelle, Damme, Sandwich, Lübeck and Gdańsk, attests to certain practices of naval construction and enables us to follow its evolution from the twelfth to the seventeenth century; political and economic ambitions were asserted in legends and emblems.

Commemorating an event or a personage by fixing its image on a medal was a practice handed down from Antiquity for maritime subjects as well as for others. The classical renewal of the Renaissance, aided by the technical progress of stamping, stimulated its use. France, England, Spain, princes and cities of Italy and Germany vied with each other in this practice. Born out of an initiative of Louis XIV in 1663 the Académie des Inscriptions et Belles-Lettres was given the task of preparing legends for medals and checking the quality of the impression. The numerical importance of medals with a maritime subject is revealed in the work of

M.–J. Jacquiot; the choice of marine themes and personages thus promoted to the first rank of national consciousness shows well the attention paid to affairs of the sea. Thus medals commemorated the naval battle of Cartagena (1643), the fortification of Dunkirk (1671), the battles in the English Channel in 1690 and 1694; they also offered ambitious images of the globe illuminated by the royal sun, under the saying 'Nec pluribus impar'; the glorification in 1668 of the restoration of the navy included on the obverse the representation of a vessel accompanied by the legend *Navigatio instaurata*. There were also medals celebrating overseas expansion. These examples are representative of a common practice of political propaganda on the part of European states.

On a popular level, but very widespread, and without artistic pretensions, another form of representation present in the most diverse places – churches, towers or simple houses – was *graffiti*, engraved with rudimentary means, and representing boats, mariners and nautical scenes. The spontaneous sincerity of these fragile testimonies of maritime life arrests our attention. In France, Normandy (Dieppe, the lower Seine), La Rochelle and Beaucaire, on the Rhône, offer examples of this rudimentary aesthetic, where former mariners, prisoners of memory, thus clumsily freed themselves of their memories and yearnings.

Marine painting

The same commemorative intent explains the diffusion of painted marine votive offerings. Considered to be naive works by mediocre dabblers, they were discredited during the Age of Reason. In the *Encyclopedia* Diderot asserted their decadence, even in Italy, where, according to him, there were no longer anything but 'poor painters reduced, to survive, to producing them for miserable pilgrims'. What would he have said, this chronicler of the Salons, if he had seen the Paris Salon of 1831 accept the works of Jugelet from Dieppe? Disdain for an 'obscurantist' practice gave way before the indisputable merit of certain authentic artists: Bommalaer in Dunkirk, Grandin in Fécamp, Adam in Honfleur, Pajot in Sables-d'Olonne, and especially the Roux dynasty in Marseille. Several exhibitions mounted during the last thirty years in the latin countries of Europe have brought them out of the shadows and have even made them known (those from Livorno, for example) across the Atlantic. These works, due to their fragility, rarely go back beyond the seventeenth century, unless they are attributed with certainty to great artists such as Nicolas da Fabriano (*St Nicholas Saving a Ship in Distress*) or preserved in a famous monument (the *Virgin of Mariners*, in the Alcazar at Seville).

Without belonging to the votive genre, the suite of scenes from *The Legend of St Ursula* in Venice shows what an attentive observer was Carpaccio, of whom it has been said that he was a 'parenthesis' in the history of marine painting; thus the heaving over onto its side of a large boat with highly complex rigging is imposing in its technical veracity.

Indeed, as in all areas of pictorial art, two principal tendencies characterize marine painting. One aims at a representation of reality which is as exact as possible; the other internalizes observation. Each one of these orientations involves different nuances. The first often corresponds to a specialization. Whereas in general the great Renaissance painters saw the sea from afar, the Flemish and Dutch in the seventeenth and eighteenth centuries brought true marine painting to life. That genre erupted into European art 'with the impetuosity of a great spring tide'. Certain names are in everyone's memory: Van Dyck, Van de Velde, Vermeer, Ruijsdael, Backhuijsen, de Hooghe; but any list is incomplete. Regarding these prestigious schools, one critic has written that: 'a seascape painter knew boats like a constructor and a mariner, and, if he painted naval combats, he had naval experience of them.' Marine painting produced portraits of ports, fleets, shipowners and mariners from the United Provinces which were true historical documents.

Another current was a reflection of the classicism of literature and imprinted an academic character on the images of the sea. The sea, certainly luminous, appeared in majesty in a frame of 'manufactures', that is, of porticoes and columns; but it took a lot of imagination to regard as ancient the vessels, equipped with portholes, from which the artist had Ulysses or Aeneas disembark in the company of Nereids. It was a mixture of genres, and the sea seen thus had only an indirect relationship to life. Claude Lorrain might have illustrated the pages of *Télémaque* and the same critic, himself 'a painter of the Navy', might find it difficult to consider Lorrain as a painter of the sea.

The eighteenth century cultivated the exactitude of the seascape. Venice had the distinction of producing the *veduta* [view], whose name conveys the wish for a visual image, in which Canaletto, Guardi and Zuccareli excelled. The genre was very successful in France. Claude-Joseph Vernet, trained in the Venetian style, introduced his countrymen to their seas and ports. In his series of fifteen ports in France, he conscientiously followed the suggestions dictated in the name of Louis XV himself by Marigny, the General Director of Ships. His attention to detail enables one to follow, for example, the construction of a vessel in Rochefort and the bustle of men on the quays of Toulon. This type of painting was immensely successful and helped to interest the French in their navy. The catalogues of the Salons – annual art exhibitions held in Paris – notably of 1763, testify to this, as does the diffusion of engravings by Ozanne.

Academicism did not prevent Vernet from being attentive to the natural forces of the marine universe, in contrast to the peace offered by harbours. He also came under the influence of a contemporary of Lorrain, Salvator Rosa, a Neapolitan, famous for his theatrical representations of tempests and shipwrecks. The French thus became accustomed to a wider view of marine horizons.

Vernet had close relationships in England, where the realist vision of the sea was to reach its heights. The sea began to be the spectacle to which romanticism was to give full emphasis. Two names dominate the end of the eighteenth century and the beginning of the nineteenth. First, that of J. M. W. Turner, whose considerable work (principally in the Tate Gallery in London) is characterized by an exceptional vigour of line and use of shadow. No one has ever been better able to observe, feel and express a tempest. Turner, who at the end of his life claimed to be a professional sailor, experienced a sort of obsession with water, rendering the contrasts of colour, shadow and light with a consummate art of composition: 'premonitions of impressionism', as has been said of his work. His *Death of Nelson* (1808) is a fine example. His contemporary John Constable was a seascape artist; he perceived it as more peaceful, on the beach at Brighton and in Weymouth bay, although his skies are often tormented.

On the French side of the Channel pictorial representations of the sea were also shaped by romanticism. What painters made their

French public witness of the sea was marked both by a classical dramatization and by violence of gestures and colours. These were the academic turmoils represented by Louis Garneray, a disciple of Vernet, a veteran of the campaigns of Robert Surcouf in the Indies and the first official painter of the French Navy. The same could be said of Eugène Delacroix (*La Barque de Dante*) and of Théodore Géricault (*Le Radeau de la Méduse*).

A final remark might express the intimacy with the marine universe which the impressionists were able to share with their audience. All the same, a distinction seems to impose itself and still to be valid up to the present time. Without being insensitive to the savagery of the wind and the sea, some of them saw and felt them only from the shore; in general they portray ports and boats, but rarely set sail themselves. We can cite, for example, Adam, Braque and Dufy on the one hand, Pissarro, Baboulène, Monet and Buffet on the other. Signac, however, did sail.

The truth is that the perception of life at sea is indeed more faithful when the artist is also a mariner. Let us recall someone who has now been forgotten, who contributed in making the sea known: Pierre Fleury, who sensitively and with an infinity of nuances interpreted and translated the play of physical forces in the wind and the waves, as well as the symbolism of their power. We thus understand that in the nineteenth century France endowed itself with a Corps of Navy Painters, whose mission was not just aesthetic. They worked in close connection with officers of the bridge and hydrographers, which connected them to specifically scientific tasks.

Echoes in musical art

Quite naturally, music has been associated with the artistic symphony inspired by the sea. This has been true since ancient times. From the Athenian galleys to their distant eighteenth-century heirs in the Baltic, songs have sustained the rhythm of the sea. On the sailing ships the mariners' songs accompanied the gestures of the topmen. Mariners brought along rustic instruments to chase away their nostalgia. Likewise, from the start passenger boats offered concerts for those on board. And all fleets had their music of the

crews, appreciated for their artistic quality as much as for providing moral support for the troops. This support also came from the
lyrical music of the theatre; a famous example is the finale of the
opera *Alfred*, performed in London in 1740: *Rule, Britannia!*,
which was taken up throughout the Victorian era as the ultimate
expression of England's maritime pride.

The sea's contribution to European symphonic composition was
once again the fruit of romanticism. As Monique Brosse has
observed, it is curious that the sonorous depths of the sea,
off-shore and even more on the rocky coasts, has not found more
of an echo in travel tales and ship's logs. They laconically mention
the whistling of the wind in the sails and the shrouds, the spouts of
rain streaming onto the decks and into the gangways, the rattling
of chains, the cracking of wood, and finally the cries of fear when
the ship touches. Are mariners more visual than auditory? It is
notable that certain poems authentically evoking the voices of the
sea are the work of blind landsmen.

Romantic sensitivity sharpened by Germanic national awakening found in ancestral traditions rich sources of inspiration, and
thus served as an example to Europe. Mendelssohn's *Fingal's Cave*
was one of the first to signal a rupture with customary insipidity.
But it fell to Richard Wagner to exploit, in an heroic tone, the
violent grandeur of the sea. His *Flying Dutchman* (1843) borrows
from the legend of the same name the tragic story of a shipwreck
where all hands were lost. His *Tristan* exploits the old Nordic
maritime depths, an inexhaustible vein which surfaces again in the
middle of the twentieth century in Sibelius, who was inspired by
the Finnish epic poem, the *Kalevala*, and entitled a symphonic
poem *Oceanides*.

The theme of the tempest, taken up in every generation, lends
itself to the most varied effects of instrumentation; we know how
it was used in the seventeenth century by Henry Purcell in
England, in the eighteenth century by Luigi Caruso in Italy, and in
the nineteenth century by Antoine Thomas in France and by
Tchaikovsky in Russia.

The traditional use of themes has blended with those of nations,
as Sibelius shows. Sir Edward Elgar, too, in his *Sea Pictures*
(1897–9) borrowed a large number of their subjects from the Celtic
antiquities of Britain as well as from the daily life of the port of
London. Benjamin Britten later presented a similar reflection of

British reality, in *Billy Budd* (1951), evoking the Navy of the eighteenth century.

The relationship between European music and maritime inspiration was not confined only to the use of old national themes. The sea has exercised an influence, sometimes a fascination, which belongs to it alone, over composers as well as painters. Albert Roussel served several years at sea after his passage on the *Borda*. At the other end of Europe Rimsky-Korsakov left active duty after seventeen years only to become the inspector of the military band of the Imperial Fleet for eleven years. His talent for orchestration constructed 'moving symphonic tableaux' in which some have recognized a sensitivity to the incessant movement of the sea. And as the editor of Mussorgsky's work, we owe to him the publication of *The Seagull*, an indication of harmonic changes.

To sum up, the power of the contemporary symphony conveys the personality of the sea, with the curling of its waves, the movement of the tide, the anger of tempests accompanied by the violent blowing of the wind. In it composers find an inexhaustible field of expression. Maurice Ravel, for example, with *Une barque sur l'Océan*, knew just as well how to interpret vivid sensations as he did to evoke sentiments and arouse emotions. For his part, Claude Debussy first benefited from contact with the sea in Cannes before staying in Russia at the home of the Tchaikovsky's patroness. It was on that trip that he met Mussorgsky, who exerted a strong influence on him. The very personal character of his evolution explains that at risk of an initial scandal, his three symphonic sketches, composed in Dieppe (1903) under the title of *La Mer*, evoke like a burst of light the ever-renewed movement of the ebb and flow; boldly for his time, he recalled with a baffling variety of tones the moment, in constant flight, of the Ocean. It is the sea in itself, and for itself.

The sciences of the sea

The European presence on, and its domination of, the seas of the world are associated with a continuous scientific and technical progress. Without devaluing China's contribution to the techniques of maritime navigation, that of Europe has been served by an inventive spirit, a sense of initiative, by far-reaching means and resources. Unfortunately, in the present study we cannot go beyond a rapid glance at the issues raised and the solutions adopted. Nor will we consider the origins and the details of their development; it suffices, on the European level, to consider the principal stages. The stimulus came from the conjuncture, but the source was curiosity, imagination, reflection and research; social conditions played no less a role than did economic and political circumstances.

The phases correspond to the noteworthy stages of European civilization, the twelfth, sixteenth and eighteenth centuries, when the great issues of maritime navigation were raised. Although research was abundant, development did not progress at a constant speed towards more capacity, speed and security. However, the appearance of the three-master and of partitioned sails in the fifteenth and sixteenth centuries paved the way for a perfecting which was later brought to its height in the middle of the nineteenth century. Navigation in European waters did not pose the great careening problems which appeared later in the tropical and equatorial waters. In the second half of the eighteenth century a solution to this was the doubling of hulls with copper plating, in England and in France, then in the nineteenth century iron, then steel, construction. On the way naval construction underwent several great developments. The work of Frederic C. Lane has brought to light the medieval conceptions of the Venetian genius, but true plans for ships did not appear with any regularity until the eighteenth century. Now computers, by working with numerical data taken from texts, can reconstruct the lines and profiles of ships. The sixteenth century had produced technical treatises, but it was in the eighteenth century that in England and especially in France scientific training enabled builders to visualize their concepts through diagrams, to calculate the characteristics of ships and to diversify the types of vessels and frigates. The role of the Grandes Ecoles (in Paris, that of the Travaux Publics, which became the Ecole du Génie Maritime in 1765) and the Académies (the Académie de Marine in Brest in 1752) contributed to developing the art of ship-building into a science. It was a long way from the tentative steps achieved locally in the sixteenth century (for example in Dieppe and in Le Havre), and praised in the seventeenth century by a few authors, such as Father Tournier. The *Encyclopedia*, responding to maritime concerns, to which a colloquium was devoted in 1984 in Brest, could not neglect such an important realm of human knowledge. It called upon almost all the maritime specialists of the time, notably the members of the Académie de Marine, Sébastien Bigot de Morogues, Aymar de Roquefeuil, Henri Duhamel du Monceau, Pierre Bouguer, Honoré Vial du Clairbois, Philippe Buache, Jacques Bellin. In England, a sort of response to Diderot's initiative appeared in the *Encyclopedia of Method*, which appeared in 1786.

Europe was to supply the models to be followed for more than a century, until the new states (the USA, Japan) presented their own: huge combat ships or light vessels, large trade boats or average or small cargo boats. The 'Jeune Ecole' was born in Europe at the end of the nineteenth century. And it was in Europe that prototypes of submarines were conceived and built. This progress was achieved through competitiveness, indeed in competition, undoubtedly with the awareness of common scientific knowledge, but not with a view to cooperation.

The navy and science went hand in hand in all areas, and in a very remarkable way in nautical skill. Despite the knowledge gained in the age of the Great Discoveries, the impossibility of determining longitude for one's position at sea persisted. A competition was set up between the Board of Longitudes in London, stimulated by the attraction of a prize of £20,000 established by Queen Anne, and the Bureau Français des Longitudes, in its early form in the Académie des Sciences, which had also established a prize. The big event was the invention of a chronometer, which was substituted for the calculation of distances between the moon and the fixed stars. The perfecting of lunar tables was the object of the calculations of both Frenchmen (Borda, Romme, Delambre, La Caille) and Englishmen (Maskeline, the author of the *Nautical Almanach*). As for the invention of a marine chronometer, the credit goes to an Englishman, John Harrison, and to the Frenchmen Pierre Le Roy and Ferdinand Berthoud, whose discoveries were tested at sea in 1761–4 and in 1768. Navigation became an 'exact science' when the navies of the two kingdoms were endowed with those chronometers, and the end of the Middle Ages can be determined, from a nautical point of view, from that innovation.

The scientific fruits of such inventions benefited primarily hydrography and cartography. In France both disciplines found favour with the king, Louis XVI, who had learned them from Buache. The General Bureau of Maps and Plans, Journals and Studies Dealing with Navigation was created in France in 1720, seventy-five years before the establishment of an analogous service in England. Louis XVI is credited with having a cousin of Buache's, Beautemps-Beaupré, join it: he renovated the methods of hydrography at the moment when there was need of exact readings, notably in the Baltic and in the North Sea, and especially for the great voyages of exploration.

Before sharing primacy in the techniques of navigation with the United States, in the nineteenth century Europe preserved its priority in major inventions, which for a long time maintained, particularly in England, its lead among maritime nations. Steam propulsion in France and England had been the object of experiments (Denis Patin in 1690, Jonathan Hulles in 1736, and especially Jouffroy d'Abbans in 1783) which came before those of the American, Fulton. In the middle of the century, the adoption of the propeller and that of metallic construction in French, English and Swedish shipyards gave birth to the first great modern ships, capable of linking Europe to America with increased speed (the *Napoléon*, built in Le Havre in 1841, sailed at 11 knots), larger dimensions (the *Great Eastern*, in 1843, was 210 metres long) and greater fire power (the *Gloire* in 1859 was the first armoured ship).

Hygiene and health on board ship constituted a third major aspect of European scientific research. The interest of the Age of Reason in the natural sciences contributed to this, but so even more did the very serious epidemics on board ship and in the ports. The Marseille plague (1720) was not new, and it was not a discovery to note the disastrous conditions of hygiene on the ships. Typhoid ravaged the fleets of the duke of Anville and of Emmanuel Dubois de La Motte in 1746 and 1757–8 to the point of preventing their voyages to Canada. Thus the Académie de Marine and the young Ecole de Médicine of Brest began studying two serious problems. For drinking water, ship's doctors and surgeons proposed, without great results, different ways of treating the fresh water brought on board; a Danish process consisted of filtering it over sand and gravel. A process of distilling sea water was achieved through the use of the cucurbit, a kind of retort, in particular for very long voyages such as that undertaken by Bougainville. The best solution, for lack of anything better, remained to choose clean water and conserve it on board.

More serious were the human losses due to epidemics, particularly during the Seven Years' War. In twenty years the Royal Navy lost 80,000 men to illness, a little more than one-tenth of its numbers. Ill-health cost France several squadrons and lost it Canada. Along with typhoid, scurvy was a menace to all seamen. Its symptoms had been known for centuries: Joinville had described them in the fleet of St-Louis in Egypt; the tales of the voyages of discovery made mention of them among the companions of Vasco da Gama, the Parmentier brothers from Dieppe, and Jacques Cartier. Without being able, before the end of the nineteenth century, to attribute scurvy to a lack of vitamins, they attempted to prevent and cure it with palliatives. The slaughter produced by scurvy on Anson's seven ships between 1740 and 1744 stimulated efforts in England and France.

Tentative steps were taken in therapeutics. A Scottish doctor in the British Navy, James Lind, having succeeded in 1747 in saving those suffering from scurvy by using lemons, that fruit, not without some difficulty, became the panacea. Paradoxically, the attitude of Cook himself and of the Royal Society in encouraging the use of malt and sauerkraut with vinegar and vitriol, halted the consumption of lemon juice, which only became obligatory in the Navy in 1795 – mixed with 10 per cent brandy to overcome the repugnance of the sailors. On the contrary, the French royal navy continued to use vinegar and cabbage. It was thus that Sicilian lemons, of which the British Navy consumed thousands of tons, were the true victor of Trafalgar over the Franco-Spanish crews decimated by scurvy. After so many delays, scurvy only disappeared when long sea voyages became quicker, with the embarking of stocks of potatoes, and especially with advances in cooling techniques. Another scientific breakthrough subsequently resolved the medical problem, serious on ships, posed by the use of lead for drainage on board. Lead poisoning caused serious illness on the allied Western fleets during the Crimean War. Research was necessary to detect and eliminate the origin of it through a change in installations.

For the time being, Europe, which remained attentive to the technical and scientific progress of naval construction in particular – the dreadnought, the first submarines, of telecommunications and of naval medicine, had to share the initiative with the United States and soon Japan. Europe had set an example, but had not kept the privilege of its earlier efforts.

The sea and social life: modes of interaction

The promotion of the sea in European social life is recent. Until the nineteenth century, outside the ports, many coasts were almost empty, and in certain regions they remained so until the present time. Clearly, this was not because people were unaware of the sea, but their attention was fleeting and was sometimes limited to simple aquatic frolics, games and festivals of landsmen on the water.

In the second half of the fifteenth century, the sea formed part of one of the rituals of the court of Anjou: King René went for rides on the sea with his court, and Charles of Maine kept a boat for his diversion. The sea was used above all for the movement of those of princely rank: certainly between the British Isles and the continent, but also between the Iberian peninsula, Brittany and the Low Countries; the daughter of the king of Navarre, for example, arrived in Saillé near Guérande on a 'completely gold-covered boat' for her marriage to Duke Jean IV of Brittany. Equally lavish was the boat which carried the doge of Venice at the time of the 'Wedding of the Sea'.

The Renaissance developed that social role. When Francis I came to Lyon in 1515 a procession took him to the banks of the Saône for a nautical spectacle in which 'a large vessel like a sea ship' figured largely. Two years later in Marseille, a mock sea-battle using oranges preceded the king's review of the arsenal and the fleet of galleys. When the king returned to Marseille in 1533 to meet Pope Clement VII it was an occasion for more nautical festivities. But to what extent can we see in this naval aspect of ceremony more than symbolic manifestations of prestige? In 1518, at the time of the engagement of the young Prince Francis to Mary, the daughter of Henry VIII, a spectacle organized by two Italians, Visconti and Rincio, was given under a blue canopy portraying the celestial vault; the royal emblem of the salamander took the place of the Constellation of the Great Bear, guiding the king, the pilot of the kingdom. The king's mother, Louise de Savoie, had chosen a ship's anchor as an emblem.

In mystery plays, in the commedia dell'arte as in the classical plays of the seventeenth century, maritime subjects included an appropriate setting, and the directors' playscripts conformed to the professional language of mariners. Similarly we know of the nautical festivals at Versailles on Neptune's Fountain and the Grand Canal, with the Plaisirs de l'île enchantée.

The eighteenth century followed this example and the sea was in fashion. It was considered well-bred to be interested in tales of maritime voyages and to have a 'cabinet' in one's home, that is, a collection of stones and of stuffed animals brought back from distant voyages, and to enrich one's herb garden with exotic plants. The *Encyclopedia*, with accurate illustrations accompanying articles on indisputable areas of competence, initiated the 'enlightened' milieux to disciplines, practices, customs and professions of the sea of which they were often unaware. The learned societies with a maritime character recruited their adherents from among the merchants of Rouen, Nantes, Bordeaux, Marseille, Lisbon, Seville, Amsterdam and London. People willingly went to visit ports, for example, Bernardin de St-Pierre to Lorient. If one could not go on an excursion, one frequented the Salon which Diderot commented on and, in the second half of the eighteenth century and at the beginning of the nineteenth, there was no aristocratic or bourgeois home which did not have engravings by Ozanne.

Great personages made voyages on the coasts. Louis XV visited Le Havre and Louis XVI passed by there on his return from his trip to Cherbourg. Brest received, besides the count of Artois (the future Charles X), the Emperor Joseph II and the heir of Catherine the Great. The American War of Independence contributed to French society's infatuation with the navy and fashion launched the fad of a strange hairstyle which, under Louis XVI, put the replica of a vessel on top of piled-up hair, calling it 'à la Belle Poule' or à la Frégate'. One episode which became legendary expressed the passing fashion: 'I have three hats', said a young elegant woman, 'and like navy warships I've baptized them, the *Court-toujours*, the *Va-t-en-Ville*, and the *Glorieux*.'

The Revolution and the wars momentarily suspended the fashion for the sea. It was later taken up again with even more enthusiasm in France after the Restoration, following the English example. The beach at Brighton was all the rage in 1781. Dieppe was its French counterpart, for there the duchess of Berry introduced, even for ladies of 'high society', the custom, though very discreet, of sea bathing. That beach was then to benefit from the proximity of the princes of Orléans in Eu. Some twenty years later the Empress Eugénie initiated the autumn season in Biarritz on the Basque coast at the doors of her native land. For its part, the British gentry frequented the beaches of southern England. This social phenomenon is European. The sea appeared as a discovery. Chateaubriand went swimming out at sea. Roscoff attracted those who were from among the worldly and literary milieux of Paris. Heinrich Heine went swimming in Norderney. Curiously, the fashion reached the Mediterranean and the Asian shores relatively slowly. Flaubert liked the 'great blue sea'; before him, in 1810, it is believed that Lord Byron indulged in the pleasure of swimming across the Dardanelles. Michelet appreciated the mildness of winter in Hyères in 1858; but if he found the Inland Sea beautiful, he judged it 'harsh'. The 'Côte d'Azur' became fashionable towards the end of the century with an influx of British. For them the Channel played the role of a *cordon sanitaire* exempting their islands from continental influences; but for all that they did not forget that it was a link, which the Anglomania of the Belle Epoque illustrated by inventing 'franglais', the sign of a civilization of the Channel.

Painters have fixed the lofty marine environments of the European upper classes on their canvases; photographs, invented by Daguerre and disseminated with the first postcards, initiated the general public into the joys of the beach and of yachting. The latter was designated internationally by its Dutch name by reason of the origin of its development. The first regattas had begun in the eighteenth century, even in 1718 in Russia; the fashion reached England, where the name of Cowes recalls the first regattas of Europe (1775), followed by those, no less famous, of Tor Bay. Victorian England saw in marine sport the symbol of its imperial vocation.

Two expressions formulate this in a significant way. One defines the very profession of a mariner: 'to follow the sea'; the other conveys the intimacy of the mariner and his ship, two inseparable companions ('The Ship and I are two brave fellows'). The English example gave rise in the middle of the nineteenth century to an emulation which spread over all of Europe. Authors, involuntarily turning into publicists, spread the opinion that crossing the sea was an initiation. Flaubert devoted part of his royalties to pleasure boating, and Maupassant acquired the *Bel-Ami* in the same way. As for Jules Verne, the construction of his three *St-Michels* shows that he joined, with passion, action to words.

From social to sportive, the rivalry passed on to a national and political level around 1900. This broke out at the time of the regattas at Kiel in 1912, when the yacht *Grille*, the pride of Kaiser William II, claimed the right to compete with the *Victoria and Albert* owned by his cousin Edward VII.

From that time, and especially since the Second World War, Europeans have proved the extraordinary attraction of the sea in their summer migration, facilitated at least in France, Belgium and Germany by social legislation on vacations, but also by the no less important efforts to market all floating devices. Clearly, in the great tourist spots many comfortable boats scarcely ever sail and serve as vacation homes for their rich owners. If they do set sail they carry a clientèle of organized cruises on luxury passenger boats; and yet marine tourism seeks to reach the general public. If it cannot have direct access to the sea, that public has a growing interest in competition and nautical performances, in which Europe continues to share the initiative. A promising sign for the future is the taste young people have for the sea; although it is not true sailing, windsurfing can give a familiarity with, if not an initiation to the sea, to its risks and its joys. There is a maritime Europe of leisure and sport. However, the sea should not be considered only as a space for sport or an occasion for profit. Events continually remind Europe that the sea, or rather the seas, all connected throughout the world, have an infinitely greater importance for its future.

11

Conclusion: And Now?

At the end of this rapid journey through the past Erasmus may again formulate a final question for us. 'Oh, misfortune!', he cried, 'only the name of their countries separate the peoples. Why do so many common things not reconcile them?'

Of all the things common to Europeans the sea is certainly one of the most constant and most fertile. History recognizes the double mission of joining and separating which geography has assigned to it, but peoples have given priority to one or the other, according to their interests, without claiming the constraints of determinism. Historical experience offers an approach to the opportunities and the obstacles presented by the sea to those who wish to 'make Europe'. The sea – that is, the Mediterranean and especially the Atlantic Ocean – provides useful observatories: one can agree with Edgar Morin that 'it is difficult to see Europe from Europe and even from a particular point in Europe.' A certain distance is necessary, the sea provides one.

The positive contribution of history: the sea, a common heritage

In the historical construction of Europe the sea has been a decisive factor. It has worked on it in fits and starts, but with perseverance, locally or on a vaster scale, and for centuries. In the past Themistocles was the first to dare to say to his co-citizens that 'it was necessary to be attached to the sea' (Thucydides, I, 93–4), and the sea made possible Athenian thalassocracy. Then, rid of pirates by Pompey, the sea offered Rome an empire. Later it contained the 'barbarian' invasions. Unfurling from the Orient, the sea brought

227

the Christian faith destined to give Europe its first unified face, *Christianitas* – the same sea whose angers the apostle Paul had to overcome in order to bring his message. It was again the sea which brought the influence of the oriental monks from the Desert as far as the tip of Ireland. The sea formed the foundations of the Danish and Norwegian kingdoms, and the path of the Normans who, moving around Europe via the Atlantic, founded the Sicilian state and formed the advance guard of the crusades. To their brothers who remained in the country the sea served as a link between Normandy and England, then as a centre of gravity for the Plantagenet monarchy between the British Isles and Aquitaine. The destiny of England at that time was fixed by the sea, for England, rejected by the continent at the end of the Hundred Years' War, found in its island position the basis for an unequalled maritime power in the modern age.

The political configuration of Europe was in large part the result of Mediterranean predominance. Without the sea Venice and Genoa would not have existed as we know them, nor would the crown of Aragon, which in the fourteenth and fifteenth centuries turned the western Mediterranean into a Catalan lake. Without the sea Portugal would not have been in the fifteenth and sixteenth centuries the European figurehead in the discovery of Atlantic and Indian worlds.

On the political level, the image of Europe has depended upon the conjunction of its two maritime faces. Thus the monarchy of Charles V succeeded in dominating simultaneously the Hanseatic region, Flanders, and the Spanish and Italian coasts. Similarly, following a timid beginning in the thirteenth century, the kingdom of France enlarged under Louis XIV its two maritime façades, in the Ponant and the Levant, from Dunkirk to Bayonne and from Port-Vendres to Toulon. Beyond continental disputes, the control of the sea formed the crux of rivalries. The English hold on Gibraltar and later on Trafalgar imposed the conditions of British dominance over European maritime routes. Other possibilities depended on 'sea power'. Napoleon himself made this pledge to Las Casas: 'I threw the handle after the axe at the time of the disaster of Trafalgar; I could not be everywhere'; undoubtedly he thought of Villeneuve what in Egypt he unjustly reproached the mariners for, who, in his opinion, 'understood nothing of what is great'. In any event Napoleon's unmerited opinion of mariners and his discouragement after Trafalgar confirm the importance of the role of the sea in the destiny of states.

Indeed, the analysis of which we have attempted a sketch has noted certain definite facts, of two types. First, similarities among European maritime countries. At a higher level, Europeans have gradually become aware of what they have in common, despite rifts, competition and conflicts. Some examples of similarities can be cited. The condition of Mediterranean and Atlantic salt workers bears comparison, although the fortunes of each group have differed. The fate of fishermen, more differentiated, includes analogies between groups, types and zones of fishing, as well as in the function of the countries and their laws and customs. The problems of deep-sea fishing include many matters common to Norway and Portugal, for example; on the other hand, deep-sea fishing, as in earlier times in the Middle Ages – in different conditions, it is true – produced conflicts between the French and the Spanish in the Bay of Biscay. The heritage dates from a long time ago.

On the contrary, other sectors had certain experiences of cooperation. The presence of Italian and Iberian merchants on European commercial sites had a decisive influence on the formation of an international commercial environment at the end of the Middle Ages; French, Dutch, English and Germans joined each other there. The practices of fitting-out, of financing and of insurance experienced at that moment a beginning of unification, the progressive adoption of Italian techniques by Germans, for example. Correspondence between merchants' bank regulations from market to market and from port to port give proof of this. Family alliances were formed. Networks of cousins stretched from Seville to Genoa, from Lisbon to Antwerp, from Bilbao and Burgos to Nantes and Rouen, as well as from Florence, Genoa and Leghorn to London and Southampton, and from London to Hamburg, Bremen, Lübeck and Gdańsk. A Europe of merchants was formed, capable of not turning up its nose at political conflicts, but of living with them and surviving them. The mutual acceptance of tradesmen beyond maritime borders had repercussions in the realm of recruitment. In the sixteenth century crews were made up of a composite range of mariners of different origins and languages, able, despite their diversity and sometimes animosity, to feel their common adherence to the world of the sea.

It thus does not appear surprising that with the increased frequency of maritime relationships in Europe resemblances were perceived as much as oppositions were experienced. Those oppositions were relaxed, if necessary, in the face of a third player, the continental, a foreigner to all things of the sea. Cohesion in maritime life was natural among the English, for no one lived more than 150 kilometres from the coast, whereas among the Germans or even the French there were those who, even in modern times, had never seen the sea.

On the other hand, overseas expansion stimulated the awakening of a European consciousness. In the nineteenth century as in the sixteenth and seventeenth centuries, Europeans projected on to the new worlds an image of their native land, but at the same time they transferred their rivalries there. Granted, it was not a proof of cohesion, even less of cooperation, but can we not find there nevertheless the proof of origins in the same world? By keeping their distances from their respective homelands overseas, Europeans had the opportunity to discover what was common to them as much as to feel what set them apart.

... But a disputed or misunderstood heritage

The heritage in question is a disputed heritage, because its great value is set upon it by all having rights in it, beginning with those most prepared to dominate the sea, the English. England's ambition, starting in the Elizabethan era, incited the envy of its rivals; Philip II, in his will, advised his successor 'always to have his eyes and thoughts turned towards the British islands and seas'. But Cardinal Richelieu understood and expressed the problem particularly well in his *Testament politique*:

> The sea is one of the heritages to which all rulers claim to have the greatest share, and yet it is the one in which the rights of each person are the least clear. The empire of this element was never well assured to anyone ... One must be powerful to claim that heritage.

But, as he explains in his 'Advice to the King' (Louis XIII), 'the first thing to do is to make oneself powerful on the sea, which gives an entrance to all states in the world'.

The disputes concerning this inheritance need be described no further. Without any doubt their root lies in the opposition of interests, but, seen from the sea, oppositions also reveal attitudes based on different concepts. This is noticeable in past competitive and hostile behaviour, but also in the contemporary verbal and diplomatic confrontations on the organization of Europe. Jacques Pirenne writes that throughout history the maritime countries have proven to be individualists and liberals, whereas the continental countries, social and authoritarian, have a taste for hierarchical organizations. This being so, discussions on the theme of Europe convey deep rifts, in which the sea has a share of the responsibility. This is not new. In English political literature of the end of the Middle Ages, Europe is almost absent, although travellers crossed the Channel; increasingly in the sixteenth century Europe, a tributary to English negotiations, appeared like another world. This current, having come from far away, was fully manifest by the time of the formation of the free exchange zone, some forty years ago. Having reservations with regard to the Community, there pierces through a deep individualism and above all the British attachment to the countries of the Commonwealth, themselves worried about agricultural competition on the European continent. In his *Mémoires* Jean Monnet reports 'very strained conversations' with regard to the Schuman Plan, and the caricature representing two old English ladies on a boat in the Channel, observing the horizon with longnettes, is self-explanatory. One of them says: 'In clear weather one can see the common market.' These respectable ladies are expressing their concern about the questions they consider essential. On the contrary, Jean Monnet, on the occasion of a press conference given by General de Gaulle in January 1963, declared himself shocked by the possible failure of negotiations on issues 'ultimately secondary compared to the objective of the union of Europe'. The difference in appreciation was serious. They were perhaps secondary for the continentals, but the issue of maritime trade could not be so for the British. The sea thus weighs heavily on the inheritance of history, and cannot be ignored. Is it a coincidence that Thucydides' *Peloponnesian War* is commended to the meditations of future naval staff officers in the same breath as the most modern scientific reasoning, right now in the twentieth century? And that is on the other side of the Atlantic, in the American Naval War College! So what can one think on the 'old' continent?

In fact, a list of misunderstandings and incomprehensions concerning the issues of the sea might risk halting the unification of Europe. Curiously, again in his *Mémoires*, Jean Monnet is quite silent on maritime issues; perhaps a systematic examination of his abundant correspondence preserved at the Foundation that bears his name in Lausanne will break this silence. For it is unimaginable that he should not have evaluated the importance of the sea for Europe, he who, working in 1917–18 for the organization of American aid, wrote at that time: 'the nerve of the war is henceforth tonnage'. It is true that the Treaty of Rome, while it organized a common market, did not foresee common waters. This gap perhaps results, at least partially, from atavistic mental attitudes. Very few authors of the abundant contemporary literature relating to Europe have a thought or a line for the sea. It is also rare for the numerous colloquia relating to Europe to give a little space to the sea. Let us at least point out, in France, the triple initiative of the Ecole Nationale d'Administration, of the Institut Français de Recherche pour l'Exploitation de la Mer, and of the Société Navale Française de Formation et de Conseil, which in 1987 resulted in the publication of *La Mer – Hommes – Richesses – Enjeux*, the fruit of seminars and scientifically based consultations.

... and threatened

The work just mentioned contains depressing reflections: 'European institutions have only been interested in transport since 1974, although it was within the competence of the Treaty of Rome.' Further, 'Maritime Europe currently [1987] forms more of a zone of free exchange than a true common market.'

The maritime decline of the West is inscribed in statistics. Between 1977 and 1987 the registering of ships of the EC fell from 30 per cent to 17 per cent of world tonnage. The end of the great colonial empires brought about the appearance of the flags of states which had attained independence and which preferred separatism to cooperation with other navies. Great Britain once controlled 22 per cent of world tonnage; this has decreased to 2 per cent; at the same time the USA has dropped from 33 per cent to 5 per cent. These observations allow us to perceive the nature and origin of competition. What is most serious is that for the competitors

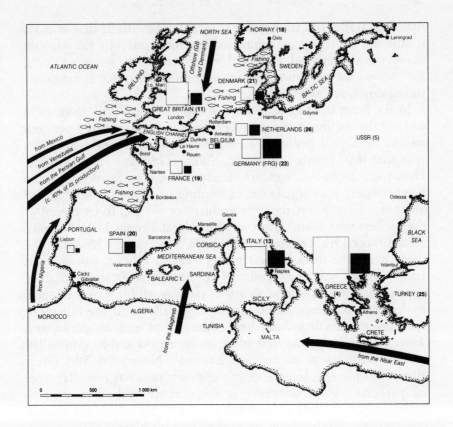

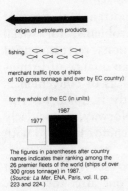

origin of petroleum products

fishing

merchant traffic (nos of ships
of 100 gross tonnage and over by EC country)

for the whole of the EC (in units)

1977   1987

The figures in parentheses after country
names indicates their ranking among the
26 premier fleets of the world (ships of over
300 gross tonnage) in 1987.
(*Source: La Mer*, ENA, Paris, vol. II, pp.
223 and 224.)

*Figure 11.1   The maritime economy of Europe towards the end of the
twentieth century*

maritime traffic is a tool rather than an end in itself; that in itself means an endemic weakening of maritime life. In the face of competition in general, Europe does not manage to renew its fleets, for various reasons among which economic ones, that is manufacturing costs, are not the least.

In the heart of the European Economic Community from 1977 to 1987 the decline in the number of merchant ships was 2 per cent and in tonnage 1 per cent, Great Britain maintaining first place, followed by France, Portugal, West Germany and Greece. However, the fall-off appears clearly in the classification of trade fleets under a national flag according to *Lloyd's Register of Shipping*. Greece was the only country of the EC to be placed in the highest ranks (4th); Italy is 12th, Great Britain 14th, Norway 18th, France 19th, Denmark 20th and West Germany 22nd. On the other hand, the three highest places went to Liberia, Panama and Japan. True, one must consider another classification, that of controlled fleets, which add various flags, notably of convenience, to their national flags. Although not especially good, the European position appears less weak here, though not without paradoxes. Thus Greece holds the first place in the world and its controlled tonnage remains at 50 per cent national; Norway is 5th; Great Britain is only 6th, but the fleet it controls raises its own flag over 60 per cent; West Germany is 9th, France 10th, but, true to tradition, it maintains its own colours on 85 per cent of the ships it controls; the Netherlands are ranked in 12th place.

The numbers emphasize the growing importance of flags of convenience and the incidence of social problems; for social burdens, notably in France, heavily restrict national recruitment of labour. The 'unflagging' weakens the European quality of fitting-out, even where, without resorting only to flags of convenience, national flags are doubled by using apparently fictional inscriptions on the *Registres bis*, for example for Norway, particularly liberal, for France with the flag of the Kerguelen, for England with those of Gibraltar or the Isle of Man.

Equally serious for European maritime interests is the issue of naval construction, for shipyards are closing one after the other. England lost the preeminence that around 1960 still gave it fifth place in world naval construction. The Asian shipyards, in South Korea, Taiwan, Hong Kong and Singapore, have an abundant and cheap labour force; they compete with Europe in its own market.

This reality links with another: the displacement of the centre of gravity of international exchange towards the Pacific and the Indian Ocean, accompanied by the appearance of a new type of ship, the very large oil tanker, only in part under European control.

As much and even more than trade, the European heritage of fishing is a misunderstood and long mistreated inheritance. 'Blue Europe' suffers from a laborious gestation, despite the interventions of the EC, and is coming up against a short-sighted exploitation, 'overfishing', and against the sometimes unbridled competition of fishermen; the system of quotas is attacked by local egoisms, the rights of sovereignty of the states over fishing zones and the sacrosanct principle of the freedom of the seas. The development of the new international law of the sea in this realm strikes a delicate nerve.

The issue of territorial waters in Europe is more complicated than elsewhere; the most characteristic example is undoubtedly that of the Aegean Sea, where the distribution between Greece (35 per cent) and Turkey (8 per cent) continues to cause disputes. The international convention of Montego Bay (1982) distinguishes the territoriality and the sovereignty of marine waters, but the ratifications did not have the unanimity which would give strength to the convention; certain jurists continue to believe that the competence of the state over the territorial sea is a right of jurisdiction, but not of sovereignty.

In a completely different view, the naval issue from the military point of view raises its head within the European framework. The political fragmentation of Western Europe and, until recently, the East–West opposition and the integration of part of the Western naval forces into NATO prevented even the conception of a European fleet. Historical memories, conceptual divergencies between staff members as to the use of various types of ship, such as aircraft carriers, above all divergencies of national interests, have halted experiments and true efforts at cooperation. Certain recent colloquia have demonstrated research into a definition of 'the European identity of security'. Some would like to see a European navy; but that ambition, formulated in a convincing way in principle, is far from being realized, for its application would raise enormous difficulties. European multinational cooperation is one approach, for, from all the evidence, freedom of navigation implies quasi-permanent consultations. The intensity of maritime circulation and the multiplicity of straits are for Europe an incontrovertible imperative. Even distant maritime interests impose it, and one may justifiably think that perhaps the problems of the Middle East will have as a result at least a more lively awareness of the commonality of the maritime interests of European states.

The chances and possibilities of the sea

The conceivers of the unification of Europe do not seem to have taken greatly into account its maritime possibilities. Everything proves, however, that the sea is a component, both historical and current, of its identity. That identity must be adapted to the extension of maritime activity outside the geographical frameworks to which it has been accustomed, in large part because they have been formed by it.

In the present conditions, both inherited from the past and imposed by the transformations of the decades gone by, two lines of conduct seem to offer possibilities and open up perspectives. One, of general importance, is the structural change in maritime circulation. The other, of a more specifically European character, postulates a geographical rebalancing of that activity on the shores of the continent. In this connection, one might wonder, without prejudging the response, what effects the Channel Tunnel will have in the long term on the maritime future of Western Europe, when Britain is connected to the continent.

The first observation to make is that the individualistic era of isolated ports has evolved into chains of transport functioning on criteria of profitability and competitiveness. On the European scale that implies the freedom of transport, and disturbs the habits of national competition. Thus those from Antwerp like to say that their port is the first French port, because it siphons off a sizeable portion of French traffic from the North and the East. But Antwerp is not alone and shares with Rotterdam a tendency towards a concentration of traffic in the northern ports.

This chance, however, counterbalances the measures taken by the EC in favour of the maritime countries of Southern Europe in order to rebalance the maritime landscape. These countries benefit from long traditions, from professionally competent maritime populations, as well as from competitive navigation companies. This is the case with Greece, whose position in the statistics is so favourable that it holds third place in the world, and with Italy, Portugal and Spain, about which it has been written that it is a 'fishing giant', from the number of its boats and the experience of its crews. The Mediterraneans have not forgotten that for centuries they were the animators of European trade; the Mediterranean makes up 12–13 per cent of the world's traffic, and its median location remains just as valuable through its marine relationships as through its continental surroundings.

To preserve its chances and benefit from them, Europe, however, must harmonize the conditions of competition in traffic and in fishing, encourage the modernization of its ships, normalize the social conditions of the crews and the technical training of its administration, and stimulate among them the knowledge of foreign languages. On that point already the diffusion of English is an undeniable international commodity. Under these conditions, as under many others, the building of a Europe of maritime transports appears inescapable; but it will be slow.

To accelerate it there has been talk of adopting a European flag. That will not happen overnight. A flag is the expression of the sovereignty and the power of the state, whose ship itself is the symbol of its territorial reality. It is difficult to see how France, Great Britain, Italy and Spain would agree to give theirs up. More reasonably, it has been proposed that European ships add to their national flag a pennant, which would be the symbol of their European connection.

Other possibilities offer Europe opportunities for a future and a presence on the seas. Without promising it unlimited autonomy in matters of energy, the off-shore exploitation of oil from the North Sea by Britain and Norway places Europe among the notable producers of a product for which it possesses, in the English Channel, a major arterial route, and in the Netherlands, in Rotterdam, one of its world regulatory markets. In the investigation of the ocean depths, the Europeans have their opportunities, whether it be for the exploitation of plankton or prospecting for minerals. We must not forget that in 1948 Auguste Piccard's invention of and experiments with the bathyscaph were the fruit of a European cooperation between France, Belgium and Italy. Since then, even if the size of the necessary financial investments has transferred the most important technical achievements across the Atlantic, Europe and notably the military navies take their part in them. Above all the placement of zones of oceanic exploitation foreseen by the United Nations Conference on the Law of the Sea, through the intermediary of France and Great Britain, reserves considerable possibilities to Europe throughout the world. Clearly Europe has lost world predominance, but we may hope that the authorities which are preparing its unification consider its historical roots, pledges to its future, both on the water and on the continent.

Let us conclude. The excuse, if not the justification, for the reflections of an historian pushed beyond the limits of the medieval waters familiar to him, is that history knows no hiatus. In my eyes, at least, it is in the scope of its history that the sea is an opportunity and a promise for the solidification of a European identity. That identity rests upon a common culture, of which the sea is an essential element.

Glossary of Technical Terms

carack: well-armed three-masted ship of relatively heavy tonnage.

caravel: small sailing vessel, usually lateen (triangular) rigged on two or three masts, known for its speed.

carvel: small fishing or coastal vessel, differing from the above-mentioned caravel by its square rigging, its shallower hold and its lesser speed.

carvel built: denotes a hull whose shell is formed of planking or plating laid close on the frames so as to present a smooth exterior.

caulker: worker specializing in caulking.

caulking: procedure used to make a vessel water-tight by filling the seams between its planks with oakum (loose rope fibres) or other materials.

clinker built: denoting a hull whose shell is formed of planking in which each strake overlaps the next one below and is overlapped by the next one above.

cog (coca, coque): a round, decked boat sitting high on the water; also (*cogue, kogge*) a large, heavy cargo boat, rigged with square sails.

heave to/lying to: to stop the headway of a ship by bringing the bow to the wind and trimming the sails so that they act against one another.

hulk: a heavy cargo ship, flat-bottomed with a round poop deck, two castles and square sails.

knot: measure of speed at sea, equal to one nautical mile per hour (approximately 1.15 statute miles per hour). The term 'knot' is believed to result from its former use as a length measure on ships' log lines, which were used to measure the speed of a ship through the water. Such a line was marked off at intervals by knots tied in the rope. Each interval, or knot, was about 15 metres (47ft 3ins) long.

landmark/seamark/leading-mark: a prominent or conspicuous object on land that serves as a guide to ships at sea.

lateen sail: a triangular sail set on a long, sloping yard.

plating: the planking of a ship serving to cover the hull of a vessel.

port of order: port where instructions were given for the next stage of a voyage.

239

RAIL: accepted convention and international usage for distinguishing sea passages ('up' and 'down' routes to avoid collisions, for example around the point of Brittany).

stay: amount of time a ship remains in a port of call to load or unload there.

stern post/rudder-post: a strong upright piece of wood rising from the after end of a keel.

strait: a narrow passage of water connecting two large bodies of water (between islands or between an island and a continent).

tiller: a bar or lever fitted to the rudder head used for turning the rudder in steering.

Bibliography

General works

Braudel, Fernand et al., *L'Europe. L'Espace, le temps, les hommes*, Paris, Arts et Métiers Graphiques, 1987.

Bywater, M., 'La Mer européenne: patrimoine communautaire ou ressources côtières', *Revue du Marché Commun*, 1976.

Chaunu, Pierre, *European Expansion in the Later Middle Ages*, trans. Katharine Bertram, Oxford, North-Holland, 1979.

Concina, Ennio (ed.), *Arsenali e citta nell'Occidente europeo*, Rome, NIS, 1987.

Conrad, Joseph, *The Mirror of the Sea and Personal Record*, ed. Z. Nadjer, World's Classics, Oxford University Press, 1988.

——*Typhoon*, World's Classics, Oxford University Press, 1986.

Duroselle, Jean-Baptiste, *Europe: A history of its peoples*, trans. R. Mayne, Viking, 1990.

——*L'Idée d'Europe dans l'histoire*, Paris, Denoël, 1965.

Gast, René et al., *Des phares et des hommes*, Paris, Éd. Maritimes et d'Outre-Mer, 1985.

Godino, V. Magalhães, *Mito e mercadoria utopia e pratica de navegas seculos XIII–XVIII*, DIFEL, Lisbon, 1990.

Grotius, Hugo, *Mare liberum. De la liberté des mers (1609)*, Paris, CNRS, 1990.

Hague, D. B., and Christie, R., *Lighthouses: Their architecture, history and archaeology*, Llandysul, Gomer Press, 1975.

Hocquet, Jean-Claude, *Le Sel de la terre*, Paris, Du May, 1989.

Lecerf, Jean, *Histoire de l'unité européenne*, Paris, Gallimard, 1965.

Le Pinchon, Y., *La Mer sous le regard des peintres de la marine*, Paris, Berger-Levrault, 1989.

Lewis, Archibald R. and Runyan, Timothy J., *European Naval and Maritime History*, Bloomington, Indiana University Press, 1985.

Lucchini, Laurent and Voelckel, Michel, *Les États et la mer*, Paris, La Documentation Française (Notes et études documentaires), 1978.

McKay, Derek, *The Rise of the Great Powers 1648–1815*, London/New York, Longman, 1983.

Mahan, Alfred T., *The Influence of Sea Power upon History 1660–1783*, London, Sampson Low, 1890.

——*Naval Strategy*, London, Sampson Low, 1911.

Masson, Philippe, *Marines et océans, ressources, échanges, stratégies*, Paris, Imprimerie Nationale, 1982.

Mollat du Jourdin, Michel et La Roncière, Monique de, *Sea Charts of the Early Explorers, 13th to 17th Century*, trans. L. le R. Dethan, New York, Thames and Hudson, 1984.

Morghen, R., *L'Idea da Europa*, Rome, ERI, n.d.

Monnet, Jean, *Memoirs*, trans, Richard Mayne, London, Collins, 1978.

Morin, Edgar, *Penser l'Europe* Paris, Gallimard, 1987.

Roskill, Stephen W., *The Strategy of Sea Power*, London, Collins, 1962.

Rougemont, Denis de, *The Idea of Europe*, trans. Norbert Guterman, London, Collier-Macmillan, 1966.

——*Vingt-huit siècles d'Europe. La conscience européenne à travers les textes*, Paris, Christian de Bartillat, 1990 (preface by Jacques Delors).

Simpson, B. Mitchell (ed.), *War, Strategy and Maritime Power*, New Brunswick, Rutgers University Press, 1977.

Villain-Gandossi, C., Borhemans, K., Metzelin, M and Schäffner, C., *The Concept of Europe in the Process of the CSCE*, Tübingen, Gunter Marr, 1990.

Vogel, Walther, 'Zur Frösse der europäischen Handelsoflotten im 15. und 17. Jahrhundert. Ein historisch statistischer Versuche', in *Forschungen und Versuche zur Geschichte der Neuzeit* (Festschrift Dietrich Schäfer zum 70. Geburtstag), Jena, 1915.

Weiss, Louise, *Un combat pour l'Europe*, Lausanne, 1984.

Wilson, David, M. (ed.), *The Northern World: The history and heritage of Northern Europe AD400–1100*, London, Thames and Hudson, 1980.

Periodicals

The American Neptune, Salem, MA. (from 1941).

Hansische Geschichtsblätter, Leipzig (from 1872).

International Fishing News, London (from 1960).

The Mariner's Mirror (International Journal of the Society for Nautical Research), London, National Maritime Museum (from 1911).

Marins et Océans. Études d'histoire maritime, Paris.

Neptunia, Paris, Revue de l'Association des Amis du Musée de la Marine (from 1946).

Relations Internationales, Paris (special numbers on European maritime problems: 1988, 1989, 1990).
Revista de Historia Naval, Madrid.
Revista Marittima, Rome (from 1868).
Tijdschrift voor Geschiedenis, Amersfoort (from 1886).

Symposia and collections

Accera, Martine, Merino, José, Meyer, Jean (prés.), *Les Marines de guerre européennes XVIIe–XVIIIe s.* (Colloquium, 1984), Paris, Presses de la Sorbonne, 1985.
Les Aspects internationaux de la découverte océanique aux XVe-XVIe siècles (5e Coll. Int. Hist. Mar., Lisbon, 1960), Paris, SEVPEN, 1966.
Balard, Michel (dir.), *État et colonisation au Moyen Age et à la Renaissance* (Colloquium, Reims, 1987), Lyon, La Manufacture, 1989.
Balcou, Jean (prés.), *La Mer au siècle des encyclopédies* (Actes colloque, Brest, 1984), Paris/Geneva, Champion-Slatkine, 1987.
Cabantous, Alain and Hildesheimer, Françoise (eds.), *Foi chrétienne et milieux maritimes XVe-XXe siècles* (Actes colloque, Collège de France, 1987), Paris, Publisud, 1989.
Céard, Jean and Margolin, Jean Claude, *Voyager à la Renaissance* (Actes colloque, Tours, 1983), Paris, Maisonneuve-Larose, 1987.
Course et piraterie (15e Coll. Int. Hist. Mar., San Francisco, 1975), Paris, CNRS, 1975.
El Estrecho de Gibraltar-Ceuta (Actas del congreso internacional, 1987), Madrid, 1988, vols I–III.
L'Europa. Fondamenti, formazione e realta (Colloquium, Rome, 1983).
L'Europe et l'océan au Moyen Age. Contribution à l'histoire de la navigation (Colloquium, Nantes, 1987), Nantes, CID, 1988.
Les Gens de la mer en société (18e Coll. Int. Hist. Mar., Bucharest, 1980), Paris, 1980, mimeo.
Le genti del Mare Mediterraneo (17e Coll. Int. Hist. Mar., Naples, 1980) Naples, 1981, 2 vols.
Les Grandes Escales (10e Coll. Int. Hist. Mar.), Brussels, 1968, 3 vols.
Groshens, J.-C. (dir.), *Cartes et figures de la Terre*, Paris, Centre Georges Pompidou/Centre de création industrielle, 1980.
Guerres et commerces en Méditerranée, IXe–XXe siècle, prés. par M. Vergé-Franceschi, Paris, Kronc, n.d.
Guerres et Paix 1660–1815 (Journées franco-anglaises d'histoire de la marine, Rochefort, 1986), Vincennes, Service hist. marine, 1987.
'Les Hommes et la mer dans l'Europe du Nord-Ouest de l'Antiquité à nos jours' (colloquium, Boulogne-sur-Mer, 1984), *Revue du Nord*, special no., 1986.

Il Porti come impresa economica (Atti della 19° settima. di Storia economica F. Datini, Prato, 1987), Florence, Cavaciocchi, 1988.

Istanbul à la jonction des cultures balkaniques, méditerranéennes, slaves et orientales aux XVIe-XIXe siècles (Actes colloque de l'AISEE, Istanbul, 1973), Bucharest, 1977.

Méditerranée et Océan Indien (6e bis Coll. Int. Hist. Mar., Venice, 1963), Paris, SEVPEN, 1970.

La Mer. Hommes. Richesses. Enjeux, Paris, IFREMER, 1989, 2 vols. (co-dir. ENA, IFREMER, NAVFLO).

Mollat, Michel (ed.), *Les Origines de la navigation à vapeur* (Actes colloque, 1960), Paris, PUF, 1970.

Les Navigations méditerranéennes et leurs liaisons continentales (11e Coll. Int. Hist. Mar., on board the *Ausonia*, 1969), Naples, 1981.

Le Navire et l'économie maritime du XVe au XVIIIe siècle (1er Coll. Int. Hist. Mar.), Paris, SEVPEN, 1956.

Le Navire et l'économie maritime du Moyen Age au XVIIIe siècle principalement en Méditerranée (2e Coll. Int. Hist. Mar.), Paris, SEVPEN, 1958.

Le Navire et l'économie maritime du Nord de l'Europe du Moyen Age au XVIIIe siècle (3e Coll. Int. Hist. Mar.), Paris, SEVPEN, 1960.

Palacio, Atard Vicente (coord.), *España y el mar en el siglo Carlos III*, Madrid, 1989 (collected papers).

Poleggi, E. (ed.), *Citta portuali del Mediterraneo* (Atti del Convegno Internazionale, Genoa, 1985), 1989.

Quand voguaient les galères, Rennes, Ouest-France, 1990 (catalogue of works on the occasion of the exhibition at the Musée de la Marine, Paris, 1990).

Renouard, Yves, *Études d'histoire médiévale*, Paris, SEVPEN, 1968, 2 vols.

Les Sources de l'histoire maritime en Europe du Moyen Age au XVIIIe siècle (4e Coll. Int. Hist. Mar., CNRS, 1959), Paris, SEVPEN, 1962.

Les Villes portuaires (16e Coll. Int. Hist. Mar., in association with the Commission Internationale d'Histoire des Villes, Varna, 1978), Sofia, Academy of Sciences, 1985.

Specific topics

Albion, Robert G., *Forests and Sea Power. The timber problems of the Royal Navy 1652–1862*, Cambridge, MA., Harvard University Press, 1926.

Balard, Michel, *La Romanie génoise: (XIIe–début du XVe siècle)*, Rome, École Française, 1978, 2 vols.

Bernard, Jacques, *Navires et gens de mer à Bordeaux (vers 1400-vers 1550)*, Paris, SEVPEN, 1968, 3 vols.

Bournaz-Baccar, A., *La Mer et l'aventure marine dans les genres narratifs et dramatiques français de 1640 à 1671*, doctoral thesis, University of Paris III, 1988, typescript.

Braudel, Fernand, *The Mediterranean and the Mediterranean World in the Age of Philip II*, 2 vols, trans. S. Reynolds, Fontana Press, 1986, 1987.

Braunstein, Philippe and Delort, Robert, *Venise. Portrait historique d'une cité*, Paris, Éditions du Seuil, 1971.

Bresc, Henri, *Un monde méditerranéen. Économie et société en Sicile 1300–1450*, Rome, École Française, 1986, 2 vols.

Brezet, F. E., 'Une flotte contre l'Angleterre. La rivalité navale anglo-allemande 1897–1914', *Marins et Océans*, Paris, 1990.

Brosse, M., *La Littérature de la mer en France, en Grande Bretagne et aux USA.*, thesis, Paris, Lille, Presses Universitaires, 1983, 3 vols.

Cabantous, Alain, *La Mer et les hommes: pêcheurs et matelots dunker-quois de Louis XIV à la Révolution*, Dunkerque Westhoek-Éditions, 1980.

——*La Vergue et les fers. Mutins et déserteurs dans la marine d'Ancien Régime XVIIe–XVIIIe siècles*, Paris, Tallandier, 1984.

——*Le Ciel dans la mer. Christianisme et civilisation maritime XVe–XIXe siècles*, Paris, Fayard, 1990.

Carus Wilson, Eleonora, *Medieval Merchant Venturers*, London, Methuen, 1954.

Coornaert, Émile, *Les Français et le commerce international à Anvers. Fin du XVe–XVIe siècle*, Paris, Rivière, 1961, 2 vols.

Coutau-Bégarie, Hervé, *La Puissance maritime soviétique*, Paris, Economica, 1983.

Czaplinski, Wadyslaw, 'Le Problème baltique aux XVIe et XVIIe siècles', in *XIe Congrès international des sciences historiques. Rapports, IV, Histoire moderne*, Göteborg-Stockholm, Uppsala, 1960.

Delumeau, Jean, *L'Alun de Rome XVe–XIX^{e}s.*, Paris, SEVPEN, 1962.

Dollinger, Philippe, *La Hanse XIIe–XVIIe siècles*, 2nd edn, Paris, Aubier, 1988.

Doria, G. and Pergiovanni, P. M. (dir.), *Il sistema portuale della republica di Genova*, Genoa, 1988.

Ferreira Priegue, Elisa, *Galicia en el comercio maritimo medieval*, La Coruña, University of Santiago, 1988.

Fleury, Pierre, *Les Amours du vent et de la mer*, Tours, Éd. du Cercle, 1984.

Glykatzi-Ahrweiler, Hélène, *Byzance et la mer*, Paris, PUF, 1966.

Gravier, Maurice, *Les Scandinaves*, Paris, Lidis, 1984.

Heers, Jacques, *Gênes au XVᵉ siècle*, Activité économique et problèmes sociaux, Paris, SEVPEN, 1961.

Houtte, Jan A. van, *Bruges. Essai d'histoire urbaine*, Brussels, La Renaissance du Livre, 1967 (coll.Notre Passé).

Israel, Jonathan I., *Dutch Primacy in World Trade 1585–1740*, Oxford, Clarendon Press, 1989.

Jeannin, Pierre, L'Activité du port de Königsberg dans le seconde moitié du XVᵉ siècle', *Bulletin de la Société d'Histoire Moderne*, 56, 1958.

Jenkins, Ernest H., *A History of the French Navy: From its beginnings to the present day*, London, Macdonald and Jane's, 1973.

Kerhervé, Jean, *L'État breton aux XIVᵉ et XVᵉ siècles: les ducs, l'argent et les hommes*, Paris, Maloine, 1987, 2 vols.

Ladero-Quesada, Miguel Angel, 'L'Espagne et l'océan à la fin du Moyen Age', in *L'Europe et l'Océan au Moyen Age*, Nantes, CID, 1988: pp. 115–130.

Lane, Frederic C., *Venice, a maritime republic*, Baltimore, Johns Hopkins University Press, 1973.

Lebecq, Stéphane, *Marchands et navigateurs frisons du Haut Moyen Age*, Lille, Presses Universitaires, 1983, 2 vols.

Malowist, Marian, 'The economic and social development of the Baltic countries from the XVth to the XVIIth centuries', *Economic History Review*, 2nd ser., 17.2, 1959.

Melis, Federigo, *Aspetti della vita economica medievale* (Studi nell'Archivio Datini di Prato), Siena, Monte dei Paschi, 1962.

Merino, José, *La Armada española en el siglo XVIII*, Madrid, 1981.

Mollat, Michel, *La Vie quotidienne des gens de mer en Atlantique (Moyen Age-XVᵉ siècle)*, Paris, Hachette, 1983.

——(dir.), *Histoire des pêches maritimes en France*, Toulouse, privately printed, 1987.

——*Jacques Coeur ou l'esprit d'entreprise au XVᵉ siècle*, Paris, Aubier, 1988.

Mülhenraun, R., *Die Reorganisation der spanischer Kriegsmarine in XVIII. Jahrhundert*, Cologne, Vienna, 1975.

Musset, Lucien, *La Tapisserie de Bayeux: oeuvre d'art et document historique*, St Leger-Vauban, Zodiaque, 1989.

Reddé, Michel, *Mare nostrum. Les Infrastructures, le dispositif et l'histoire de la marine militaire sous l'Empire romain*, Rome, École Française, 1986.

Roover, Raymond de, *The Rise and Decline of the Medici Bank 1397–1494*, Cambridge, MA, Harvard University Press, 1963.

Rougé, Jean, *Recherches sur l'organisation du commerce maritime en Méditerranée sous l'Empire romain*, Paris, École Pratique des Hautes Études, 1966.

Seyssel, Claude de, *La Monarchie de France*, Paris, Librairie d'Argence, 1961 (ed. J. Poujol).

Spratt, Hereward P., *The Birth of the Steamboat*, London, Charles Griffin, 1958.

Taillemite, Étienne, *L'Histoire ignorée de la marine française*, Paris, Perrin, 1988.

Thrupp, Sylvia L., *The Merchant Class of Medieval London 1300–1500*, University of Michigan, Michigan, 1962.

Treppo, Mario del, *Il mercanti catalani e l'espansione della Corona d'Aragona nel secolo XV*, Naples, Libreria scientifica, 1968.

Villain-Gandossi, Christiane, *Le navire médieval à travers les miniatures*, Paris, CNRS, 1985.

Vogel, Walther, *Geschichte der deutschen Seeschiffahrt*, Berlin, 1915, vol. I.

Index